NOTES FROM THE
CHALKBOARD

To Charlotte

NOTES FROM THE
CHALKBOARD

TEACHER TALES FROM THE MOUNTAINS OF
NORTH CAROLINA

Thank you for reading my book

J. TERRY HALL

J. Terry Hall
2018

authorHOUSE®

AuthorHouse™
1663 Liberty Drive
Bloomington, IN 47403
www.authorhouse.com
Phone: 1-800-839-8640

Published by AuthorHouse   07/12/2012

ISBN: 978-1-4772-3249-1 (sc)
ISBN: 978-1-4772-3251-4 (e)

Library of Congress Control Number: 2012911614

This book is printed on acid-free paper.

Life is like juggling five balls-work, religion, family, health and friends and, you are keeping them all in the air at the same time. One day, you finally understand that work is a rubber ball; if you drop it, it will bounce back. The other four balls-friends, health, family and religion are made of glass. If you drop one of these, it will crack or be shattered beyond repair.

Paraphrased from:
Suzanne's Diary For Nicholas, James Patterson,
Warner Books, 2001, pp. 23-24

This Book Is Dedicated To Ben Frank Hall
Son, Husband and Father
"All things work together for good to those who love the Lord"
Romans 8:28

AUTHOR'S NOTES

There were many people who provided support and encouragement in the process of compiling this book. Thanks to all the educators who related their many wonderful stories and are mentioned in the biographical section. To my wife, Patricia, a special thank you for all the hours she spent alone while I worked late into the night. And especially, I want to thank our son, Ben Frank Hall, for not only his encouragement but for the many stories he remembered from his school days in Asheville City Schools where I served as an administrator. Ben suffered in silence as other children and even some teachers mistreated him because of decisions his father had to make.

CONTENTS

FORWARD

Something very special happens when a wonderful book such as this one by Dr. J. Terry Hall falls into the hands of readers who are interested in local life and culture as described herein. Insightful books such as this one are based on utilizing oral history methodology as a means of writing history at the grassroots level. Oral history is not the falsehood of history as defined by some scholars. As I personally say, "Oral history typically represents history of the multitude of the world's population whose names never get into formal history books." People like to relate personal experience memories about their own activities across the years, about friends and community members, also about their ancestors who are typically known only by traditional stories told about them.

Stories and descriptive commentaries included in this book focus on education, school administrators, teachers, and students in the beautiful mountain area of North Carolina during the past half-century, and early times as well. The truly wonderful memories herein, as provided by persons who typically experienced them on a personal level, will thrill future readers who know little to virtually nothing about earlier school times. And to all readers, whether your roots are in the mountain region or not, may you find your mind filled with personal nonforgettable menories.

Dr. William Lynwood Montell, Ph.D.
Author of twenty-seven books
based on oral history methodology,
and emeritus professor at Western Kentucky University

INTRODUCTION

Retiring from public education after forty years as a teacher and administrator, I realized one of the saddest things I could conceive of was for a person to serve in the American public schools for many years, live to a ripe old age of eighty, ninety, or even one hundred years, and, when they die, for all their wonderful tales and experiences die with them. I began attempting to remember as many of personal and others' tales as possible that had happened through the years. While in my home office, I would begin laughing out loud about some event that had long ago been forgotten. My wife, Patricia, would come in and say, "What in the world are you laughing about?" and I would share some memory of long ago to which we both would laugh. Within a few days, I was waking in the middle of the night, jumping out of bed and rushing into my office to make a note of some event I had just dreamed or remembered.

As my thinking and enjoyment continued, I realized that I was probably not alone in my desire to share with the world experiences from long ago. I began to seek out other school teachers and school administrators that I had crossed paths with through the years, discussed my project with them and asked if they would consent to be interviewed for inclusion in my book. I was thrilled at the positive response I received and began immediately the task of picking their brains for tales they had encountered over the years.

Many people shared both positive and negative accounts they had encountered. Some of their tales involved themselves and children they had served over a long career, while others were accounts involving fellow teachers and administrators.

I used the following criteria for choosing potential storytellers for this book. First, I sought out people who had been in education for several years and had time to gain years of experience. There was one exception: My grandchildren asked me if I would include their favorite teachers in the book. What is a grandfather supposed to do when his grandchildren say, "Pretty please Papaw?" For the most part, those interviewed were either retired or very close to retirement. Second, I attempted to seek out educators from a broad spectrum of the profession. The storytellers taught in preschool, elementary, middle school, high school, college and/or were administrators. Third, I limited my selection of storytellers to teachers and administrators who either taught in small mountain communities of North Carolina or had connections with the mountainous area in the western part of the state. In addition to tales received from personal interviews I included tales of educators who are no longer living and their tales were either related to me by others or found in archives. One more advantage of sharing educators' accounts from other generations is that it allows one a perspective from which to view the present. If the tales were not personal but are about some other person in the profession, these accounts are considered folk tales, (stories assumed to be true when they are told). Also, I included personal tales based on my forty years in the profession.

The procedure used was to present the storytellers with a list of questions to help jump start their memories of tales experienced during their careers. These questions would later be used to organize the chapters of my book. Questions for consideration were: deciding to go into the field of education; experiences in college; experiences during the first years in the profession; most influential people; funny experiences that happened along the way; experiences of other educators; most fearful experiences; fights and discipline; most rewarding experiences; office politics; and winds of change in the profession. At the time these questions were delivered, the storytellers would be given a choice to either schedule a taped interview or to respond in writing to the interview questions. Following the interview, I transcribed and paraphrased the interview before sending a written copy back to the person for editing. Upon approval, a written copy would be filed to later be included in my book.

Although many of the storytellers were personal acquaintances whom I had worked with over the years, there were several I had never met. The procedure for the interview was to spend a few minutes visiting with the storytellers and getting to know them on a personal level before turning on my digital tape recorder. After the small recorder was turned on and put aside, we carried on an informal conservation. Within a short time, the storyteller would become so caught up in their tales that the recorder would seem to be forgotten.

The purpose of this book is to present in written form tales experienced by educators throughout their careers. These tales constitute the great majority of personal and human experiences that never get into history books. For a generation or two, some of these tales may be passed down from parents to their children, but in a short time, these wonderful tales would be forgotten and a very important piece of history would be lost. My hope is that through this book an important piece of history can be retained.

CHAPTER ONE

CHOOSING THE PROFESSION

MY GUIDANCE COUNSELOR TOLD ME
I WOULD NEVER SUCCEED

When I started college at Lindsey Wilson College in Columbia, Kentucky in the fall of 1961, I had no idea what I wanted to do with my life. I chose Lindsey Wilson because it was the closest to my home, only forty-five miles as the crow flies. Also, the only plan I had in life was to attend Lindsey Wilson for one semester in order to see what college was like. I had absolutely no thought of finishing college and obtaining a degree in the two year school. After all, my guidance counselor in high school had advised me not to go to college, she realized how hard my parents had to work to make a living and I would just be wasting my time and their money as I would never succeed in college. My plan, if one could call it a plan, was to go to barber school and take a job working the empty barber chair in the only barber shop in Tompkinsville, Kentucky. I had previously checked with the barber, Fred Downing, who informed me if and when I received my barber's degree, he would let me have his empty chair.

On the first day at college during registration, a young teacher by the name of Catherine Rodgers walked up and asked me in what my major was going to be. I had never been asked that question and did not know what she meant. She explained she was the teacher of the Elementary Education Training Center on campus and wondered if I was planning to major in elementary education. After explaining that all students had to declare a major area at registration, she asked me to consider majoring in elementary education and signing up for the "Fundamentals of Education" class which she offered. I decided that since I had to declare a major Elementary Education was as good as any. Later, I found out that she was the only Elementary Education teacher at Lindsey Wilson;the Training school consisted of only four grades with from three to four children in each grade, and, all those were students of fellow college teachers at Lindsey Wilson.

This seemingly accidental encounter was the genesis that molded the rest of my life. I attended the "Fundamentals of Education" class and loved it. The children actually looked up to me just like I was a "real" teacher. They even called me Mr. Hall! I had never felt like I was successful at anything because I had always been put down; and after all, even my high school counselor told me I would never succeed in college. With Mrs. Rodgers' loving guidance, I completed the first semester with good grades and returned home, telling my financially-stressed parents that I really wanted to continue college to become an elementary school teacher. My parents never let me know of their sleepless nights worrying about the next semester's tuition. They did without, or whatever was necessary, but they always had the tuition when it was due.

At the beginning of the second semester, Mrs. Rodgers came to me and asked if I would consider working with her as a teaching assistant in the Training School for a stipend of seventy-five dollars for the semester. To say I was thrilled would have been an understatement! No one, except my parents, had ever made me feel successful in life. Now, here was a college professor who was willing to pay me for doing what I loved. Not even having my wife, son and parents see me walk across the stage at the University of North Carolina in Greensboro, North Carolina and receive a Doctor of Education degree forty-five years later was as rewarding as receiving that seventy-five dollar stipend.

J. Terry Hall, Scott Mountain,
Buncombe County,3/3/11

TEACHING—THE JOB THAT WILL CUT THE CAKE

I majored in pre-engineering when I started college, but when I had to take calculus and physics and was confronted with four hour math problems, I decided that was was not how I wanted to spend the rest of my life. I left Clemson University after the second semester and moved back to New Jersey to become a dental assistant. During this time, I found out the head dental assistant was making only twelve dollars an hour and I said, "That's not going to cut the cake if I ever need to take care of someone other than myself." I decided I would go back to school since my dad was going to help me out and I realized what I enjoyed most in dental assistant school was working with young children. I thought, what can I do that will put me in contact with kids? I finally realized I really wanted to become a school teacher. I then went back to school at UNCA in Asheville and earned my degree in psychology because UNCA did not have a degree in teacher education at that time. I finally finished my teacher certification and started working at Candler Elementary Schools. I now have my gifted certification and my goal is to teach the gifted class; but I also realize those teachers do not let go of their positions very lightly. I will just have to be patient while I work on my master's degree. I guess one could say I am an elementary school teacher because I like young kids more than grown-ups for the most part.

Elizabeth Middleton, Candler,
Buncombe County, 10/21/10

A MOUNTAIN BOY FOLLOWS A CROOKED ROAD

As I started college, I had several people encouraging me to go into teaching, although I had in mind to go into the Forest Management area.

Once I had entered college and realized how many requirements there were for science courses in Forest anagement I decided the teaching profession didn't seem all that bad.

I came from a mountain high school in Madison County with a senior class of eleven. Our agriculture teacher usually taught us the sciences and we spent most of our time working in the shop area. This did not give me a very good background in the sciences and I realized I did not have the foundation necessary for a degree in Forest Management, and I was not willing to apply myself to proceed in that area.

I had two teachers who helped me make the decision to go into teaching. One taught English and the other taught social studies and Spanish. The Spanish teacher was also a Priest and a minister at our local Catholic Church in Hot Springs. After I began college, I realized that teaching was the area I needed to pursue, and I studied Middle Grade Math. Although in my second year of college, I took a course in Library Science and realized that this was the area where I best seemed to fit. Following undergraduate school, I received a master's degree in educational media, and was certified in grades four through nine. My first year teaching assignment was a fourth/fifth grade combination class. A few years later, I was hired as a Media Coordinator, and, after three more years got into school administration in Haywood County. One of the many duties in which I was involved was helping develop a personnel office for the county. Following this assignment I served two years as Assistant Principal at a local high school which turned out to be the busiest two years of my career. After having as much fun as I could stand in that position, I came back to the Central Office and began working with Federal Programs where I have been for the past eighteen of my thirty-six years in the profession.

Fred Trantham, Waynesville,
Haywood County, 11/11/10

YOU REALLY GOT A HOLD ON ME

I went to a little Union school and had the same principal all the way from first through the twelfth grade. Mr. Charles A. Parlier patted me on the head as a first grader and gave me my diploma when I graduated twelfth grade. Mr. Parlier was destined to be a principal because his parents gave him the name Charles Aycock, and the Aycock name is well known in the mountains of western North Carolina as an outstanding educator.

One day, a couple of us boys were skipping class and when Mr. Parlier came looking for us, I slipped under the stairwell. It was dark under the stairwell and he came around and looked into the darkness. I could see him because of the light behind him, but he could not see me. He was feeling around in there and he grabbed me by the arm and started to pull me out; I couldn't think of anything to do but to sing a song that was out at the time, so I began to sing, "You really got a hold on me." He had a notebook in his hands and he swatted me about three times on the butt and took me back to class.

Dorland Winkler,
Malvern Hills, 8/12/11

A DEFICIENCY IN MUSIC
LED ME INTO TEACHING

I always loved school and I loved every teacher I had in elementary school. My favorite teacher was Helen Cathey, and she encouraged me to become a teacher. We had to memorize poems in her class. She was a beautiful woman inside and out; I really looked up to her and whatever she asked me to do I did. There was never a time when I didn't want to become a school teacher. I loved school and played school often. I was always "the teacher." Since I loved teaching and music, I decided to become a choral music teacher in high school. Although when I was young and had access to piano lessons, I didn't practice like I should. When I tried out for music at the Woman's College (now University of North Carolina) in Greensboro, I was told I had a deficiency in piano, so I decided to become a primary school teacher, which is what it was called back then.

Julia Clark,
Biltmore Lake, June 2, 2011

A MAYBERRY RFD LIFE

I have always enjoyed being around people and consider myself a people person. I grew up in a little valley between Lenoir and Blowing Rock, North Carolina. It was deep in the mountains or foothills, as they call it, and about the only employment was either the furniture business or teaching. My dad worked for the Broyhill Furniture Company for about forty years and I had an opportunity to learn the value of hard work.

Mostly, I have fond memories of roaming around the mountains with my brother and sisters. My sisters were eight and nine years older than I and they taught me how to read before I started first grade. I guess my first grade teacher thought I was smart because I came to first grade already reading. We spent many a day sitting on the creek bank fishing, or down by the river, exploring our mountain world. We would leave home in the morning and our mother would tell us we needed to be back home about dark thirty because that was when supper was going to be on the table. I guess you could say we lived a Mayberry RFD kind of existence. It was a simple world back then. We hitchhiked about everywhere we went and no one ever heard of a pedophile. We never even considered being out alone as being dangerous. The entire community watched out for us. They may not have known which one I was, but they knew I was one of Carroll Winkler's kids and word of my behavior always managed to get back to my mama before I arrived home. I also loved sports and took part in football, basketball and hiking, but my favorite was baseball, and it still is. I am an avid supporter of the Asheville Tourist Baseball Team and can usually be found at the park every time the Tourist are in town.

I was fortunate enough to have several good teachers in elementary as well as in high school who served as positive role models. Most of my teachers had high expectations and that was what I needed. I needed someone to put the yoke around my shoulders and steer me in the right direction. They said they recognized in me some type of quality and suggested that I should pursue that and become a teacher. I have no idea what they saw; maybe they suffered from some type of astigmatism or something; but I attempted to follow their suggestion. Someone asked me once how old I was when I decided what I wanted to be when I grew up; my reply was that I have never actually grown up. In fact, I have been told that several times over the years.

Dorland Winkler,
Malvern Hills, 8/12/11

TEACHERS WITH BIG HEARTS

In the sixth grade, I had a wonderful teaching principal; she was so kind to my family and I. Mrs. Burdette selected me to be a patrol and would stop by my house in the morning about 6:30 to take me to school. Arriving so early in the morning allowed me to pop popcorn for the school. She also put me to work in the cafeteria washing trays so I could have a hot meal. I loved to grade papers after school. Mrs. Burdette was a tough teacher, but had a big heart.

In high school I had an awesome shorthand teacher. She often told me that I would make a wonderful first grade teacher because my handwriting was so large and clear.

Miss Lee would take her lunch time to visit and discuss with me about any concerns or problems that I might have with homework.

Dr. Judy Pierce,
Winston Salem, 6/15/11

THE RIVER RUNS THROUGH IT

As a kid, the highlight of the week was going to Marshall. My Granny and I would often walk or hitch a ride. Marshall was the main gathering spot for many families. The benches in front of the courthouse were all filled with people catching up on the latest news. I still have fond memories of getting a hamburger or a milkshake at the Rexall Drug Store lunch counter . . . they were the best.

One interesting place in Marshall was the school on the island. Marshall High was another school in Madison County. I am sure you have heard the saying "The river runs through it." Being surrounded by the French Broad River on two sides was both wonderful and dangerous. When we would get a big rain and the river got up, it would literally run through the middle of the school. Since then, they have closed the school, but it is still open for retail stores.

Charles Cutshall, Sodom Laurel,
Madison County, 7/14/11

I LEARNED TO FOLLOW THE RULES

In high school, a group of choral singers of which I was a part, decided to stop for lunch before returning to school. This proved to be a bad decision and we all got detention for that one.

Julia Clark,
Biltmore Lake, June 2, 2011

I GREW UP A LONG WAY FROM ANYWHERE

I grew up living with my grandparents in the Mt. Sterling area of western North Carolina which was a long way from anywhere. This was before I-40 was built through the mountains, and the only way to get to Waynesville, North Carolina, which was across Catalochee Valley, was to travel through part of Tennessee on a narrow mountain road before heading east into North Carolina. Oddly enough, my dad's family went to Western Carolina College which was a teachers college at that time. My aunt and uncle were school teachers, but my uncle was killed during World War II and I don't think he got to teach very long. My family valued education very highly and my dad had to board with people in the Finds Creek community in order to attend high school and graduate. There was a one room school in our area, but it was only a one through eighth grade school with only one teacher. I never went to that one room school since we had moved to Waynesville by the time I started first grade. In Waynesville the school was just across the creek from my grandmother's house and the big kids would wade across the creek and carry me over when I was very young so I could go over there and have lunch with them. That was a very good experience for a little girl.

Sandy Caldwell,
Waynesville, Haywood County, 11/11/10

An Unusual Gym

Growing up in the Sodom Laurel Community, I attended Laurel School which was a grades 1-12 school. Most of us started together in first grade and then graduated together as seniors, all 24 of us. The total school population was about 250 to 300 students. The thing that really got me going was playing basketball in high school. Our gym was not a regular size gym. It was probably about half to three-quarters the size of a regulation gym. The odd thing about the gym was it had exposed support beams that supported the roof of the gym. At one end of the gym, the support beams really didn't come into play . . . however, the other end of the gym had a support beam that was directly above the foul line. It was interesting to watch the opposing team member get set and launch their foul shot only to have the ball hit the beam and fall harmlessly right back at their feet. At first, he didn't realize that the beam was our sixth man. Not only did we practice our plays, but also practiced shooting over and under the beams. As a team, we could really play competitively with any team in that small gym, but when we went to their gym, we were already blown out and winded by half-time because of running up and down a regulation court. Another lesson we learned early on was when we were fast breaking, we had to learn to put the brakes on really fast or we would be up on the stage with the fans. Well, one night we were fast breaking and one of the referees was back-peddling, thinking he was in a regulation size gym, he didn't brake, and knocked himself out as he hit the wall full force. The next time he refereed our game at our gym, he ran slower and faced the wall to avoid the same outcome.

Charles Cutshall, Sodom Laurel,
Madison County, 7/14/11

SOMETIMES WE JUST GO WHERE WE ARE LED

I really never intended to get into the field of education. I majored in Bible at David Lipscomb College and was working with the church full time. When a principal friend of mine who was a member of the church, had a teacher get fired about three days before school was supposed to start for stealing gas out of a state motor vehicle. He asked me if I would come and help him by teaching in his school. I had a degree, but I didn't have teaching certification; but I worked with him for three years. It was a very small school of about seventy-five kids in one through twelve and I taught nearly everything in grades nine through twelve. During that time I decided that if I was going to stay in education, I would at least have to get my teaching certification.

I enrolled in Western Carolina University to work on my certification since I had grown up in Sylva, North Carolina, about ten miles from the university and it felt like going back home. One of the professors there was Dr. Kilpatrick and he talked me into continuing to get my masters degree. I received my masters as well as my principal's certification.

Next, I took an assistant principal's job at Pisgah High School in Canton, North Carolina and only stayed there one year before moving on to the University of Tennessee in Knoxville and receiving my Doctor's degree. Following my degree, I worked at an architectural institute in Nashville, Tennessee, designing school buildings. After building a couple of buildings in western North Carolina, I accepted a position as high school principal at East Henderson High School in Hendersonville, North Carolina.

So, you can see I didn't start out to make a career in education. But I had several family members who had graduated from Western and were in education, so it was a likely choice that I would end up spending thirty-three years in the profession.

Thomas Ledbetter,
Hendersonville, 4/ 13/ 2011

THESE ARE FOR OLD PEOPLE

In the mid to late 1950's, my siblings and I attended elementary school in Rocky Mount, N.C. My younger sister was extremely shy, obedient, and never gave my parents any problems. However, she was very nervous upon entering the second grade and was having trouble with her class and home work. Upon learning that she required glasses, she went into a "meltdown" and refused to wear them. My parents tried everything from my father getting a pair of glasses to punishing her, but nothing worked. Her glasses either broke or disappeared and could not be found at home, school, church, relatives' nor friends' homes. My parents finally gave up (which was very unusual for my parents—no such behavior was every allowed at our home!) and the teacher moved her to the front of the room. Imagine everyone's surprise at the end of the school year, when four pairs of glasses mysteriously were located in the cloak room among other lost items!

Beth Carter,
Garner, 5/1/2011

ON THE ROAD AGAIN

I began my career in the public schools of North Carolina. During that first year, we missed the entire month of January because of snow and I had two accidents during that winter. It was very dangerous for anyone to drive in that type of weather, but especially for a twenty-one year old girl driving alone through those lonesome mountains. After one year, I moved to South Carolina and taught for three years.

Although I enjoyed living in South Carolina, I was assigned to six different schools and was on the road continuously. Three years later, I moved back to North Carolina and took a job where I taught for the next five and a half years. It was a good thing that gas was not as expensive back then as it is now.

Anonymous,
Western North Carolina, 5/6/2011

I DREAMED OF SCHOOL

The desire to teach was with me from my very first memories. I loved playing school when I was a little girl, even "rock school," and my teachers were my idols. Most kids in my classes counted off the days until summer vacation each year, but not me. I dreaded summer vacation because I would not be allowed to attend school. Going to school was wonderful and I could hardly wait to see the sign on the door telling me who my teacher would be, who would be in my class for the upcoming school year, and to smell the clean building and the newly oiled floors. By the time school started, I had arranged my pencils and paper a million times, just dreaming of the action the new year would bring.

Sue Harris,
Hominy Valley, April 26, 2011

THE GIRL WAS NOT LAUGHING

When I was in third grade, a group of my "buddies" and I decided to tie a girl up to a tree in the woods behind the school for a joke. When our exploit became public, we all had to sit in the principal's office after school for a week. NOT FUN!

Julia Clark,
Biltmore Lake, June 2, 2011

UNCLE BOB WAS MY ROLE MODEL

I had a very close knit family and they always expected me to go in the field of education. Whenever anyone in the family would have a birthday, we would all get together for a meal and celebrate his or her birthday. I had an uncle Bob who was a principal and everyone held him in high regard. He was sort of a role model for the family and I always wanted to be like him. I didn't question the fact that I was supposed to go into education. Although, I wanted to be my own person and since I was attending a Methodist school, I decided to become a Methodist minister. So, after graduation, I attended a Methodist College with plans to become a minister. While there, I had a miserable experience with a minister at my home church. He was kind of a crazy guy and nobody liked him and I don't think he liked being a minister. After my experience with him, I decided that being a minister was not for me. Therefore, I fell back on my respect for Uncle Bob and decided to become a teacher. That worked better for me anyway because at College in Ohio, I decided to major in mathematics. Although when I hit the higher math courses, I decided that I just didn't want to spend my life studying math and changed my major to comprehensive science and became a biology teacher.

Larry Liggett,
Skyland, Buncombe County, 7/21/11

GROWING UP AS A MOUNTAIN BOY

When I was in the lower elementary grades, I attended a two teacher school that was about a hundred yards from my house and served around sixty or seventy children. Several of my relatives had taught at this school in earlier years and my aunt was one of my teachers. My uncle said he could never get away with anything at school because his teachers were always his relatives. Although, being a very small school had its advantages. For one thing it was close to my home. I could walk home for lunch each day. When I was in fifth grade I had the job of building fires in the big pot bellied stove in the middle of the room. Another part of my job was to go over and check on the school during Christmas breaks. I remember one year I went over to check and a pipe had broken in the kitchen and there was about six inches of ice on the floor. They had to redo everything before school started back in January. I believe we got along as well if not better than some of these fifteen hundred or two thousand student schools that we have today.

Thomas Ledbetter,
Hendersonville, 4/13/2011

I DREAMED OF BEING A TEACHER

I can't tell you exactly why I got into teaching, but I have thought about it just about all my life. I figured when I started that I would teach music but, after we moved up here from Florida and applied for a job, they said I would have to be certified in the classroom. I started traveling to Western Carolina University at night to get my hours and became certified. I was hired to teach fourth grade at Rankin Elementary in Asheville and that became my favorite grade.

Sue Harris,
Hominy Valley, April 26, 2011

I REACHED OUT TO A CHILD IN NEED

Back when I was still a kid living in the project over in Shiloh, I knew this kid who just needed a friend. He was a kid who everybody wanted to pick on; they made his life miserable, always beating him up and calling him names. He looked funny too, with big feet. Others in the projects made his life miserable. Looking back, he was like those boys at Columbine who came to school and killed all those people. He was a crisis waiting to happen. The only thing I could do at the time was to just be his friend. He and his sister lived with a woman there in the projects and they were even poorer than my brother and I. The foster "mom" would get money for taking care of them, but she never packed them much lunch and they never had what that needed. He always had knots on his head where his "mom" had hit him on the head. She eventually sent him off to a boys' school even though he was always a good boy. He spent over a year there and when he came back my brother and I were still his friend. I felt sorry for him and went out of my way to be his friend. Whether our unconditional friendship made a difference in his changing his stars or not, but he was able to turn his life around and is now a manager of a large McDonald's restruant chain.

I had this Latino boy when I was working at the Swannaoa Juvenile Center that I really feel I made a major difference in his life. He had a lot of problems and I let him know that I believed in him and showed him how he could become a leader and not a follower. When he realized I really cared, he changed his life and now has several businesses in south Asheville and is very successful. Every time I meet him, he gives me a hug and lets me know that he will always be there for me if I ever need help.

I remember this one boy, I will call him Mack, who was at the Detention Center and when he got out he came back to campus and asked to speak to me. We had a rule that once a person left the center he could not come back on campus; so I sent him word to wait outside and I would come out to see him. He asked me if I would let him come live with me. I realized that to do that would encourage his dependence on me rather than accepting responsibility for himself. I did take him home with me and made him a bologna sandwich and took him out to a bridge and gave him two dollars. I told him he could go over to the store on the other side of the bridge and buy himself a coke and eat his sandwich, pick up a box and come back up on the bridge and beg for money; or he could hitchhike back to Hendersonville like he got over there and go back to his job. I felt that if I gave in to him, I would enable him to not face his own responsibility. Sometime one has to know when to use tough love. He went back the way he had come over and succeeded once he accepted his own responsibility.

Ron Lytle,
Woodfin School, Oasis program, April 28, 2011

If I Became a Teacher I Could Go Into The Teachers' Lounge

I grew up in a little mill town called Lawndale, North Carolina where almost everyone worked at the cotton mill. The school was the main part of the community. It was a very small community where everything was close together; like here was the school, here was your home, and here was your church. People just didn't go into a big town because everything one needed was close by. There was no kindergarten at that time and there was only one teacher for each grade one, through six. The only children who went to pre-school were the more wealthy children who may have attended a private kindergarten, but I wasn't one of those. My family had everything we needed, but we were a mill worker family.

The thing I remember most about when I started school was how the teachers looked, acted and dressed. It was as if they were special and everyone respected their teacher. There was no teacher assistant at that time, just the teacher in her room and everybody had great respect for that teacher. Also, most parents told their child's teacher that if they got into trouble at school they would be spanked and if they got a spanking at school, then they would get another one when they got home. I remember as I walked down the hallway at school I would pass by the teachers' lounge. The door would be open just a little and I would take a peek inside; I could see the drink machine and the chairs where the teachers sat and talked. I knew, even at that time, I would become a teacher so I could go into the teachers lounge. Years later, after I became a teacher, I realized what drew me to the teaching profession was the teachers' lounge. I know that the teachers' lounge is the place one should avoid because that is where most school problems get started, but at that time in my life, it was where I wanted to be. As I got older, I just felt like I really had a gift to work with children, especially children who had problems; so I decided that was what I wanted to do with my life. I knew I did not want to do what most people in the community did and work in the cotton mill. I did that as a teenager and realized that I did not want to do that for the rest of my life.

My family's house was right next door to the church where my daddy was the caretaker. That was a big part of my life. We went to church regularly and I taught Sunday School every Sunday. I felt, since I wanted to teach and with my church background, that I would go into Christian education. My mom and dad told me they would send me to college for free if I wanted to go and if I did not get married until I finished. I just couldn't make myself let my parents pay two thousand dollars a year to go to Gardner Webb College, so I decided to attend Western Carolina College, where it was cheaper. My parents knew the value of having an education. My mom went through eighth grade and my dad maybe went through fourth grade. Mom and Dad grew up way up in the North Carolina foothills where there was very little value for education. Almost everyone had to work on the farm in order to help make a living so they wanted me to get an education. I was the only one of their children who went to college. One of my brothers went to work at Pittsburg Glass Company and worked himself up to a very high position. Two of them were drafted into the army and one took advantage of the GI Bill after he left his tour.

I believe teachers coming out of college today are so much more prepared than they were when I finished school. They have a much stronger support system and are more open to learning new things, especially technology. There are some older teachers in the profession today who are not open to change. In today's world, one must be open to trying new things if he is going to succeed in helping children; mainly, because children and families are constantly changing and so are their needs.

Jan Lunsford,
Averys Creek, Buncombe County, 12/2/10

WHEN THE CAT IS AWAY THE MICE WILL PLAY

In Junior High School in rural N.C. in the early 1960's, my eighth grade classes were separate from the rest of the first through twelfth grade school. One day, some students arrived at school before our three teachers. As a result, we became slightly rambunctious and started throwing a softball back and forth in one of the classrooms, breaking a window. Upon being caught by a very frustrated and outraged (it was the 1960's) teacher, we were required to write—"The mice will play when the cat is away! I am a RAT!!"—two thousand times. I never played in a classroom again.

Beth Carter,
Garner, 5/1/2011

I HAVE ALWAYS ENJOYED WORKING WITH KIDS

Back when I was fifteen or sixteen years old, I began to have some interest in becoming a teacher. I had an uncle who was Superintendent of Schools in Eden, North Carolina who kept encouraging me. Also, I was working with some children in a program from the Lions Club where they actually paid me some money to go there and basically play baseball with them. I really enjoyed working with those children and from about sixteen years old, I knew I wanted to be a teacher. I never wavered from that as I attended college, nor when I got my first job teaching. I realized that a lot of teachers give up their profession in a short time, but I have always enjoyed working in the educational profession. I have always enjoyed working with kids and still do. Even though I am retired, I still work with an after-school program.

Charlie McConnell,
Sylva, 6/17/11

I REALIZED MY MISSION WAS TO HELP A CHILD

When I was fourteen years old, I worked in a recreational facility where we offered kids positive activities. One thing which helped me greatly was serving in the Jr. Elk's drill team. The experience with the Drill Team helped me develop much needed structure in my life. Growing up in Kingsport, Tennessee, the drill team allowed me to travel all over the state preforming with the team. Later, I attended Warren Wilson College just east of Asheville, North Carolina and have been in and around Asheville ever since.

Early on, I worked construction for three years and that taught me a lot, but most of all it taught me I didn't want to spend my life working construction. I admire people who work in construction, but I found it was not where I needed to be.

When I began my college education at Warren Wilson College outside Asheville, I was planning to major in math. I loved working in the area of math even in high school and had taken all the higher level math courses available, but Warren Wilson did not have a strong math program so I ended up taking several social work classes. Once I got into the field of social work, I knew this was where I belonged. I ended my work at Warren Wilson with a triple degree, sociology, psychology and elementary education. Following graduation in 1974, I was hired by Asheville City Schools where Dr. Holcom and I formed the Optional School for Asheville City Schools to help curb dropouts or to work with those who had already dropped out of school. After about six months, I was informed that the budget would have to be cut, and since I was paid with half state and half federal, I was concerned my position would be cut, so I left. The way it worked out, everyone was hired back but I felt I needed more security with my family and all, so I took a position at the Juvenile Detention Center in Swannaoa near Asheville. I worked there until I retired in 2005 after thirty-two years.

Working in the facility at Swannaoa took a special breed of people. To quote my secretary, "When you work in a place like this you get locks, clocks and broken hearts." One must remember when working with this type of children, that they come from abused or neglected situations or they have been influenced by others in their peer group and then they go down an avenue of criminal behavior that winds them up with us at Swannanoa. But, some of the most wonderful people I have ever worked with were some of the children who had to spend time at the Detention Center and later turned their lives around. Looking back over the years, the little children I now work with in the Oasis program are like little angels, and that is how I see them.

There have been many programs employed across the nation to help the at-risk child. I remember the "Scared Straight" program where we used to take our kids from the Detention Center down to Morganton to visit the state prison, hoping that seeing the reality of prison life would shock them into getting their lives in order. But, what I found out was that these children actually looked up to the prisoners as role models due to their backgrounds on the street. They actually wanted to go to prison because they had so many people in their backgrounds from their families and the streets who were there or had been there that they looked forward to the experience. In my opinion "Scared Straight" did not work. They seemed to look at the trips as "old home week" and it became like a revolving door for many of those children. Our success rate was not very good. We had about a third who changed their lives, a third who we did not know if it made a difference or not and a third who went directly into the prison system. In my opinion, one of the reasons they shut the Detention Center down was due to the lack of success.

Although, there were success stories during my time at the Detention Center. One kid I remember got his life straight after he got out and is now a millionaire. He has his own business of laying fiber-optic lines across the state.

Another thing I learned was that most people who came out of the Detention Center would offer me respect whenever we would meet on the street. There seemed to be no hard feelings against me because I always tried to show them respect and for the most part they showed respect in return and call me "Mr. Ron" whenever we met.

Part of my job at the Detention Center was to work in a camping program where I could teach life skills. Programs such as this teach the person to plan and make decisions. For example, if the kid eats all his four day supply of food in three days then he would get really hungry on the fourth day because he would have no food. If I showed him how to put up his tent and he decided to put it up wrong, when the rain came, he was going to get wet. My job was to teach the kids life experiences and that they were responsible for the decision they chose to make in life.

I had this one kid who really impressed me by wanting to turn his life around. He had a drinking problem and had been in and out of the local jail several times for disorderly conduct. I had met his daddy and he also had a drinking problem. The young man did turn his life around and now has his own business. He still respects me, and although he is close to fifty years old he still calls me "Mr. Ron." The camping program was a huge success. Most of the children who completed the program had success. They learned a lot about life and a lot about themselves.

One part of the camping program involved a solo night hiking trip where the kid would hike for an hour or two down a trail by himself in the dark. It is interesting how much he would learn about himself by just being out there alone and having time to think about himself and to contemplate his future. For some, it may have been the first time they had ever had a quiet time to really think about who they really were.

Ron Lytle, Woodfin School,
Oasis program, April 28, 2011

LOOKING UP TO AUNT MURIEL

Growing up in a rural part of Madison County called the Sodom Laurel community, I had several community adults who served as role models in addition to three of my aunts who were school teachers. I had an opportunity to spend a lot of time with my Aunt Muriel during summer and Christmas vacations and she proved to be my main mentor in becoming a teacher.

Charles Cutshall, Sodom Laurel,
Madison County, 7/14/11

HELP A CHILD FIND HIMSELF

I worked thirty-two years with Swannanoa Valley Youth Development under the direction of the Juvenile Justice system. When I retired, I started transporting kids all over the state of North Carolina; but feeling I had more to offer than being a bus driver, I accepted a position with Families Together Counseling where I could teach life and social skills to children. I realized this was an area where many kids needed support. After a while, a position with the Oasis Program opened up and I felt like I could provide more help to children in this position. The Oasis program has been going on for five years under the direction of Families Together and I have been with them four years. The Oasis program is an alternative class for children who need extra support in order to succeed. A child is allowed to attend the Oasis class for a specific period of time instead of attending his or her regular classroom. During this time, the child is provided individualized instruction with emphasis on behavior control.

Ron Lytle, Woodfin School,
Oasis program, April 28, 2011

GOD'S CHILDREN KNOW NO COLORS

I worked sixteen years as a secretary at Asheville Hosiery Company when I was just starting out; the hosiery company did not offer a retirement plan and I finally realized I needed to be building for retirement. I left the hosiery company and began work as a secretary in Doctor Daniels' medical office in Asheville for a while. While there, Joe Ramsey, a good friend of mine, suggested I explore working as secretary in Asheville City Schools where his wife Peggy was a teacher and he described the procedure needed to apply for such a position.

To make a long story short, I was hired as secretary and assigned to Hill Street School in downtown Asheville. The main reason I decided to work in the school system was the opportunity to be off in the summer with my six-year old daughter Lynn, who had just started school and I could drop her off at her school on my way to work and pick her up as soon as school was dismissed. Also, I would have a state retirement for my later years.

At that time Hill Street School was an all black school with Jim Penley, Principal, and a few teachers being the only members of the white race in the building except me. I never had any problem as secretary at Hill Street. I have always loved children and white or black made no difference. To me they were all sweet children and race made no difference what-so-ever. Later, Mr. Penley was transferred to South French Broad Jr. High School and Mrs. Bovine was assigned as Principal and I worked a year with her before being transferred to Vance Elementary school in West Asheville only a few blocks from my home. I remained at Vance Elementary until I retired in 1991.

Dot Bryson,
Malvern Hills, Buncombe County, 1/12/11

FALSELY ACCUSED

I attended high school in the early 1960's where "Miss Beulah" taught Latin. "Miss Beulah" was tiny but with the nature of a bull dog and we were all terrified of her. One day in her 9th grade class, during a Latin vocabulary pop quiz, "Miss Beulah" stomped to my desk, grabbed and shredded my paper, and threw it into the trash can, telling me to see her immediately after class. I was mortified, ashamed, crying, and utterly terrified. After class, I explained that I was not cheating but working on my Algebra homework from my previous class (I wanted to attend a game that night and my parents required all homework to be done before we went elsewhere). "Miss Beulah" gave me a hug, told me not to work on other subjects in her classroom and graciously explained the situation the next day in class. Thereafter, "Miss Beulah" was one of my favorite teachers.

Beth Carter,
Garner, 5/1/2011

THE YOUNG THINK THEY KNOW IT ALL

Back in high school I remember sitting in my biology class, and like an arrogant teenager, thought I could teach this class as well if not better than he's teaching. So, I decided I wanted to be a teacher. By the time I was a student at the University of Colorado, I decided I wanted to be an engineer until I realized that I did not feel comfortable with biology and really wanted to major in English. And as an English major it remotivated me to follow my original dream of becoming a teacher.

Darren Barkett,
Canton, Haywood County, 1/23/11

CHAPTER TWO

College Experiences

A Farm Boy Has Responsibilities

When I started college there were no co-ed dorms. Although, I remember in my second year I was at least in a building next door to a girls dorm. Nothing really stands out during those years since I wasn't much of a risk taker. There may have been a few weekends that I stayed on campus, but most of the time I went home to Madison County to help my dad on the farm. We had tobacco, hay, corn and cattle and I was needed every chance I could get to help out with the farm work. Of course, later in college I had a girl friend, but I won't go into that.

Fred Trantham,
Waynesville, Haywood County, 11/11/10

Living with The Hippies

I attended Western Carolina College in Cullowhee, North Carolina. They changed it to Western Carolina University when I was a Junior. I was unable to get in a dorm when I began college so I stayed in a small shack off campus with some other boys and we ended up staying there the full four years. This was during the 1960s and the "Hippie" movement was well underway. I remember one time I walked into the house and smelled something. I thought someone was burning something. It was the first time I had ever smelled pot being smoked. I walked on into the room and found them sitting round a strobe light quoting poetry.

The place was raided a time or two and the Jackson County Sheriff's Department knew all about the little shack. I never got into trouble, but a couple of the guys got into some serious trouble by breaking and entering up around Cashiers, North Carolina. The Sheriff raided the shack and they were arrested and finished their education in prison in Raleigh.

It was during that time that I became an early riser because that bunch of boys would party and raise hell until about two O'clock in the morning. So I trained myself to wake about three in the morning after they had passed out and there was quiet in the house as well as some hot water, in order to shower and get my studying completed before they awoke.

It was during this time that some students at Western began to wear their hair long and wore beads around their necks and sandals on their feet. There were two who drove this old hearse and slept in the back during the night. They had dyed their hair purple which was an oddity back in the day. Today if one goes to Pack Square in downtown Asheville and does not see at least one person with purple hair it is odd.

Dorland Winkler,
Malvern Hills, 8/12/11

THE STORM

I did not get to go home very often while I was in college. East Carolina was a long drive especially since I-40 was not completed at the time. I made many friends while at East Carolina College. One is my best friend ever and I really feel a part of her family. When I attended East Carolina we had a curfew where we could not be out after a certain time and were required to study a certain number of hours each night.

Since there were no phones and, of course, no cell phones we were pretty much isolated from our families. I remember one time there was a hurricane that came through the area and, being from the mountains, I had never experienced even a tornado much less a hurricane. I got really scared and a little homesick and walked to a local phone booth and called my mom crying and asked her to come get me and take me home. She said for me to give it a day or two and then we will decide. By that time the storm had passed and I had calmed down.

Sandy Caldwell,
Waynesville, Haywood County, 11/11/10

CARRYING THE JAPANESE

One time we had these Japanese foreign exchange students who lived in the dorm where I was counselor. Being foreign exchange students they had different rules than the regular students on campus. Since we were a Methodist college, drinking alcohol was prohibited. Although, since there was a liquor store right around the corner from campus, the Japanese students bought themselves some liquor and, when I did my night inspection of the dorm, I had to carry one of them inside. He was smashed and I had to lay him down in the bathroom on the cold floor, face down, so he would be as comfortable as possible and let him sleep there through the night.

Larry Liggett,
Skyland, Buncombe County, 7/21/11

COW PATTIES IN RADIATORS?

The Mars Hill College Upward Bound program helped me adjust to college life prior to graduating from high school. This program was held each summer at Mars Hill College and served high schools students from several districts. It was there that I met many adults who still are heroes to me: Dr, John Hough; Dr. Bill Sears; Dr. Vernon Chapman and Charlie Phillips.

Following my senior year in high school, I entered college at Montreat Anderson Junior College and then finished my BA Degree in Education at Mars Hill College in 1975. Both schools were very strict in nature. However, it never kept us from midnight raids on the girls' dorms, short-sheeting beds with raw eggs in the foot of the bed, placing cow patties in radiators of rival students, putting dead snakes in desk drawers and stealing all the trays from the cafeteria to use as sleds when it snowed.

Charles Cutshall, Sodom Laurel,
Madison County, 7/14/11

Now This Was Bad

The college where I attended was a ministerial school as well as a music school. I had the privilege of hearing some wonderful concerts while attending school.

I joined a fraternity while I was in college and of course I had to enter as a pledge. One time a group of us pledges took all the toilet paper out of the fraternity house. Also, before we did that, we presented all the active fraternity members a big plate of chocolate chip cookies. Instead of chocolate chips we substituted X-Lax. When the active members came in they pigged out on those delicious cookies before going to their meeting. After they left, us pledges decided to move all the commodes and proceeded to take all the commodes out of the house. So, when they returned to the house there were no commodes and no toilet paper. We pledges just sat back and enjoyed the show. Most of them ended up the next day sitting in the infirmary taking paregoric. As soon as they got back to the house the announcement came over the speaker, "All pledges to the porch!" That was also when they made paddles and drilled holes in them to paddle the pledges. We were told to stand up and take our punishment, but when it came to me, since I was a track member, the fraternity member who was assigned to paddle me told me to start running and every time I stopped he would swat me with the paddle. I stayed ahead of him most of the time but he did catch up with me and I got a few licks on the butt.

Larry Liggett,
Skyland, Buncombe County, 7/21/11

I WENT FOR THE GOAL

I attended Western Carolina College from 1974-1978 and had to work very hard to succeed. I have always thought that today they would have most likely classified me as having a learning disability because I had to read things over several times in order to learn. I had to work harder than many others in order to succeed, but I did succeed. My only regret is that I did not continue on to get my Masters Degree. When I finished my undergraduate degree I was tired and also planning to marry. Of course, after my son Elliot came along, I didn't want to give up the time I needed to spend with him. I always encourage my student teachers to finish their Graduate Degree before they stop.

Jan Lunsford,
Averys Creek, Buncombe County, 12/2/10

I Became BMAC

While I was in college I was elected president of my senior class and also inducted into Pi Delta Kampa which was the educational honor society. Being a member of all the activities, I soon became the BMOC-Big Man On Campus, and as such, I was able to gain the attention of a beautiful young lady by the name of Dixie whom I later married and have lived happily with ever since.

Larry Liggett,
Skyland, Buncombe County, 7/21/11

Holding Off The Panty Raiders

My college experience was wonderful. When I went to college I wanted to be a part of everything going on and I signed up for track and cross country. One of the privileges of being an athlete was that I got to eat at the training table. So for the first two years in college I ate, and ate, and ate, but running for twenty miles daily kept my weight under control. Although, when I stopped competing in track, I began to put on weight because I continued eating everything around and with little exercise, I began to have a weight problem.

In college, I was appointed adviser and counselor of several things including dorm counselor. As with most colleges, there was an occasional panty raid. So, when there would be a panty raid, as counselor, I would have to go down to the girls' dorm and stand between the raiders and their target, as if we could really make a difference.

Larry Liggett,
Skyland, Buncombe County, 7/21/11

First Time On TV

I will never forget the first TV to ever be placed in a school room in Western Carolina University was in my classroom. Teachers from the Department of Education at Western came down and asked for a volunteer to have an Interactive TV placed in their classroom and be observed continually throughout the school day. No one volunteered and I held up my hand and said, "Turn it on and leave it on I don't care!" I was boastful back then. If I had it to do over, I wouldn't have said that. So, they placed the TV in my room. They placed a camera in my classroom and the college students would be on campus watching my teaching and then critique what I did. Well, after awhile, they got tired of watching me teach and wanted to watch other teachers teach. So, I had to pack up my kids and move to the music room or somewhere while the music teacher would come to my room to teach in front of the TV. One day they had wanted to watch the music teacher teach a music lesson and when I got there early one morning, she was already in the room sitting up for her music lesson. She plugged in something and the plug was dead. She went to the next outlet and plugged in and it also was dead. After trying all the outlets and finding them all to be dead, she, not realizing the TV was already on placed her hands on her hips and said, "This damn lesson is shot all to hell!" Some of the college students had already arrived to class and heard what she said. I think the teachers at Western handled it very well; they said, "Hey, these are humans too and we all make mistakes."

Charlie McConnell,
Sylva, 6/17/11

It Helps To Have Friends In High Places

I remember one time I got into trouble during my freshman year. We had very strict rules at the school and one of them was be be in the dorm by a certain time. A group of us girls came back to the dorm late. We returned a little late and I was called before the judicial board for a hearing. It wasn't all that bad because I had been sitting at the table with the chairman of the board. I never made that mistake again and was always in the dorm on time.

Julia Clark,
Biltmore Lake, June 2, 2011

MOUNTAIN MEN ARE TOUGH

When I was in school at Western Carolina University, I had an uncle who loved to fight. He ended up being a teacher, basketball coach and later a superintendent, but, early on, he really loved to fight. One time while he was a coach, a boy jumped on him as he was leaving the gym and a free-for-all took place. My uncle told me later he had never seen so many stars in his life, but when the fight ended and the combatants separated, they had to carry the boy who started the fight up the hill to his dorm and put him to bed.

Thomas Ledbetter,
Hendersonville, 4/13/2011

GIRLS WILL BE GIRLS

When I was in college, I attended a few parties during my first year since I had never been away from home before, but I soon learned that I needed all my time to finish my work. After all, I had been brought up in church and realized that the party life was a waste of my time. One of the wildest things I did was a bunch of us girls would have water fights on the fourth floor of our dorm. One time water had run all the way down to the third floor and they came up and made us stop. Another time we short sheeted another girl's bed several times and she was so gullible she would always believe us when we told her we had not done it.

Jan Lunsford,
Averys Creek, Buncombe County, 12/2/10

STUDENT TEACHING

When I was doing my student teaching, I worked at Little Canada School way up in the mountains. We were not wealthy when I was growing up, but the people in the Little Canada community were so poor that they hardly ever left the community. They were so far back in the sticks that you could almost hear the "Deliverance Theme" as you went up the road. I was convinced that a lot of people up there probably married their cousin. Many families still had homes with dirt floors. The children were expected to attend school, by their parents, through the sixth grade, but when it came time for them to go down the mountain and attend the school in Cullowhee, they were not for it at all. Going down the mountain to Cullowhee was "going to town," and none of the children I had in my class ever attended school higher than what was offered in the community because the parents didn't want their children under the influence of the town folks. When they were assigning schools for our student teaching, no one wanted to go to little Canada. Two other girls and I volunteered to work in that school. Even then I realized those children needed my help. When I got to the school, my room was a K-one-two classroom with twenty children-three grades and only twenty children. One day children started running up and down the halls screaming at the top of their lungs. I asked what in the world was wrong and found out that a weather balloon had landed in the school house yard. Some of the teachers were as afraid as the children. We had to explain to them that we were not being attacked from outer space.

Another school I worked in during my student teaching was the Log Cabin School located up toward Cherokee. The winter I worked at the school it snowed almost every day. I had to either learn to drive my sixty-four Chevy in the snow over those mountain roads or I would never get back to campus.

Jan Lunsford,
Averys Creek, Buncombe County, 12/2/10

SOMETIMES IT JUST DON'T PAY TO CHEAT

One of the funnest stories that happened while I was in college-well, it wasn't very funny to the boy I will tell you about was when I was working on my masters degree at Western. There was this young man in class who was from western North Carolina, but was living in Florida. He needed a class for Florida certification and he had come back to the mountains to get it. Well, he was just a little lazy to say the least. He did nearly nothing. If he could get another person's work or anything he would copy it and turn it in as his own work. One day he got a chart from me and just traced it exactly without making any changes. He couldn't have taken a test on the material because he didn't know anything about it. It wasn't long before he was required to complete a problem that would take about four hours to complete, if you knew how to do it. He then had to present his work in front of the class. Dr. Kilpatrick had told me in private that the young man was going to find out how easy it was to fail in graduate school if he continued cheating. Well, he handed his paper, torn out of a composition book to Dr. Kilpatrick in front of the class and Dr. Kilpatrick took it and ripped it right down the middle and handed it back to him saying, "This is not acceptable." The young man was flabbergasted. He just turned around and stared at the class as if he didn't know which way to go. I think he ended up getting a "D" in the class which received no credit. But, he deserved it by not being willing to work.

Thomas Ledbetter,
Hendersonville, 4/13/2011

A Great Man And A Great Friend

One of my professors and friend was Dr. Trever who later became one of the people to travel to the middle east as an archeologist and had a part in the discovery of the Dead Sea Scrolls. My college experience was a very good experience and I met many good people who helped me along the way and helped me find my true path in life.

Larry Liggett,
Skyland, Buncombe County, 7/21/11

When Kennedy Died

In November 1963 I traveled to an elementary school in Charleston, WV to complete field experience. While there, we heard that President John F. Kennedy has been assassinated. It was so terrible. All of the children and teachers were sad.

Dr. Judy Pierce,
Winston Salem, 6/15/11

BASKETBALL WAS MY LIFE

I never wanted to go anywhere but to Western Carolina University. Back in the 1960s Western was booming and the attendance was running over. There was no room in the dorms so I had to live off campus which was bad. I wasn't prepared for college. I had goofed off in high school and it was tough when I started college. I went back home on the weekends which I really do regret that now. I remember how wonderful it was to eat in the cafeteria. I loved cafeteria food. Being a country boy, I had never eaten French toast. I kept seeing what I thought was a piece of bread with syrup on it and when I tried it, it was good.

I remember this one boy, Henry Logan who played basketball at Western, and he was probably the first black to play basketball at Western Carolina University. He was like a little Michael Jordan. I remember when Western played in a tournament in another southern state and they would not allow Henry to play in the tournament because he was black.

My life just revolved around basketball. Jim Gudgger, our basketball coach, was such a great guy. We loved him and would have done anything for him. I had this desire to be the one who rang the victory bell after we had won a game. I would leave the gym early in order to rang the bell, but before I could get there someone would ring it. I finally got my chance to ring it and did probably three more times. It was nothing spectacular; I was just enjoying life and would like to do it again. Some people say they are glad to get out of college, but I really enjoyed it and would do it again in a minute.

When it came time to graduate, I was afraid I would not make it. I had heard stories about some students being pulled out of the graduation line at the last minute and I was terrified that this might happen to me. During our practice for graduation, I was told that I would be standing right here and I knew I was going to make it. I let out a big sigh of relief.

Charlie McConnell,
Sylva, 6/17/11

THUNDER ROAD

There was this one boy who attended Western Carolina University who was a pretty good old boy, but he had been picked up when he was younger for hauling moonshine. He had a forty-nine Chevrolet Fleet line that had the back seat out and a tank installed where the seat was suppose to be so he could haul his moonshine. That car had been souped up and could run about one hundred and forty miles an hour. That was in 1956, and nothing on the road could catch him. Finally, they caught him and he was in the penitentiary over at Craggy Prison near Asheville. They agreed to let him out of prison provided that he go back to school. While he was going to school at Western I rode back and forth to school with him for more than a year. He was a good driver. He could be going down the road about fifty miles an hour and slam on his breaks and do a 180 degree turn and proceed on in the opposite direction without ever stopping. We would cover that ten miles from my home in Sylva to Western in less that fifteen minutes on a very crooked mountain road. One day, a friend of his from Bryson City, North Carolina challenged him to a race. Of course my friend accepted. They went down the road to the only half way straight stretch of highway in that part of the mountains to prove their mettle. As they entered a curve that had to be at least a two hundred seventy degree turn, my friend was on the side near the river. As they exited the curve my friend passed him. The boy from Bryson City got out, slowly walked up to my friend and said, "Since you were on the side near the river, I eased up and let you pass me." "Oh sure," said my friend, "If you really believe that you let me pass you, let's do it again and this time you put your car title up here on the hood and I'll put mine up there and the person who wins will own both cars." After stammering around for a bit, the boy from Bryson City hung his head and walked off.

Thomas Ledbetter,
Hendersonville, 4/13/2011

A TRIBUTE TO COONY

One of the things I remember was having to wear a beanie. A beanie was a small skull cap that all freshmen had to wear as part of their initiation. We had to wear those things all the way to Homecoming, and every time we met an upper class-man we had to tip our beanies.

We had this man that would come on campus and he always acted kind of weird. Everybody called him Coony. Everybody knew Coony and he would bring big bags of candy to all the basketball players before the ball games. He thought he was sneaking in to all the games, but everybody had been told to let him in free. He would walk up to the gym door and turn and look over his shoulder to be sure no one was looking and then "sneak" through the door. He also dressed odd to say the least. He wore these two cap pistols, one on each hip and he had a beard. Well, we always hung out at the Townhouse Restaurant. It was the regular place to go and have a coke. One day I was sitting in the Townhouse with a friend and Coony came through the door with his two guns shining in the sun. I don't remember what we did, but soon we realized who he was and that he was harmless. I enjoyed going to the Townhouse. I could get a hotdog for a quarter, a coke for a dime and a pack of crackers for a nickle. We would spend our two hours between classes hanging out at the Townhouse. That is where we met our friends, who in many cases, became friends for life.

When I went to college I had no idea that we only went to so many classes during the day. I remember when my first class finished and everybody got up and left, I thought, my goodness, what do I do now?

Charlie McConnell,
Sylva, 6/17/11

I FOLLOWED THE PING–PONG TEAM TO COLLEGE

I had a math teacher in junior high school right after integration who helped me turn my life around; my brother and I had her for Algebra and she recognized we had a talent in the area of math. We had her for algebra 1, algebra 2 and algebra 3 and made an "A" in each class.

My brother and I also worked at a restaurant as bus boys and a man there told us about Warren Wilson College. He played ping-pong with us and informed us that they had a ping-pong team at Warren Wilson. He took us over to the campus where his daddy was a campus minister. We realized this was where we wanted to attend school following graduation from high school. My brother and I took out a student loan and took part in the work study program. It took us a long time to get the loan paid, but we finally succeeded.

It was a big challenge to move from the ghetto to working on a farm at the college. What did I know about a cow? I soon realized cows were not for me and I was assigned to working with the pigs. Even though the little pigs were smaller, sows and especially the big bore hogs were fierce with those big sharp tusks. I came to enjoy working on the farm and my brother still works out there to this day. While working with the pigs at Warren Wilson, we were engaged in a scientific study which followed the pigs from birth to the time when they were slaughtered.

I had no problem with any part of the study up unto slaughter time. I always became so attached to the pigs that I just could not help slaughter them; they became like my pets. I learned a lot during my time at Warren Wilson, but one of the main things I learned was that I did not want to spend my life working on a farm. I remember working on a combine machine and the dust would get in my eyes and nose until I could not see and even had trouble breathing. I finally realized that my calling in life was in a field where I could make a difference in the lives of young children.

Ron Lytle,
Woodfin School, Oasis program, April 28, 2011

LOOKING AT A HORSE'S ASS CHANGED MY FUTURE

My wildest experiences in college at Western Carolina University was working three hours a day in the gym for Coach Guddger. In high school, I was a pretty good basketball player and I got an invitation from Duke and also Wake Forest Universities, trying to recruit me to play for their teams. I was averaging about twenty-five or thirty points per game at the time. Midway through my senior year I got the worst case of the flu I ever had and had to stay in bed for a week. When I came back and started to play, I was still very weak. Well, of course, that was the time recruiters from both universities came to watch me play. I was so weak I could hardly make it up and down the floor and that was the last I ever heard from them.

After that experience, I was so discouraged I decided not to go to college, but to get me a job. During the summer I got a job with Mr. Brown who was Vice President at Western Carolina University at that time and he gave me a job working on his farm. One part of the job was to take this old horse and ride right through the middle of the campus and go plow out a corn field on the other side of the college. It was so big it took me three days to finish plowing. Every afternoon I had to ride right back through that campus. I would be soaking wet with sweat and that old horse would be lathered up with gnats swarming around his rear end, and, as I rode through campus I could see my high school buddies sitting around and I got to thinking that I had better go to college. So I went over to the Registrars Office and told the Registrar, Ms. Addie Beam that I knew I was too late to sign up for this first quarter, but I would like to go ahead and get my paperwork started for the next quarter. She said, "You are already enrolled." I interrupted her and said, "No, I haven't done one thing." She said, "Your guidance councilor has already brought all your paperwork over here and all you have to do is go to registration tomorrow and sign up for classes." I will never forget Dr. Mary Wayte for doing that. She always believed in me and believed I had potential. So, I ended up going on to college.

Charlie McConnell,
Sylva, 6/17/11

POSITIONED FOR AN OPPORTUNITY

Soon after I started at Western Carolina University, I went down to the gym and, although I didn't have a scholarship I played on the freshman team. I asked the coach if I could stay and practice with the varsity team when our season was over. He agreed to allow me to practice with the varsity team and that was the year they won the district championship and went to Kansas City and finished second in the nation. As I had been practicing with them for about three weeks after our season was over one Saturday morning, Coach Guddger called me and asked me to come on down to the gym to practice. I said, "Oh, are you practicing today?" He said, "Yes, we have to get ready for Kansas City and you're going. One guy just flunked out and you got his slot." So, I have been very fortunate. I could not make three pointers consistently, but if there had been a three point line, I would have been much more wealthy than I am today.

Charlie McConnell,
Sylva, 6/17/11

THE PANTY RAID

When I was at Mars Hill College, we had a panty raid. Though funny to some of us, it was not very funny to Dr. Jolly, and professor at the college. He said, "If you have time for such foolishness you can do some extra credit work." Everyone in each of his classes had to research and write the platforms of everyone who had run for president all the way back to the Whigs and Tories. It took forever, but I suppose we learned a lot.

Sue Harris,
Hominy Valley, April 26, 2011

DON'T JUDGE A BOOK BY IT'S COVER

One time at Mars Hill College, I came in to find everything in my room upside down. Someone had short-sheeted my bed and filled the bed with locust shells. I later found out that this was done by my room mate who looked like an angel, was a top honor student and a hall monitor. The house mother would never have believed she was so full of mischief.

Sue Harris,
Hominy Valley, April 26, 2011

BELLY UP TO THE BAR

At Women's College (University of North Carolina at Greensboro), my friend and I met two soldiers from Fort Bragg who took us to dinner at the corner diner. We ordered our dinner and they ordered a beer. My friend and I looked at each other and excused ourselves to go to the restroom. From there we were out the back door and ran back to the dorm. They had ordered a beer. "Yike!" We thought they must be horrible, dangerous people. Oh, how times have changed!

Sue Harris,
Hominy Valley, April 26, 2011

A MOUNTAIN GIRL GOES OFF TO SCHOOL

When I started college, I didn't really know what I wanted to do with my life. Being from a small mountain community, I didn't know what opportunities were open for girls. I know that sounds kind of nuts, but I had to think, "what am I going to do with my life?" That is always a difficult decision, but especially for a girl who had very few experiences outside the mountains. There are so many areas that are available today that were not available when I began college. I decided on the teaching profession because I had an aunt who was a teacher and it felt like the right path, but I didn't start out thinking I wanted to be a teacher. I see these young girls today saying I want to teach even in elementary school, but that wasn't the way it was with me. Looking back, I realize it was the best decision because I love teaching and I love kids. I went to East Carolina College for the first two years which is on the other side of the state and that was a long way from home for a mountain girl like me. I enjoyed my time at East Carolina, but decided to transfer to Appalachian College at Boone, which was closer to home to finish my undergraduate degree before going to Western Carolina University to complete my graduate work.

Sandy Caldwell,
Waynesville, Haywood County, 11/11/10

My Job Provided a Training Ground

In preparation for employment, I took shorthand and typing from a private teacher and then completed some secretarial courses at Asheville-Buncombe Technical Institute. Most of the training was on-the-job as I worked day in and day out with children and teachers.

Dot Bryson,
Malvern Hills, Buncombe County, 1/12/11

Reminiscing With An Old Friend

When I began college at Western Carolina, I had decided to major in physical education, but they had this physical education club on campus that met on a Monday night and I didn't know about the meeting and missed going. So, the next morning Dr. Sawart a retired military man called me and spoke with a very gruff voice. He said, "You missed this meeting and if you miss another one, you are out of the department for good." I said, "What if I am a senior and miss one?" To which he replied, "You are out of the department." I went that day and changed my major to elementary education.

I really enjoyed college and made many good friends. I ran into some of them a few weeks ago at a baseball game and it had been forty years since I had seen some of them. We reminisced a lot. One thing we did was to take canoes and paddle over to Goat Island and camp out over night and come back the next morning like boys will do. I asked one of my friends, "Glenn," I asked, "Do you remember Goat Island?" He said, "Not much, I was usually pretty drunk." He was right, he had drank beer all night on Friday and then went down to the baseball field on Saturday and tried to pitch in eighty degree weather. I will never forget it; he threw sixteen straight balls-walked the bases full and walked in a run. The coach went out to the pitcher's mound and, about that time, the sweat broke and the beer smell was coming out of him. The coach said, "Glenn, you are going to stay out here and pitch this game. I don't care if the score is one hundred to nothing. What is the matter with you?" Glenn, looking pretty green by that time said, "I'm having trouble seeing my catcher." Well, the sweat broke and he won the game eight to one.

Charlie McConnell,
Sylva, 6/17/11

SQUARE DANCING

While I was a student at Western Carolina University several boys would drive over to Clyde, North Carolina and get tanked up on beer and get back to the dorm about two or three o'clock in the morning. They would get my popcorn popper and cook soup when they came in. They would eat the soup and then start square dancing. They would always drag my roommate out of bed and he would have to be the woman in the square dancing.

Charlie McConnell,
Sylva, 6/17/11

My First Love, Or At Least I Thought So At The Time

Once I decided to actually go to college and not just try it out for a semester, I began to realize college could be a lot of fun, especially the girls. I had never had the confidence needed to get into a boyfriend/girlfriend relationship in high school. I was always the wall flower whenever I was around members of the opposite sex and always felt rejected. This all changed when I entered Lindsey Wilson College. During the first week of school, the college provided a hay ride one night with a wagon piled with loose hay being pulled by a tractor. Shortly after boarding the wagon, I met a cute blond who seemed to occupy my time the rest of the ride and for most of the following year. I remember the ride stopped at a local restaurant on the way back to campus for sodas and the blond and I were so engrossed in talking that we just stayed on the wagon and held each other. By the end of the night, this country boy thought he was in love.

J. Terry Hall,
Scott Mountain, Buncombe County, 3/3/11

When We Heard Let It Rip, We Did

As a freshman at Lindsey Wilson College, I was assigned a room on the third floor of the old dorm with three other boys. There were four of us in a twelve by twelve foot room. There was a small table with a lamp and four bunk beds stacked two high. Just outside our room, there was a fire escape that led down to a side street that came onto campus. Someone had a bright idea that if we took a container, filled it with a little water and poured it over the fire escape just as a car came up the drive, it would be fun. Well, as freshmen often do, we gave it some thought and decided if a little water would be a little fun then a lot of water would be a lot of fun. We set upon a plan. We would fill a twenty gallon trash can with water and three of us boys would carry it to the fire escape window while the fourth boy would be the lookout. His task would be to watch for a car entering campus and give us the signal where we would empty the can of water over the fire escape. It sounded like a good idea at the time. When the lookout gave the word, we heaved the heavy can over the edge just as an upper class man passed under driving his father's new Chevrolet convertible. Needless to say, the boy most likely felt like the Egyptian army felt when God Almighty allowed the Red Sea to crash back down on them as they followed Moses toward the Promise land. He waded out of his father's car and rushed to the third floor with malice in his heart. When he arrived, all guilty students were working hard at their desks trying to prepare for the next day's assignments.

J. Terry Hall,
Scott Mountain, Buncombe County, 3/3/11

Some People Are Beyond Gullible

I guess we are all gullible to a certain extent, but some folks seem to be wearing a big sign saying, "Sock it to me!" There was a boy named Dick in my freshman class who was so gullible that he would believe anything he was told. In addition to that particular trait, he was a small framed boy who wanted to be the king of the walk.

One day some boys decided to set him up. They told Dick that he was the strongest, most fearful boy in the dorm. They told him they just wanted to be sure he never got mad at them and tried to fight. They said they recognized his strength and just didn't want him to hurt them. He puffed up his chest and said he didn't have any reason to hurt them, but others better watch out if they messed with him. This went on for a couple weeks and Dick kept walking around with a swagger.

After about two weeks they said, "Dick, we heard that Joe down on the second floor said he could take you and you better not set foot on their floor." Now the second floor was where the upper classmen were housed and Joe happened to be a big old boy. One night they said, "Dick, I hear Joe is out in the hall bragging about how he is going to whip you. We think you need to go down there and teach him a lesson." Dick was enraged! He stormed out of the room and went straight to Joe's room. Keep in mind no one had told Joe about the ruse. Dick rushed up to Joe's door, banged on it and shouted for Joe to come out in the hall and fight like a man. When Joe opened the door, Dick charged him like a raging bull, knocking him against the wall. Joe grabbed Dick by his shirt collar with his left hand and the back of his belt with his right, picked him up and shoved his head through the sheetrock on the hall wall. All of us boys looking on were so shocked that we were ashamed and terrified that if Dick's head should have hit a two by four stud he could have been killed.

J. Terry Hall,
Scott Mountain, Buncombe County, 3/3/11

The Day My Future Became Clear

During my second semester at Lindsey Wilson College in the spring of 1961, I had an experience that made a major impact on my life. My education teacher and mentor, Catherine Rodgers, was always taking her future teachers to educational conferences across Kentucky. She had taken us in her own car at her own expense to conferences in Somerset, Bowling Green and Louisville. I especially remember her taking us to the Kentucky Education Association Conference in Louisville.

Growing up in the small town of Tompkinsville, Kentucky, I had never experienced the thrill of being in a big city for a purpose other than to visit a relative. Now here I was going to Louisville to attend the KEA conference. It is hard to put into words the awe I felt as I followed Mrs. Rodgers into that huge auditorium that day and took my seat among the hundreds of teachers and administrators from across Kentucky. Even though I had previously decided, with Mrs. Rodger's help, to make teaching my life long career, it had never really come home to me that I, James Terry Hall, could become a teacher just like these professionals and maybe, in some small way, have an impact on future generations. Although, over the next twenty-seven years, I completed many degrees including a Doctorate in Educational Administration, I never again felt as proud as I did on that day.

J. Terry Hall,
Scott Mountain, Buncombe County, 3/3/11

Hobnobbing With The In Crowd

During high school, I loved singing and participated in all the choral groups and sang in all the contests across the state and, especially, the Woman's College in Greensboro, where the state contest was held. So, when I began college it was only natural for me to go there. I really loved college and everybody seemed interested in me as a person. At that time, they had family style meals where everybody sat together and had their meals. They assigned my seat and I happened to be sitting at the table with the senior officers and the chairman of the Judicial board and got to know them on a personal basis. Being a lowly freshman and being able to sit with all these upper class girls, I thought it was fantastic.

Julia Clark,
Biltmore Lake, June 2, 2011

A Good Teacher Makes Her Class Fun

I had this one teacher who was retired from the military and she always called me "Red" because of my red hair. I had never liked to be called that, but with her it didn't really matter. She gave me a hard time. I remember one time she measured everybody's wrist and I had the biggest wrist of anybody in the class. I still have no idea what she was trying to teach by measuring our wrists.

Another teacher I had was Dr. Rodgers, who taught science. He was like a father to me and I took every class he taught.

Julia Clark,
Biltmore Lake, June 2, 2011

CHAPTER THREE

TEACHING EXPERIENCES

The Unique Principal

After I graduated and Mark and I married, I got my first job at Fairview Elementary. At that time, Fairview was a small mountain community and I was so happy there because I loved the mountains. This was the same school Mark had attended as a child and my mother-in-law was the school secretary. I felt like I was going home to be working at Fairview. Back then we could have fun at school. I remember one time I dressed up as a witch with a green face and went to school. It was amazing at some of the things we did to keep the children interested. The main reason I got a school at Fairview was because of the principal, Ronnie Sams. I always liked Ronnie because he was an old country boy who spoke his mind. Sometimes that got him into trouble, but you always knew where Ronnie was coming from and, what you saw was what you got. Most of what was wrong with Ronnie was he played favorites with his teachers and that is something that doesn't work with a bunch of women. Ronnie was one of a kind; one day he came on the intercom in the middle of the day and announced, "Ladies there is a truck load of watermelons out in the parking lot if any of you want to buy some." There we were teaching and he was selling watermelons.

Jan Lunsford,
Averys Creek, Buncombe County, 12/2/10

Here I Am Send Me

During my senior year at Western Carolina University, Dr. Ben Battle, Chairman of the Education epartment at Western, called everyone in who was scheduled to do their student teaching during the spring quarter and said that there was a schedule conflict. There were too many students scheduled to complete their student teaching in the spring quarter and, if anyone was willing to do their student teaching now, he would be able to place them in Asheville. That was very lucky for me because at that time I had a sister who lived in Asheville and that was free room and board since I could stay with her. I quickly raised my hand and was placed at Vance Elementary School in Asheville. I had no idea where Vance was located, but my sister and brother-in-law took me by the school and when school began, I walked up to Mr. Harold Haden, the principal, and said, "Here I am."

My experience during student teaching was very good. One thing I remember was that it snowed often during that winter and we only went to school about three days each week. The rest of the time I just kicked back and enjoyed it. When spring finally came I went back to Western and completed my classwork.

Dorland Winkler,
Malvern Hills, 8/12/11

AM I THE HEAD?

In addition to teaching, I also worked as supervisor of the gym for youth leagues and adult basketball teams. I was in the gym one afternoon when a man walked up and asked me if I knew where the "head" was. I really had never heard that term, so I thought he was looking for me . . . so I told him I was the head. Looking confused, he said, "I need to find the bathroom." Red faced I showed him to the bathroom.

Charles Cutshall,
Sodom Laurel, Madison County, 7/14/11

The Young Will Change The World

When I first moved to Buncombe County, I was young and headstrong and thought I was going to change the whole teaching world. My principal at Erwin Middle School, Andy Peoples, who was in his first year as principal, was patient with me and helped me realize that my task was to teach the students and not attempt to change the world. Although I had always thought I would teach in high school, I began to realize that middle school was where I seemed to best fit. Working in middle school is a special calling. It is a time in the child's life where they are thinking with their hormones much more than their brains. It is a time of turmoil and searching for their place in the world and it definitely takes a special type of person to work with middle school students. The middle school child has so much enthusiasm and if a teacher can channel that enthusiasm in a positive manner, the child will succeed. I have learned that students at this age need someone to hold them to a higher standard and to acknowledge their work and achievement of that standard in a positive manner. They need someone to guide them and to praise them for the successes in their lives.

Darren Barkett,
Canton, Haywood County, 1/23/11

The Teachers' Lounge Is A Dangerous Place

During my first year of teaching, I grew to hate the teachers' lounge. Every time I entered the lounge they were always complaining about their kids or someone else on the faculty. I decided early on to stay out of the teachers' lounge.

Larry Liggett,
Skyland, Buncombe County, 7/21/11

Let Me Think About That

After three years, I returned to the mountains of North Carolina. Looking for a job, I was set to interview at an elementary school in the Asheville City School System. I was ready, or was I? Joe McGuire, Principal at Jones Elementary at that time, was a wonderful man. Little did I know that Joe marched to his own drum beat. I prepared in advance for my interview and studied up on all the latest education trends of the day. I really went into the interview feeling prepared for whatever was to come. I took a seat and had all of the knowledge stored in my brain and ready to impress when Joe looked at me and said, "Charles, what would you do if one of your students told you to go to hell?" That just blew me out of the water and I could not remember a thing. I must have said the right thing. I got the job. Mr. McGuire gave me great support in growing my wings more as a teacher. One peculiar thing though, that Joe did was, in the middle of a conversation in the hall, he would just start walking away. I learned to get my important points or questions in at first before he started his journey. The teachers at Jones Elementary were fabulous! Through watching their teaching methods, I gained so much as a teacher.

Charles Cutshall,
Sodom Laurel, Madison County, 7/14/11

A Biology Teacher In Ohio

When I began teaching, I taught biology in a middle school in northeast Ohio. In my class, I had a black snake in a terrarium that I had named "Asphalt." I chose the name because it was his own fault that he got his ass caught.

As part of my biology class, I taught different phylum. I explained to my class that before we studied each phylum we would have to eat that particular animal. When we studied ants, we would eat chocolate covered ants. When we studied mollusk, we would eat squid. When we studied foul, we ate chicken. My rule was before we dissected the animal, we would have to eat it. I had a friend who would cook each animal and always fill it with garlic.

Beginning my teaching in northeast Ohio every time the wind blew across Lake Erie during the winter, we would get snow. This was before I was married and I rented a room in the upstairs of Ms. Wright's house. Being away from the main part of the house allowed me to slip in and out unnoticed any time I wanted; although, when it would snow, I would leave tracks and Ms. Wright would always know when I had been out.

Later, when Dixie and I decided to be married, we set a wedding date as soon as school was out for the summer. Well, the winter before we were to be married, we had even more snow than normal and all the snow days we missed had to be made up. Every time we had a snow day, the end of school was pushed farther and farther into the summer. When we were finally married, on a Saturday, I had to go back to work on the next Monday. So much for a long honeymoon.

Larry Liggett,
Skyland, Buncombe County, 7/21/11

Paying My Dues

Following graduation in 1975, I received my first teaching job at North Canton School, teaching a fourth/fifth grade combination class. When I walked into the classroom, it was not even set up for a classroom, just one large room. It wasn't a bad experience because they had set it up where I had advanced fourth graders to work along with the fifth graders. Another positive was they provided me with a couple of mentors and the principal provided me with the support I needed. There was also another male teacher in the school, which was rather unusual for that day and time.

Fred Trantham,
Waynesville, Haywood County, 11/11/10

A COUNTRY BOY GOES TO THE CITY

When I first drove through downtown Richmond, I thought this is great I could drive and not have to worry about traffic lights, or so I thought. Little did I know that the traffic lights were on posts along the side of the streets. I went all the way through downtown Richmond running every traffic light and, luckily, not being pulled over by the police.

We had twelve hundred middle school students at Hermitage Middle School, which were more people than any town in which I had lived at that time. My science room was wonderful. It had been a home economics room and was very large. The teachers were also very supportive and made me feel welcomed. They were like family.

Charles Cutshall,
Sodom Laurel,Madison County, 7/14/11

A HIPPIE COMES TO THE MOUNTAINS

Growing up in Colorado, it was understandable that I would attend college at the University of Colorado in Boulder. Although it took a large adjustment since I came from a small high school and there were classes at the university that were larger than my entire high school. After two years of having "fun" in my fraternity and Air Force ROTC, I realized I was not really going anywhere and didn't really know what I wanted to do; so I dropped out of school. During that year and a half, I sold shoes, worked in a hotel and waited tables. While that was all fine, I realized I was not going anywhere so I decided to go back to school and finish my degree in teaching. When I returned to school, I completely reinvented myself. I shaved my head and wore a bandana and people I had run around with didn't even recognize me. I went on to grow my hair in dreadlocks and continue the "hippie" look until I graduated. It was fun because for once I looked tough and I really wasn't tough; I just wanted to be different.

Following graduation, I bought a VW bus and my younger sister and I hit the road to discover what I really wanted to do with my life. After traveling the west coast a couple of times, the gulf coast, and then traveling up the east coast we arrived in Asheville, North Carolina, a town of which we had never heard. Continuing to travel north to Boone, I realized that this was where I wanted to live. During my traveling, I realized that most of the people I met along the road were really looking for someone to listen to them, understand them, and to help guide them toward a better life. I further discovered that I was able to give them something they had not thought of or give them information they needed at that point to help them find their way. It was at that point in my life that I realized there was something in me that wanted to help people by teaching them a better way to look at their life and that my road was leading me to be a teacher. After making my decision, I applied in Boone for a teaching position and was hired at Maple Elementary School in a fourth/fifth grade position. It is unusual I was hired since I still had my dreadlocks, but they most likely hired me because of the uniqueness of having a "hippie" working in a country mountain school.

Darren Barkett,
Canton, Haywood County, 1/23/11

AT LEAST I HAD A JOB

My first year as a teacher was pretty crazy because I was hired in an intern position without knowing it. In my interview, they failed to explain that the lady I was replacing was on maternity leave and, once she had her baby, I was to be paid as a substitute teacher for six weeks and then I was paid as a substitute for the rest of the school year. This affected my pay and caused a lot of confusion about whether I should work on teacher work days or stay at home like a regular substitute. Being classified as a substitute did not even allow me to have health care. I learned during that year the importance of not going over people's heads to try to get what you want. The action I took at that time made me look like I was going to be hard to get along with which was not the case. I soon learned that my experience was not too far out of scope as to how things are during the first years of teaching.

Elizabeth Middleton,
Candler, Buncombe County, 10/21/10

SHOOTING FROM THE HIP

I taught school for five years before I got my first principal's job. I taught in the Lab School at Western Carolina University and had fifth grade for the first two years; I taught seventh and eighth grade for the last three years. During the first year, I taught I did not have one clue about what

I was doing. I just tried stuff. I tried grouping kids: I had this one group over here doing this and another group over there doing that. The teacher who had the kids before must have done a good job, because at the end of the school year someone came in and said, "Charlie, your fifth grade kids scored better than any fifth graders in the county." Well, I just stuck out my chest and said, "Well, we work hard and bla-bla-bla." It felt good although I had no idea what I was doing. I went home that night and said to my wife, "Can you believe it, my class scored higher than any class in the county and I didn't know what the hell I was doing." In addition to teaching that first year, I coached junior varsity and varsity basketball after school. So, I spent every Sunday afternoon preparing lessons in order to be ready for my classes Monday morning. I worked very hard during that time, but I enjoyed teaching and the teachers I worked with were wonderful and helped me a great deal. I knew almost all the kids' parents and the kids knew if they got into trouble at school, they would get straightened out when they got home. I really enjoyed those years working at the Lab school.

Charlie McConnell,
Sylva, 6/17/11

EDGAR, HIRE THIS BOY

I did my student teaching at Laurel Elementary where I had attended school. My supervising teacher, Mrs. Rena Shelton, was a fantastic teacher! I still can picture her free handing all of her bulletin boards (true masterpieces) . . . alas as a teacher I bought mine commercially.

As I neared graduation at Mars Hill College, there was a major teacher glut with very few jobs available. To my rescue came Mrs. Rena again. She called her nephew who was a principal in Richmond, Virginia and said, "Edgar, you need to hire this young man." Now keep in mind that the largest city I had been to was Marshall, NC which at that time had one red light and, now I was going to be thrust into the big city life of Richmond. Talk about a country boy going to the city! I spoke with Dr. Wallin by phone and he invited me to come up and interview. So I loaded all my worldly possessions into my old Ford Galaxy 500 with a cracked windshield and headed out for truly worlds unknown. Following my interview, I went to work as a seventh grade science teacher in 1975. Little did I know that this wonderful experience at Hermitage Middle School would be the beginning of a wonderful career as a Teacher.

Charles Cutshall,
Sodom Laurel, Madison County, 7/14/11

ASHEVILLE VS. JUNGLE OF VIETNAM

At the time I did my student teaching in 1968, the Vietnam War was in full swing and they were drafting everyone. If you had a pulse and could walk straight, you were sent directly into the jungles of Southeast Asia. During my last week of student teaching, Harold Hayden, Principal of Vance School pulled me aside and said, "Would you like to have a job here next year?" I quickly thought, Vance Elementary in Asheville North Carolina teaching sixth grade vs. the jungle of Vietnam dodging sniper fire. I nearly hugged Mr. Hayden's neck as I excitingly said, "Yes!" He told me if I would go up to the Superintendent's office, he would have a contract for me to sign. I almost ran out of Mr. Hayden's office as I made my way downtown to the office of Superintendent, Woody Griffin. Mr. Griffin was sitting at his desk smoking his pipe when I entered his office. I had never even spoken to a Superintendent and was somewhat nervous as he slid a blank contract across his desk and said, "I have no idea where you will be placed next year but I know I will need several new teachers and if you will sign this contract, it will lock you in." I almost shouted, "Lock me in! Lock me in!" as I reached for the contract.

The day after I graduated, I was on a bus to Charlotte, North Carolina to be examined for the army. Mr. Griffin wrote the draft board a letter explaining that I was one of his teachers and was under contract and I was allowed to stay home. "Oh the joy of being locked in!" I am convinced somebody was looking after me.

Dorland Winkler,
Malvern Hills, 8/12/11

WE ALL NEED A SYSTEM

My first school was a fourth/fifth grade combination at Maple Elementary School outside of Boone, North Carolina. I was there for two years and during the first year, I had no idea how to keep control of my class. I would lose my temper and yell at kids and then go home feeling like a jerk for yelling at these sweet little kids. I will always be thankful for the principal that year. It may have been because of me, but most likely there were several teachers needing help; the principal offered a workshop on positive discipline. Most of the older teachers seemed to be bored since they had their system already in place, but this experience gave me a whole new perspective on dealing with discipline. It provided the system needed to maintain order and control in my classroom in a positive manner based on a system of rewards. It truly saved me as a teacher. In the years since, I have had so much success using this system that I have developed a workshop based on this positive reward approach and offer it to other teachers.

Darren Barkett,
Canton, Haywood County, 1/23/11

DID YOU SEE THAT BIRD?

In addition to my wonderful team members, I remember one teacher in particular named Betsy McCorkle, "Carol Burnette" reincarnated as a teacher. Once she had this boy who kept giving her a "bird" during class. Finally after several "birds," she looked at the boy and said, "Merry Christmas to you too!" A while later she was in the back of the room and heard him whisper to a boy one row over, "I'm not going to flip that teacher a 'bird' again, she thinks it means Merry Christmas."

Charles Cutshall,
Sodom Laurel, Madison County, 7/14/11

YOU ARE DIFFERENT

When I moved to Winston-Salem/Forsyth County Schools in North Carolina, I began teaching 4th grade in an inner city school in February to a group of students who today would qualify for special education. Of course, during those days, there was no special education, so teachers taught all children.

About three days into teaching, one young African-American girl stayed after school to ask me some interesting questions. She wanted to know how I washed my hair, did I roll it, and how I combed it out.

No student had ever asked me anything about my hair. Next, she asked, "Why do white people sit out in the sun?" Do they want to get black as I am?

Dr. Judy Pierce,
Winston Salem, 6/15/11

ASHEVILLE, N.C.—WAR ZONE

My first year of teaching was rather exciting. It was the year Asheville City Schools were integrated. In November of 1969 Mr. Hayden, Principal of Vance Elementary, called the teachers together and said, "They are rioting at Asheville High School. Windows have been broken and the police are roaming the halls. Lock your classroom doors and try to keep your children safe." We had known that was a possibility with African-Americans entering school with Caucasians for the very first time in history, and the name of the school having been changed from Lee Edwards High School to Asheville High School. There were bad feelings on both sides and the tension was so thick, one could cut it with a knife.

We had two such riots that spread from Asheville High to Asheville Junior High during that year, but it never spread to the elementary schools. This was when the school board announced we would have full integration in the middle of the school year. Toward the end of the school year, Mr. Hayden called us together and announced he was retiring and moving to his home in Candler, North Carolina where there would be more peace and quiet. It was also announced that all sixth grades would be moved to Hill Street School; therefore I would be at Hill Street. Since that was my first year of teaching, I didn't know any better; I thought every year was suppose to be like that. Little did I know that I would remain at Hill Street School for the next twenty years, first as teacher, then assistant principal and finally as principal.

This was my first time meeting Arthur Edington, Principal of Hill Street School at the time. Arthur Edington was a very unique person, an African-American gentleman in every since of the word. He carried himself straight and tall and sucked on his pipe like an English aristocrat. His language was always proper and precise.

Sixth grade teachers were transferred from all elementary schools in the school system to Hill Street School which was located in an African-American community. Many of these teachers had taught all their career in a cocoon dealing with only Caucasian children and parents. They now found themselves dealing with a situation where they had no experience and some were completely traumatized. Some of them were going to their physicians to get medication just to make it through the day. When the integrated school started after Christmas break, teachers and children were escorted into the building under police protection. It was a tense time for all.

I really did not have a problem adjusting. I had a mix of students, some from upper class homes, some from middle class homes and some from the projects, but really no problems because I always attempted to accept the child no matter the color of their skin nor from where they came. It was a challenge to bring cohesiveness to the classroom, but it was fun and I learned a lot that year.

Dorland Winkler,
Malvern Hills, 8/12/11

HELP!

My first year was a little wacky because I was hired the year the governor reduced class size in kindergarten classes. The state created a teaching position but did not create a full time assistant position to go with it. So, for the first few weeks we had other kindergarten teacher assistants rotating through to help me in the morning for academic classes while the first grade assistants would rotate through during the afternoon.

That was pretty crazy until finally the Parent Teacher Organization hired an assistant for my classroom.

Elizabeth Middleton,
Candler, Buncombe County, 10/21/10

THE NEW KID ON THE BLOCK
LEARNS A LESSON

An interesting thing happened when I was teaching at the high school. Teachers always met in the principal's office to debrief at the end of the day. One day, our principal reached over in the corner and picked up a tennis racket. He asked, "Who can tell me what this is?" Being new I said, "It's a tennis racket." The principal looked at me and said, "Well congratulation you are our new tennis coach for this semester. Also, by the way there are only three boys and ten girls signed up so you are going to have a co-ed tennis team to play against all the boys in the region."

Fred Trantham,
Waynesville, Haywood County, 11/11/10

THE PROBLEM SOLVER

During my first year, there was this one kid who had some severe discipline problems and the principal was trying to get him into an exceptional class. The kid was a runner and would run off when he did not get his way. The principal moved him into my class because I had a background in psychology. The child was able to be successful in my class and got to the point where he could make it through the day without problems. Another kid, a while later, threw a fit and punched a teacher in the stomach. This child also got to be in my class. I kind of got a reputation for being able to handle kids with problems.

Elizabeth Middleton,
Candler, Buncombe County, 10/21/10

SAYING GOOD-BYE TO A FRIEND

Another teacher I had in high school was Ms. Reems. She was my music teacher and encouraged me every step of the way. If I had spent half as much time studying as I did in the music department, I might have been a much better student. Ms. Reems and I were always very close even after I graduated. After I had gone to Greensboro and was attending Woman's College, she brought her choral group there to compete in a contest, as she always did. I was glad to see her as always and we sat together that night during the concert. I really enjoyed being with her that night and later on that night she had a heart attack and died. I did not learn about it until the next day when my English teacher mentioned that the choral director from Asheville High had passed away. It just devastated me because I had been the last person who had been with her. She was young, maybe about fifty, and that was a very traumatic experience.

Julia Clark,
Biltmore Lake, June 2, 2011

I HAVE BEEN BLESSED

My parents were very supportive of me. My mother was very insistent I go to college. I was only the second person in my family who attended college and my mother was always encouraging me to go to college and to become all that I could become.

I realize I was very blessed as a young person. There were so many people who were always there to support and encourage me along the way. I grew up in the Baptist Church and my Sunday School teachers were always providing support and encouragement. I am still very active in church and Everette, my husband and I have always taught our children to be faithful in their lives. I have been very blessed throughout my life.

Julia Clark,
Biltmore Lake, June 2, 2011

YOU CALLED ME WHAT?

Arthur Eddington, an African American gentleman, was Principal of Hill Street School during the first year of integration. He spoke in a very dignified manner and, at the end of the school year he wrote in my evaluation that I had done a very good job for a neophyte. Being a country boy from the mountains, I had no idea what it meant to be a neophyte and rushed to the library for a dictionary. The first definition was a converted heathen. I thought to myself, "What did he just call me?" Reading further, I discovered that a neophyte also meant a beginner.

Dorland Winkler,
Malvern Hills, 8/12/11

BRAVE NEW WORLD

In addition to "learning the ropes" about teaching and being responsible for those forty-two first grade children with no assistant, I was deeply in love with the man with which I wanted to spend the rest of my life. We married during my first year of teaching school in Greensboro, North Carolina where I had attended college. Now, not only was I faced with learning how to be a teacher, I was also learning how to be a wife. Even with my "Brave New World" opening up for me, it was a wonderful year. I remember it snowed from the day of my mid-year entrance in February through all of March. Since my future husband was working in Asheville and I was teaching in Greensboro, we had to catch a day when it was not snowing in order to get in the same city and get married. I was still the shy new girl on the block and I was so afraid of my principal that I could only muster up enough courage to ask for one half day off on a Friday to travel back to Asheville and get married. It wasn't that she was a hard-nosed principal, she was really a dear person, but I was so afraid of authority that I just didn't have the nerve to ask for more time off from school. I bought a wedding dress, took my one half day off, and came home to Asheville and was married on Saturday evening. Feeling guilty for even asking for any time off, I was back in Greensboro and in my classroom teaching early Monday morning. No, I wasn't pregnant, I just thought that I had made a commitment to the school system when I had signed my contract and that there was no way in the world that I could break my contract.

Sue Harris,
Hominy Valley, Buncombe County, April 26, 2011

WHAT DID HE SAY?

In this same 4th grade class was a young child who had no hair. He was as bald as Yul Brenner.

Every morning he was the first student to arrive in class (about 30 minutes early). I asked one morning why he came so early and he said, "So I can comb my hair."

Dr. Judy Pierce, Winston Salem,
6/15/11

I AM YOUR LEADER, WHICH WAY DO WE GO?

I only taught one year before I entered the principalship. I taught sixth grade in Robinsville, North Carolina. I knew very little about teaching and other teachers helped me greatly through that first year. I remember we had to turn in the "blue sheet" for attendance. I had it correct, but I didn't have it copied down correctly. The secretary had to come to see me and get it corrected.

Lowell Crisp,
Robinsville, Graham County, 6/15/11

DADDY WENT THE EXTRA MILE FOR ME

In the 1950's, I was graduating from the elementary school and my father was escorting me to my first dance, the sixth Grade Dance. As I was the oldest girl in our extended family on both sides, two aunts, my grandmother and Mama were helping me dress. One aunt fixed my hair, the other aunt provided her high school graduation dress which

Mama had altered to fit me, and my Grandmother provided me with my first hose, garter belt and heels. After much picture-taking, Daddy and I left for the dance. Now, we were Southern Baptists and not allowed to dance (when I questioned that, I got into trouble and was then told that graduation dances were acceptable!?!?). At the dance, a young man requested a dance and I refused because I did not know how to dance. Daddy took me by the hand and danced with me. In order to keep Daddy from insisting I dance with the young man, I made a bet with Daddy. I told him that if he danced with Ms. Watkins, I would dance with the young man. I was sure Daddy would not dance with this teacher because she had been his teacher in the sixth grade also and he truly did not like her. However, imagine my chagrin and surprise when Daddy danced with Ms. Watkins. I then had to carry out my part of the bet. What sacrifices daughters have to make for their Daddies, or is it—what sacrifices Daddies have to make for their daughters!!

Beth Carter,
Garner, 5/1/2011

SNAKE, SNAKE

In the second year of teaching I was assigned to teach 5th grade in a country school. The enrollment was 24 children in the classroom that included 2 brothers, Richard and Nick. Richard was referred to at the time in education as "somewhat slow." In early October, the class began a unit in science on trees and since my school was located in a rural (country) setting, I decided to take the class on a walk down a country road to collect leaves to make a scrapbook. I advised the children not to pick up anything along the road unless I asked them to do so. We were walking up the road on the left side facing any cars that might pass and of course, there were weeds and rocks along both sides of the road. Down a short embankment from the road was a creek named after the road on which we were walking. The sun was beautiful and we were just walking along enjoying the beauty of the leaves that had changed color. Richard was walking on the left side of me towards the embankment when suddenly, he bent down to pick up a stick. I just happened to look at the stick and it turns out, it was a snake. I jerked Richard all the way across the road and yelled at him all the way. That young man scared me out of my pants.

Dr. Judy Pierce,
Winston Salem, 6/15/11

SEX EDUCATION AIN'T WHAT IT USED TO BE

In Galax City Schools, Virginia, I was the Assistant Superintendent of Curriculum and Instruction. Because it was such a small school district, I wore about 15 hats. During the first few weeks of my new position, I was required to attend a state meeting on designing, implementing, and evaluating a family life/sex education program for grades K-12. This program was mandated by the Virginia legislature. I learned some very interesting ideas from many of the school district coordinators of what to do and what not to do with the advisory council. Also, I heard some interesting horror stories. The advisory council was a requirement attached to the mandate for the sex education curriculum.

About two months into the school year, I was sitting in my office one morning when the telephone rang. I answered in as polite a voice as I could and identified myself. The woman (she wasn't a lady) on the other end of the telephone shouted, "Are you that woman in charge of showing our kids how to have babies?" I said, "I am working with the teachers in the school district on writing a family life program to be implemented in the fall of the next year." She said in a very loud voice, "Well,

I just think that it is absolutely horrible that you are going to teach our kids how to have babies. You are going to teach them about that "thing." I said, "Ma'am, What thing?" The woman replied, "You know what thing I'm talkin' about." I said, "No, Ma'am, I have no idea what you mean." Well, for about five minutes we went back and forth on the telephone about that "thing." I had no clue what the woman was referring to in the conversation. Finally, she said, "You mean you are that woman in charge of teaching the kids how to have babies and you don't know what I am talking about." I responded,

"Yes, I don't know what you mean when you say "thing." She sounded very frustrated. Finally, she yelled "Well, you know that thing that a man sticks up a woman and has a "bowel movement." I said, "What?" It suddenly dawned on me what she was talking about. I responded, "You mean ejaculation."

She said, "What's that?"

Dr. Judy Pierce,
Winston Salem, 6/15/11

ADMINISTERING A KIND PADDLING

One day after I became a principal, I was paddling a boy out in the hall and I was paddling him as fast as I could. A seventh grade teacher observing me administering the paddling came over and offered some advice. He said, "Slow down and talk to the student between licks." I always tried to do that to let the student know I was not doing it because I was mad.

Lowell Crisp,
Robinsville, Graham County, 6/15/11

NOT AS MACHO AS I THOUGHT

When I moved from Richmond, VA to Asheville, N.C. I felt that I was pretty macho and decided to grow a mustache. I was feeling pretty cocky about my mustache as I was teaching my fourth grade class at Jones Elementary. I was busy teaching one day when Kevin came up and whispered to me, "I just want to tell you something Mr. Cutshall, your mustache is crooked." That afternoon as soon as I got home I shaved and have never since attempted to grow a mustache.

Charles Cutshall,
Sodom Laurel, Madison County, 7/14/11

GOOD ADVICE

When I began teaching kindergarten I loved it so very much. Kindergarten children are so honest and tell everything that they see and hear. I told my kids' parents at the beginning of the school year, that if they didn't believe everything they heard about me, then I wouldn't believe everything I heard about them.

Sandy Caldwell,
Waynesville, Haywood County, 11/11/10

ALWAYS SET YOUR CLOCK

On my first day teaching school, I overslept. My friend who lived across the hall realized I had not yet left my apartment and came over and woke me up. I ran around like a chicken with her head cut off trying to get dressed. I rushed into the classroom only about five minutes late, but all the parents were standing there with their five year old children, many of them crying because their teacher had not showed up on their first day of school. I don't think I am over that until this day.

Sandy Caldwell,
Waynesville, Haywood County, 11/11/10

BACK HOME IN NAHTAHALA

My first school was in Nahtahala, North Carolina. Nahtahala was a small mountain high school, but they could not bus students to a larger school in the county due to weather conditions. Snow would be so deep that high in the mountains that travel was impossible many days during the winter. Nahtahala would miss as many as fifteen more days due to snow as the other schools in the county. Because of the harsh weather conditions, the school is still there and it has been forty-five years since I worked there.

I had to teach almost every class since there were only three teachers, in addition to the principal, who taught half time. Nahtahala was, and I think is, still a very close knit community due to its isolation. While teaching there, I also found out that my great grandfather lived in Nahtahala just after the beginning of the twentieth century and was a preacher in the community.

Most people in the community were good people. Oh, there were some feuds going on like the Hatfields and McCoys of West Virginia, but for the most part people supported the school. One of the school board members in the county was from this community and his son later became principal of the high school there. Some people have a false idea about mountain folks. Just because they live in isolation in the mountains doesn't mean that there are a lot of dumb people living there. This is far from the truth. We had many very educated and talented people in the community who became leaders in our state and nation. Also, maybe it was because of the isolation, it seemed that almost every person had a musical ability. It was wonderful to hear the beautiful music. One year, we had a talent show and a small high school girl said she could play a guitar. We all thought that she couldn't, but she blew us away with her beautiful playing.

Several of the young people in Nahtahala would leave the community to find work in the tunneling business where they would build tunnels for water conduits or whatever. Many of these people would return to the community for part of the year and then travel to New York or Michigan or somewhere for a tunneling job for several months each year.

Thomas Ledbetter,
Hendersonville, 4/13/2011

It Can Tear Your Heart Out If You Let It

As an adult, I worked with children and adolescents at a state hospital (school) in N.C. A young teen-age girl, who was suicidal, transferred to our hospital school, needing a kidney transplant. Her history was incredibly sad and tragic; she had been found at about the age of five, prostituting herself to care for a younger sister and an infant (her mother had been missing for several weeks). All of the children were placed into the foster care system; the two sisters were eventually placed with a foster family who was in the process of adopting them. This young lady, at the time that I knew her, was very personable, lovable, smart and friendly but suicidal for obvious reasons. Her new parents, doctors, foster care system and our hospital had tried everything (including testing staff for possible transplant) but could not find a match for her transplant, so a search was instigated to locate her birth mother. The birth mother refused to even be tested. This young girl went home and, shortly afterward, committed suicide. I attended her funeral and in my twenty years at the hospital school, this was the saddest case, in my opinion, because she could have and should have been helped.

Beth Carter,
Garner, 5/1/2011

PRAYED THAT I COULD PRAY

I had my first shock when I was teaching in a literary class. We had four classrooms together and they always said a prayer at the beginning of the class. The lead teacher called on me to lead prayer. I had never lead prayer in my life and she was asking me to lead prayer in front of about one hundred people. I said a few words and a student said something to me later about the prayer, because they could tell I was really struggling.

Lowell Crisp,
Robinsville, Graham County, 6/15/11

HOW BIG IS A "BIG BOOK?"

Even though I had dreamed of the wonderful new experiences that awaited me in the teaching profession, I had no earthly idea of what I was getting into as I walked into my classroom on that very first day. I had a wonderful friend who had taught for awhile and she was a great help to me. I remember she asked me if I wanted to use the primer or the "Big Book" in my first grade class. I had no idea what a "Big Book" was. I soon found out it was just a big edition of a children's book which made it easier for the children to see the pictures as I read stories to them.

Sue Harris,
Hominy Valley, April 26, 2011

TAKE IT ONE DAY AT A TIME

Upon graduation from David Lipscomb College, I applied and was hired to teach fifth grade at Rosebank Elementary in Nashville, Tennessee. Whereas, today a new teacher is given a support system on which to rely such as mentors, intern teacher committees and follow-up from college personnel, in 1965 there was virtually no support system. A new teacher was thrust into the fire of conflict as if they were somehow miraculously changed from being a college student one day to being a teacher the next.

I remember well my first day of teaching. Harold Greenbalm was Principal at Rosebank and after one day in which to set up my room and plan all my lessons, I was brought to the classroom by Mr. Greenbalm and introduced to thirty-two wiggly fifth grade children; then he turned and walked away. I made it through that day and the day after and the day after that, but there were times when I wondered how in the world was I going to make it all the way to retirement. Now, looking back, I realize I made it by taking one day at a time and after forty years knowing when it was time to leave.

J. Terry Hall,
Scott Mountain, Buncombe County, 3/3/11

My First Exceptionally Gifted Child

One thing that has not changed over the past years is in the area of discipline. Although, there are support systems in place today that were not available forty years ago,and rules have changed in regard to corporal punishment, a new teacher cannot be prepared for the discipline problems he or she will encounter in the classroom until they meet the situation head on and then move forward.

During my first year of teaching at Rosebank Elementary in Nashville, I had a ten year old boy by the name of Jimmy. Jimmy would not follow the rules. No matter how hard I would try to make Jimmy conform to the rules of the class, he would always "win" by disrupting my class and getting all the other children to laugh at his behavior. Today, I realize Jimmy would have most likely been classified exceptionally gifted, but I was beside myself with worry and would talk to my wife Patricia most nights about what I was to do.

One afternoon as I was locking the door of my classroom, my Principal, Harold Greenbalm walked by, placed his hand on my shoulder, said, "Mr. Hall, when you lock up your classroom each afternoon, lock up the problems your children are having inside and I guarantee you that they will be waiting for you the next morning." He was wise enough to recognize I was having a problem and that I was allowing it to affect my personal life. I soon realized Jimmy was just seeking attention and if he could not obtain it in a positive manner then he would achieve it in a negative manner. I allowed Jimmy to be a class leader and to assist other children who were having difficulty with their academic assignments. Jimmy gave me no more trouble when I allowed him to "win" in a positive manner. Years later as a school administrator, I reminded many new teachers of the wise words given me by Harold Greenbalm many years ago.

J. Terry Hall,
Scott Mountain, Buncombe County, 3/3/11

A Close Knit Family

The year was 1966 and I had just graduated from college and began my first year of teaching at Flat Rock Jr. High on Sand Mountain. My first assignment was to be the teacher for the seventh grade. My principal was a deacon with one of the local churches in the area. One day as I entered the office, I was surprised to find the secretary sitting in the principal's lap. She rapidly jumped up and the principal began to explain that he and his sister-in-law were extremely close, a fact which I had quickly sumised. Shortly thereafter, the principal divorced his wife and the sister-in-law, her husband, and they got married. I met them some years later after leaving my position at the school and they were still married.

My second year teaching at Sand Hill was very interesting. I had a young girl in my class by the name of Susie. Susie was beyond her years in the flirting department and wore her skirts extremely short. I say this in order to set the stage for what I am about to relate. One day, I was showing a movie relating to our study of the westward expansion in our country. While viewing the movie one of the scenes was of a square dance in which the ladies were whirled around by their partners. As the ladies whirled and their dresses were flowing rather high, one of the boys in class said, "Hey, did you guys see her panties?", and another boy in class said, "That ain't nothing we see Susie's panties everyday!"

Also, that year the seventh grade teacher happened to be Susie's aunt (I will call her Mary Lou). She was a very lovely young lady and dressed rather provocatively. One morning Mary Lou didn't show up for work and, in fact, didn't show up for work for several mornings. I began to ask around to see what was wrong with Mary Lou and discovered that she had eloped with one of the local church deacons. I don't know what became of Mary Lour after that but I rather suspect that the deacon was only one of Mary Lou's many misguided lovers. Relating to the above event, I was unaware that Mary Lou was Susie's aunt until I decided to call Susie's mom in for a counseling session. I sent a letter to her requesting that she come in so we could discuss Susie's education. Upon arriving, I found her mom to be a nice lady who was very concerned for her daughter. I explained that Susie was wearing her skirts extremely short and creating a distraction in class. Her mother explained that when Susie left the house in the morning her skirts were knee length and the only explanation she could give for the short skirts was that Susie was stopping somewhere along the way and rolling them up. She also explained that Mary Lou was Susie's Aunt and that Susie greatly admired her Aunt. After learning that Mary Lou was Susie's Aunt the mystery of the short skirts was solved.

Every year while teaching at Sand Mountain Jr. High, our seventh grade class would put on a school play. I would write the play for the kids and I usually made them comical. This particular year the play revolved around Little Red Riding Hood. In the play we had Susie playing the part of Little Red Riding Hood and George playing the part of the Big Bad Wolf. So, in the play practice Little Red is lying in bed and the Big Bad Wolf comes in dressed as Grandma. Little Red says, "My, Grand-maw what big eyes you have!" "The better to see you with my child," says the wolf. "My, Grand-maw what big ears you have," said Little Red. "The better to hear you with my child," said the Wolf. And then Little Red says, "My, Grand-maw what big teeth you have," and the wolf says, "The better to eat you with my child!" And, with that,

Little Red jumps up and begins to run around the bed. Where upon Cleo, the Big Bad Wolf, begins to chase her all the while pinching her on the butt. While this is happening the whole class is dying with laughter. I suspected that Cleo was setting us up and decided to have a back-up for the Big Bad Wolf and sure enough on the night of the school play Cleo didn't show and Little Red didn't get her butt pinched.

Phillip Cochran,
Sand Mountain,Henderson County, 6/30/11

PUKE ON THE TEACHER

I will never forget this little kid in my seventh grade science class when I was teaching in Richmond, VA. I thought I really had my class organized and everything was going great, not realizing that half my class was really in Pittsburgh and I just thought they were listening. I was all wound up and spreading my wealth of knowledge until I got to the middle of the room when this one kid just projectile-vomited all over the table. Little did I know that that was what most of them were probably thinking about doing as I talked on and on.

Charles Cutshall,
Sodom Laurel, Madison County, 7/14/11

LEARNING TO MAKE BANANA SPLITS

During my first year of teaching 1965-1966, I was making more money than I had ever made in my life. I was taking home just a little over three hundred dollars a month. When one considers as a bag boy working in a grocery store just before college I was being paid fifty cents per hour, this was big money. But, even though we were only paying sixty-five dollars per month rent for a two bedroom house and one could buy a weeks worth of groceries for less that twenty dollars, there still was not enough left to carry us through the three months without pay during the summer.

After teaching that first year, I found a job working as a soda jerk at a drug store a couple blocks from our house. In those days drug stores had an ice cream counter where one could buy hand-dipped ice cream. Since they did not teach me to work as a soda jerk in college, I needed a little on the job training in order to serve up sundaes and banana splits. The lady who had been serving ice cream much longer than I had the job of teaching me the ropes.

During the second day of working behind the counter, a man came in and ordered a banana split. I set in to make him what I considered one of my specials. When I finished, it was a masterpiece and I served it with a smile. The man devoured his treat with great gusto and when he paid me, he gave me a quarter tip and thanked me for such a wonderful banana split. When he left the building, the regular waitress began laughing. When I inquired what was so funny, she explained that I forgot to put a banana in the banana split. The man never noticed and complimented me on a job well done.

J. Terry Hall,
Scott Mountain, Buncombe County, 3/3/11

A GREAT SUPPORT SYSTEM

When I first started teaching school in Danville, Virginia and had my very own classroom, I was nervous, but I felt I knew what I was doing. Little did I know how little I really knew and how much I was yet to learn.

I had a very neat principal in Danville who was very supportive, and I taught first grade the first year I was there. The way it was set up at that school was if you had first grade one year then you would have second grade the next year and would have the same children two years in a row; so I got to know my children pretty good by having them for two years. In addition to regular classroom teaching I taught fifth and sixth grade chorus both years. We were also fortunate to have a very good parent support group that first year, and since they were from an upper class neighborhood, they were always supportive of the school.

Furthermore, we were required to visit in every child's home during the first few weeks of the school year. This was an eye opener to see how the children lived and acted when they were not at school. It allowed me to get to know the parents better by meeting in their own homes and made it easier for them to relate to me as a person and not just an authority figure. In fact, I became very close to several of the parents and would come into their homes and keep their kids when they needed to be out for the evening or the weekends. Two of the parents were doctors and they took me out to eat and had me visit in their homes often. Times have certainly changed and I cannot imagine doing this type of thing in today's society.

Julia Clark,
Biltmore Lake, June 2, 2011

THE NEW MRS. CLARK

I moved to Virginia to began my teaching career because I wanted to be on my own, but, after two years, I moved back to Asheville and began teaching at Newton Elementary where my Principal was Mr. Clark. One interesting thing I remember at Newton was that we taught folk dancing to every class and, in the spring, we would have every class perform their folk dance. All the children would be dressed in their little costumes and I thought that was wonderful. In April of that year, my husband and I were married and his name was Everett Clark, so when it came time for Mr. Clark, the Principal, to introduce my class he introduced me as the new Mrs. Clark. That caused a commotion throughout the auditorium.

Julia Clark,
Biltmore Lake, June 2, 2011

A Need For Which I Was Not Trained

I had this beautiful blue-eyed, six year old girl in my class who had a hole in her heart and had to be watched continuously in case she developed a serious heart condition. They told me she was always in danger of death and I should always be observant of her skin color. If I should notice her turning blue, it would mean she was in serious trouble and I should immediately call for help. She made it almost through the school year with me becoming almost paranoid until one day she started turning blue and had to be rushed to the hospital. She became so fragile she had to be taken out of my class and home-schooled for the remainder of the school year.

Sue Harris,
Hominy Valley, April 26, 2011

He Was Not A Positive Leader

After one year in Asheville, we moved back to Virginia and I taught for two years. That was not a very good experience for me. I had a principal who had been a high school coach and he knew nothing about being an elementary principal. He would come into the classroom and write and write and write and then tell me all the negative things that he had observed. I don't remember any positive things he ever pointed out nor any positive suggestions he ever made.

Julia Clark,
Biltmore Lake, June 2, 2011

TIMES SURE HAVE CHANGED

One thing I remember that happened while I was back in Virginia, I had a parent who gave me her very own paddle to use on her son Sam, if the situation should ever arise. I never had to use it on Sam, but I did use it several times.

Julia Clark,
Biltmore Lake, June 2, 2011

THE OLD LADY NEXT DOOR

At the beginning of my second year back in Virginia, we moved to Chesterfield County because of my husband's work. One thing I never did understand during that year was this older lady who taught across the hall from me and, for some reason, she just did not like me and was always criticizing my teaching. Maybe, it was because she was old and I was young at the time, I just don't know.

Julia Clark,
Biltmore Lake, June 2, 2011

A High Honor

During my fourth year teaching, I was asked to leave the classroom and be a supervisor. This was a shock because, for one thing, I was not qualified to be a supervisor with it being only my fourth year teaching. I was highly honored to be asked, but we moved back to North Carolina that year and I passed up becoming a supervisor.

Julia Clark,
Biltmore Lake, June 2, 2011

A Two Year Old And A Hammer

Somewhere around 1978 when our son, Ben was two years old, I learned a very hard lesson. Each afternoon as soon as I arrived home from school, I would take time to play with Ben for a few minutes. One day I came home so tired I could hardly place one foot in front of the other. I walked into the house, fell down on the couch on my back and closed my eyes. Ben came near and expected me to take time to play with him as was my usual habit. When I did not respond he took the wooden hammer that we had bought him a few days before and, before I knew it, he raised back and hit me right between the eyes. As I came fully awake, he was raising the hammer for a second shot.

J. Terry Hall,
Scott Mountain, Buncombe County, 3/3/11

Those Were The Days

My first year of teaching was in Jacksonville, Florida. I was hired as a music teacher and I didn't have a room. I had to travel from room to room pushing a cart filled with all my music material. Not only did I have to travel from room to room, I also had to travel across town in the middle of the week and teach at another school. It was a very busy time for me. I remember teaching several little songs. One song was call the "Crocodile Song;" it went like this "A lady sailed away on a bright sunny day on the back of a crocodile. You see said she, I'm as happy as can be. At the end of the ride the lady was inside and the smile was on the crocodile." I used hand gestures as I told the story. The children loved that song.

Billie Lewis,
Enka, Buncombe County, 11/15/10

CHAPTER FOUR

INFLUENTIAL TEACHERS

An Ode To Catherine Rodgers

In my opinion, the greatest teacher I have had the pleasure of knowing was Catherine Rodgers. Mrs. Rodgers was an education teacher at Lindsey Wilson College in 1961 when I began my journey. I left the small town of Tompkinsville, Kentucky to go to college with no idea of obtaining a degree. I just wanted to attend college for one semester in order to see what it felt like to be a college student and Lindsey Wilson was the closest being only forty-five miles from home. I met Mrs. Rodgers on the day of registration when she walked up and asked about my major, a question which I had never considered. She suggested I take her class called "Fundamentals of Education" where a student actually had an opportunity to work with children from the very first day under Mrs. Rodgers' close supervision.

I followed her suggestion since I had not considered an area in which to major. From day one, I fell in love with working with elementary children. In this class under the guidance of Mrs. Rodgers, a seed was planted that continues to grow after fifty years. Not only was I prepared to follow my dream, I had found a friend.

Mrs. Rodgers, my mentor and friend, took a special interest in all her students. We were like a part of her extended family. When we had a success she was there to share it with us, and when we had a problem, she was there to console. One of the problems that often confront eighteen year old college students was dealing with members of the opposite sex. More than once I went to Mrs. Rodgers seeking advise on my love life and like a substitute mom she always took time to listen.

One time in particular, Mrs. Rodgers went far beyond the call of duty, even for a substitute mom. I had been having a problem with my girlfriend and we had broken up. On the rebound, I started seeing a freshman by the name of Jane. Well, to put it lightly, Jane was a little on the wild side back in 1962. She suggested that I get my close friend Dick and his girlfriend Sue to go with us to Lake Cumberland to stay with her uncle and aunt for the weekend. She said they had a cabin on the lake and would love for us to come. The only problem was none of us had a car to travel the fifty miles to the lake. Being a natural leader, I spoke up and suggested we try to get Mrs. Rodgers to take us over to the lake. When I approached her, she did not hesitate but agreed to provide the needed transportation. We piled into Mrs. Rodgers car and began our big adventure.

After dropping us off in front of the cabin, Mrs. Rodgers returned to campus. In an hour or so, Jane confided that she had lied and her aunt and uncle were in Florida for the week and we would have to sleep together on the beach during the night. Well, for a "good" boy who had been brought up in the church, I was not ready to lose my virginity just yet. After we had spent the afternoon playing around in the water, I walked up to a store near the lake and called Mrs. Rodgers to come get us and take us back to campus. I might add that if this had come to a vote, I would have lost. After I explained the situation, Mrs. Rodgers drove the one hundred mile round trip and rescued her precious students. On the way back to campus, not a negative word came from her mouth and it was never mentioned again.

J. Terry Hall,
Scott Mountain, Buncombe County, 3/3/11

THE MAN WHO CARED FOR HIS KIDS

Colonel Thomas was the leader of the ROTC at Asheville High School and he always looked out for his kids. There was one time when some kids were in a bad situation and were afraid to go home he allowed them to spend the night in his office so they would be safe during the night.

Larry Liggett,
Skyland, Buncombe County, 7/21/11

THANK YOU MY FRIENDS

I have worked with so many folks that I have looked up to and would like to emulate. The staffs at Jones, Claxton, Hall Fletcher, Vance and Asheville Junior High each were unique and very talented.

There were many Administrators in Asheville that served as my mentor. Some of them are Dr. Jones, Dr. Capps, Dr. Metcalf, Mr. Mitchell and Dr. Liggett. In my opinion, these people really fit the mode of what being a leader was all about; they not only were good at their job . . . but they knew and cared for their people.

Charles Cutshall,
Sodom Laurel, Madison County, 7/14/11

A GOOD TEACHER MUST BE A REAL PERSON

I had a teacher in high school, Ed Lambert, who was a role model for me. He was the first teacher I ever had who laughed with his students and made his class come alive. I have always attempted to emulate his teaching and make my classes exciting. He was an outstanding teacher.

Darren Barkett,
Canton, Haywood County, 1/23/11

MY PARENTS WERE ALWAYS THERE FOR ME

My parents were always involved with the schools as I was growing up in New Jersey. They attended all the PTO meetings and campaigned for the school board members whom they thought would make the best decisions for the children. Mom also volunteered to help in the school. When my sister was in fourth grade, my mom went to work as a school nurse and there was always school and politics talk at the dinner table.

My middle sister, also a teacher, is two and a half years younger than I. We talk a lot about our day to day challenges. I really enjoy talking to her about what she is doing in the classroom.

Elizabeth Middleton,
Candler, Buncombe County, 10/21/10

AN OLDER TEACHER TOOK ME UNDER HER WING

Miss Rose was an old maid school teacher, but she was certainly not your typical teacher. When I began teaching, she was probably in her mid sixties and extremely private in dealing with other teachers. Most teachers disliked Miss Rose due to her selfish attitude. She would have little to do with other teachers and even those who shared a relation with her because of working in close proximity found her hard to like.

She refused to share materials with other teachers even though she had more supplies than she could have possibly used. Very few people were allowed to break through the hard shell that seemed to be a defense against anyone getting too close. Miss Rose looked more than twenty years older than she was and had a face with wrinkles as deep as the red mud bank out the back of the school building after a hard rain. She always wore bright red lipstick and rouge painted on so thick and uneven that it looked like something a kindergarten child would create in finger painting class.

For some reason Miss Rose took a liking to me as a new teacher and allowed me to see beyond the veil and get a glimpse of her as a real person. My classroom was just across the hallway from Miss Rose and she would come over after school and suggest changes I needed to make in my room. I would always accept her suggestions and thank her for sharing her suggestions with me. At the end of that school year, she came into my room and, almost in a whisper, asked me to come to her room for there was something she wanted to show me. When I entered her room, she confided that she was going to retire and she wanted me to have all the things she had collected over the years. She then led me into her supply closet and motioned to all the materials that were her treasures. Construction paper was piled to the ceiling and had been there so long that the color had faded. I thanked her for her generous gift and went back to my room. When she left, I found the material in such poor condition that I had to throw it in the trash. I made sure she never learned the fate of her much valued treasure.

Miss Rose had asked me to come visit her and I made a point to go by her house which was only two blocks from the school several times for a visit. She had a beautiful rose garden in her back yard and would always take me out there in the spring and summer and show me her new treasure. As she got older, she lost touch with reality and would get lost while walking around the community. One day she lost her purse while riding a city bus and another time, she came in the school building and went up to her old room and began to prepare to teach. I felt so sorry for her and took her home. It was not long until she was placed in a nursing home where she died.

J. Terry Hall,
Scott Mountain, Buncombe County, 3/3/11

FIRE ALMOST GETS A TEACHER FIRED

. When I was teaching fifth grade at an inner city fifth/sixth school in Winston-Salem, my neighbor on the left side was a young teacher who had a very loud squeaky voice. Margaret and our principal, Mr. King didn't hit it off from day one. She was one of the teachers who was transferred from an all white affluent school to Brown due to desegregation. Mr. King would listen in on the intercom to determine what she was doing in class because Margaret had very poor classroom management skills. In the afternoon, I would literally hear her yelling at the top of her voice to the children. Well, one weekend some people broke into the primary wing of the school. They found some papers in an empty trash can in the teacher's lounge and set them on fire. Thank goodness they were not successful. The fire alarm went off and apparently scared the hoodlums away. Mr. King was immediately contacted by the police department. He came to the school at some early hour of the morning to meet the police and members of the fire department. They advised him that the fire started from his students' work in a trash can.

When Mr. King examined the papers, he immediately realized they were from Margaret's class. Well, I will tell you, I wouldn't have been in her shoes for anything in the world. On Monday morning, he called Margaret to the office and passers by could hear him yelling at her clear down the hall. He even had his office door closed. She returned to her classroom. After school, she was telling everyone what happened. Talk about someone who was mad as a hornet-Margaret was, and remained that way the rest of the week. At the end of the year, she tried to transfer to another school, but was unsuccessful. This effort made the situation worse for Margaret.

Dr. Judy Pierce,
Winston Salem, 6/15/11

LIGHTS THAT SHOWED ME THE WAY

One of the most influential teachers in my life was Ed Lambert back in high school in Colorado. He inspired the original desire in my life to become a teacher mainly because he laughed with his students and made his classroom come alive and not just a list of boring facts.

Another master teacher in my opinion that influenced my career is Bob Nolan, School Counselor at Enka Middle School in Buncombe County. He is an old hippie from the sixties with the long hair and still talks, "Man" and "Dude" and the kids love him because he is such a unique and honest person. When one talks with Bob, it is evident that what he says is heart-felt. He is a super nice guy. He had the job of doing programs during the holidays and one Christmas he asked me if I could sing a Christmas song. I tried and proved to him that I could not sing so we decided on a rap where I just spoke. We came up with this program where I dressed up as Santa and I would ride into the gym on a motorcycle. I rode into the gym on the motorcycle, revved it up real loud and we proceeded to sing a funky version of "Santa Clause is Coming to Town." Bob Nolan was the type of person every school needs to grow the spirit of the school. So many times we get lost in the pressure of testing that we lose the spirit.

Darren Barkett,
Canton, Haywood County, 1/23/11

WIND BENEATH MY WINGS

I have had several teachers who have encouraged me along the way. I had this one teacher in high school who always encouraged me to become a journalist. She pointed me in a direction where I could feel success and gave me a reason to continue with my education. Although I enjoyed writing very much, and published a couple of poems, that wasn't what I chose for a career path. Now, being a teacher, I am required to continually write goals and objectives, although I don't think that was what she had in mind.

Anonymous,
Western North Carolina, 5/6/2011

HE WAS A GOOD MAN

One of the most influential people in my life was Mr. Parlier, my Principal in elementary school. He grew up in the community and knew everyone and their kin. He was known by everyone in town and he never met a stranger as he walked down the street or shopped at the local market. He put in many many hours at the school and served in most of the clubs in the community. He was respected by almost everyone and was a very good role model.

The sad thing about Mr. Parlier was that he put in forty-two years at that school and less than two years after his retirement, he was cleaning out the gutters on his house when he fell off his roof, hit his head on the concrete sidewalk and never regained consciousness. Why he was up on the roof at his age I will never know. God rest his soul, he was a good man.

Dorland Winkler,
Malvern Hills, 8/12/11

Oops!

While I was teaching at Enka Middle School in Buncombe County they hired a new principal. As was the custom, each morning the principal would say the Pledge of Alliance over the intercom. On her first day at the school, she came on the intercom, cleared her throat and began the Pledge of Alliance About half way through the Pledge, she forgot the words and started stumbling through her words, trying to remember the rest of the Pledge. All the teachers were looking around, students were laughing and it just set the tone for a funny day when the principal blew the Pledge of Alliance on the first day of school.

Darren Barkett,
Canton, Haywood County, 1/23/11

Behave Like A Gentleman

My most influential person was probably my high school coach, Joe Hicks, who also became my boss. He became principal and gave me my first job. He believed in me and hired me. We became lifelong friends. He is down in eastern North Carolina now in an assisted living home; I have been by to visit with him. He was such a good influence for me because he always harped on having good behavior. He would always say, "Behave like a gentleman and always do the right thing."

Charlie McConnell,
Sylva, 6/17/11

A Very Dear Friend

I want to tell you about my very best friend and fellow teacher, Dianne Martin. She was a number one educator who was always loving, kind and always coming up with things to help. I would go over to her room and she would always take time to listen to any problem I might have and help me work through it. She was like my sister, my friend and she was always there for me. I always wanted to be like her. My son, Elliot, had her as a teacher and every few days he would come to my room after school and tell me I was doing something wrong because Ms. Martin did it another way. She was such a good teacher. She knew that Standard Course of Study inside and out and was the best teacher I have ever known and had great insight and wisdom as to what a child needed. We were all shocked when she found out at the end of a school year that she had colon cancer and just lived a short time. A few days before she died, she came to me and said she was planning her funeral and wanted me to be one of the pallbearers. I was glad to do what I could but I really miss her. Even after she died, she taught me something. During the following year after her death, I spent the entire year hating going to school. I realized if I was to continue teaching, I would need to move to another school. When this position at Averys Creek opened up, I applied for it and was transferred over here. That was a wonderful move for me. I have been here for seven years and they have been some of my happiest years in teaching. I have grown more professionally than at any other time in my career.

Jan Lunsford,
Averys Creek, Buncombe County, 12/2/10

Mix Um Up!

I remember this one white woman teacher in the year of integration who was a little strange. She had never had any experience working with black children and did not realize that during that period of adjustment the white students tended to group together with white students and black students tended to group together with black students where they felt more comfortable. One day, I observed her walking down the hall and seeing a group of black students grouped together, she said in a rather loud voice, "Now you all mix up. The Federal Government said we have to mix up, so mix! mix! mix!"

Dorland Winkler,
Malvern Hills, 8/12/11

To Lose A Friend

One of the teachers I remember was Madge Ferguson. She and I had gotten real close over the years. During a school year she died unexpectedly, it nearly broke my heart. It is very hard to lose a friend.

Billie Lewis,
Enka, Buncombe County, 11/15/10

DEATH BED CONFESSION

Modell Walsh was really a character in the western part of the state. He was Superintendent of Schools of Graham County, and Chairman of the Smokey Mountain Conference. He was also Chairman of the Democratic Party in Graham County. Now my good friend, Lowell Crisp, who became Superintendent, was a Republican. Modell and I had gotten to be pretty good friends and when he was on his death bed, I went to Mission Hospital in Asheville to see him. He was very very weak and I think he died about a week later. I leaned over close to him since he could barely speak loud enough for me to hear, and asked, "Modell, who is going to take your place as Superintendent?" He spoke in a voice so weak I could hardly hear and said, "Can you believe I have recommended a damn Republican?"

Charlie McConnell,
Sylva, 6/17/11

BE ON TIME FOR MEETINGS

When our large school system integrated by court order in the early seventies, there were many unhappy people: parents, students, teachers and administrators. All had to learn to work together! This was also the year our school system adopted a new reading series in Grades K-6 and hired reading specialists for each school because our school system-wide reading scores were not up to state test level expectations for our system. This was my first year as "reading coordinator" in a grades 5-6 inner city school and, not only was I responsible for the entire school's reading program, but also for Ms. Allen, a reading teacher aide, who did not like to work. The majority of students were bussed into the city from an affluent suburban area and it was in the best interest of everyone to see that these students were successful. One of my first assignments was to have a morning reading "tea" to introduce the parents to our school and to explain the reading program. We were going "all out" to have a highly,organized impressive meeting to introduce ourselves and the reading program to our parents!

On the morning of the meeting, I arrived at least two hours early to set up the auditorium, put food on the table, distribute handouts, make sure the overhead projector was in working order, and generally prepare for meeting the parents. Mr. Jacob, our Principal, had told me to ask Ms. Allen for help. After I had worked for over an hour, he arrived at school and came to where I was working hurriedly to get ready for this very important meeting. He looked around and asked where Mrs. Allen was. I told him I had not seen her. He said, "Did you ask her to help you this morning?" I said, "Yes." Without another word, he turned and hurriedly left the auditorium. A short time later, a highly angry Mrs. Allen rushed into the auditorium. She said, "Did you tell Mr. Jacob anything about me?" I said, "No." She said, "You know what that man just did to me? I was in the bathroom in the upstairs lounge and he came in where I was using the bathroom and told me to get down here and help you! He opened the door while I was sitting on the commode!" She went on spouting off about Mr. Jacob.

Together, she and I got everything ready for the presentation to be given to an auditorium full of parents. Everyone was pleased and never again did Mrs. Allen fail to do anything that I asked of her.

Ollie Hutchens,
Elkin, 2/27/11

WHEN THE CAT IS AWAY THE MICE WILL PLAY

One of the funniest teachers I have ever known taught with me at the fifth/sixth intermediate school in Winston-Salem. All of the fifth grade teachers were housed in what had been the primary wing before desegregation. The principal, Mr. Rodgers placed Nettie Fleck, down the hall from his office so he could keep an eye on her. It seems that when Mr. Rodgers was a classroom teacher he had Mrs. Fleck's son in his class. The young man apparently got into some serious trouble and his mother got into a knock down drag out fight with Mr. Rodgers. As the story goes, Mrs. Fleck ended up threatening to sue him. Mr. Rodgers would park his car under Mrs. Fleck's classroom windows in the morning and move it to the other side of the building in the afternoon so as to avoid the sun.

Mrs. Fleck always knew when Mr. Rodgers was away from school.

One day, Mr. Rodgers moved his car early in the morning due to the high humidity. Naturally, Mrs. Fleck thought he had gone to a principal's meeting. So, I was standing in the middle of the primary wing waiting on my children to return from bathroom break. All of a sudden, here comes Mrs.

Fleck dancing down the hall singing, "While the cat's away, the mice will play. While the cat's away, the mice will play." When she turned around, Mr. Rodgers was right behind her.

Dr. Judy Pierce,
Winston Salem, 6/15/11

WHAT DAY IS THIS?

One time I was at my assigned school and the telephone rang in the office. I was all the way down the hall and ran as fast as I could up the hall to answer the phone. I grabbed the phone and, out of breath said, "Hello." A teacher said, "I am so sorry. I will be late. I overslept. Have someone watch my students for me and I will be there as soon as I can get there." When she hushed I said, "Sandy, it's Saturday, hang up and go back to bed." I knew she had a bit of a drinking problem and she had waken from a stupor and couldn't remember what day it was.

Dorland Winkler,
Malvern Hills, 8/12/11

WE ARE NOT ALL CUT FROM THE SAME MOLD

It always interests me why some teachers succeed during their first few years while others just can't seem to pull it together. There was this one teacher who started teaching and had not developed a system of discipline what-so-ever. His class was utter chaos and his students had absolutely no respect for him. His students would come into my class and I would hear them telling each other how they had thrown paper wads at him when he had asked them to do something and they would just laugh at him to his face. I felt sorry for him, but there was nothing I could do. I tried to give him some suggestions but he had already lost the students' respect and there was nothing he could do. He left before the year was out.

Darren Barkett,
Canton, Haywood County, 1/23/11

MAKING DECISIONS IN SMALL COUNTIES

Jay Robertson was Superintendent of Charlotte, North Carolina and I always respected him for the way he handled that big of a school system. He told me that he never went to the school board for hiring school personnel. He said he went to the board about every three months with a list of people that he had told they had jobs and they would just approve them. He also told me that in all the years he had been superintendent, the board had never voted against any recommendation he had ever made. Now, here in smaller counties, every name has to be discussed and debated for hours before a decision is made. He was good and never brought them anything that would most likely be voted down. They were so confident in him that they just did not question his decisions.

Charlie McConnell,
Sylva, 6/17/11

THE SUPERINTENDENT STANDS ALONE

I noticed that almost every superintendent who came into a school system, saying they were going to change just about everything, ended up getting fired. You just can't go in and make all these changes with people who have lived their entire lives in that community. I remember in a school system not to far from here, a superintendent came in with the blessings of the school board and moved all the principals around. There was such a mess as you have ever seen. The people in that community came up in arms and demanded that the principals not be moved. The school board who had hired him to get this job done, as soon as it hit the fan, backed away from him and left the superintendent standing alone.

Charlie McConnell,
Sylva, 6/17/11

SUCK UP AND PUCKER UP

I was asked to come and speak to a local school board and suggest how they could consolidate one county school district and three city school districts. During the presentation, they asked me how I dealt with county commissioners. I told them I could sum it up in four words, "suck up and pucker up." They liked that and thought that was real honest. I then went on and elaborated about what I meant.

Charlie McConnell,
Sylva, 6/17/11

WELL, I WISH YOU WOULD!

The most interesting and funny teacher I ever met in my career was Lina Fortune who taught third grade at Vance Elementary School in West Asheville. Lina was a very dedicated and wonderful teacher. Some of her sayings certainly were unique, and one of them in particular almost got her into hot water. Lina had a habit when she encountered an unusual or strange situation of saying, "I wish you would!" It was just her words now and it meant surprise or something out of the ordinary. Well, one day she had had it up to her neck with this little boy Paul and wrote a note to Paul's mother, explaining all the disruption that Paul had caused during the day. Early the next morning, before children had come to class, I called Mrs. Fortune on the intercom and told her she had a phone call. Her room was only two doors from my office and she was there in just a minute and answering the phone, she said, "Hello, this is Mrs. Fortune." After a few minutes, Lina held up her hand and said, "I wish you would!" The person on the other end of the line hung up on her. Lina turned to me and said, "Can you believe that? Mrs. Smith just told me she didn't know what she was going to do with Paul, that sometimes she just felt like she would kill herself." Lina then went back to her room to greet her children as they came in the door. About an hour later, Mrs. Fortune received a phone call from the superintendent demanding that she report to his office as soon as her students were dismissed. The next morning, she told me that Mrs. Smith had called the superintendent's office crying and accusing Mrs. Fortune of suggesting she kill herself. After she explained the situation to the superintendent, he understood and suggested she call Mrs. Smith immediately and apologize.

Dot Bryson,
Malvern Hills, Buncombe County, 1/12/11

A Special Team Mate

One of the teachers who helped me a lot was Francine Delaney. Francine was teaching the fourth grade with me at Vance Elementary. This was before she was promoted to Director of Elementary Curriculum for Asheville City Schools. She and I became very close. I remember one day in particular when she took me out to lunch at TK Tripps restaurant toward the end of the year. She bought me a little gift and it was a letter opener. It was the prettiest thing and it meant so very much to me. We worked so very close together. We divided our classes and she would teach the sciences and I would teach social studies. We made a good team.

Billie Lewis,
Enka, Buncombe County, 11/15/10

GREAT TEACHERS PAVE THE WAY

During my time in public schools, I had many very good and interesting teachers. I had the same teacher for the first and second grades. She was a wonderful teacher. Like most of my teachers in the early grades, this teacher became my idol and I remember that I wanted to be just like her when I grew up. During the summer, between my first and second grade, my "idol," I will call her Miss Jones, got married and when she came back to school she was now Mrs. Smith. I was so very excited for her. Even at that young and tender age, I could see the radiance in her smile and was so excited that she was so happy.

The following year I had another great teacher, Mrs. Rodgers my third grade teacher; she would play the violin for her class. Even then, I realized that she was a bad violin player, but she was my teacher and she was doing the best she could to entertain the children. She could not carry a tune in a bucket, but I loved her anyway. I remember one year she took me to see the movie "Bambi" at the local theater and bought me a huge story book. She also took me to lunch at the S&W Cafeteria. I never forgot the many wonderful things she did for me and paid for it all out of her own pocket because she recognized I needed her extra support at that time in my life. I could never forget her and have always attempted to follow her example of kindness and empathy. I like to think I have been a better teacher and person because of Mrs. Rodgers.

Sue Harris,
Hominy Valley, April 26, 2011

A Unique And Wonderful Administrator

After thirty years working in Asheville City Schools, I retired and took a position in another state as an assistant administrator in an elementary school. The principal of the school, I will call her Mrs. Bell, was such a wonderful person. She was African-American and became such a dear friend. Not only was she a beautiful person, she was one of the best school administrators I have had the privilege of meeting.

The story of how we came to meet was one of the most unusual events in my life. To understand the story, one would need to go back forty-four years. Growing up in a small town in south central Kentucky, my parents would take me after church most every Sunday the eighteen miles to Celina, Tennessee to have lunch. At that time, most of the African Americans did not live in the small town of Celina, but up on a ridge overlooking the town called Free Hill. On Free Hill, there was a small restaurant that served the best fried chicken anywhere around and white folks would come from far and wide to have lunch. I was about ten years old at the time and while the chicken was being cooked, I would play with some of the African American children who were in the restaurant.

Forward ahead to 1997 when I was being interviewed for a position as assistant administrator. After discussing my professional credentials, we began talking about where we grew up and I discovered it was her relative who ran the restaurant on Free Hill and she was always around there on Sunday afternoons. We had played together as children and now she was hiring me as her assistant.

Mrs. Bell had a unique ability to work with all races, but she had a special technique that only she could have survived using in a school system. As her assistant, I was charged with the responsibility of handling discipline problems. There were many times when I would summon an

African-American mom to come to school to discuss a discipline issue involving her son or daughter that they would pull the race card, become upset, and accuse me of picking on their child because he/she was black. I have always been proud of my relationship with the African-American race and never allowed that fact to enter into any decision being made. But, early on I learned that when the race card was played, to step next door and ask Mrs. Bell to step into my office. She would stand above the usually young mom and, in a very intimidating voice, address the woman as an "Ally-bat" and let her know in no uncertain terms that we were here to help her child and she better shape up and support the school or her child would not amount to anything. In every case the mom would look down and quietly say "Yes Mame." One day, in private, I asked Mrs. Bell to explain to me exactly what an "Ally-bat" meant. She explained it was a woman who waited in the alleys for men to come by to pay her for sex. I took a deep breath and sat down.

J. Terry Hall,
Scott Mountain, Buncombe County, 3/3/11

My Teacher Left To Go To War

Ms. Conley, who was my first grade teacher at Aycock Elementary in Asheville in 1941, left in the middle of the school year and joined the Women's Air Core. That was just after the attack on Pearl Harbor and I still remember how shocking that was at the time.

Julia Clark,
Biltmore Lake, June 2, 2011

A Girl Has To Do What A Girl Has To Do

When I was in ninth grade, I tried out for cheerleader and my music teacher, who happened to be a distant relative, tried to talk me out of it because she thought it would hurt my singing voice. Well, I did it anyway and it did not seem to have affected my voice.

Julia Clark,
Biltmore Lake, June 2, 2011

All Teachers Are Not Positive Role Models

In junior high school, I did not have as many positive experiences as I did in elementary school. The thing I remember about my reading teacher was she looked like she came from Paris, by the way she dressed, and she always smelled like smoke due to her cigarette smoking. Even with those drawbacks, she must have motivated me in a positive manner because I still remember the poetry I had to learn.

One of the most negative teachers I have ever encountered as a child or as an adult, was my junior high school civics teacher. My father died the year I had Mrs. Kerr, and although she knew about his death the night before, she demanded that I take a scheduled civic test the following morning. It is hard even to this day to find something positive in her actions, but I think she taught me to have empathy with those who are undergoing a very difficult time in their lives. I always tried to understand the child and the situation in which they find themselves.

In high school, my most memorable teacher was Mrs. Jennings, she was the most dramatic and out-of-control person I have ever met in my entire life. When she became angry, which happened often, she would throw the nearest textbook across the classroom at some unsuspecting student. I cannot think of anything worthwhile that she taught me, except maybe to dodge. I don't remember very many funny things which happened while I was growing up. I guess I was just too serious to notice funny.

Sue Harris,
Hominy Valley, April 26, 2011

ALWAYS TELL IT LIKE IT IS

I had one teacher who just could not teach in an acceptable manner. No matter how I attempted to help him, he would not follow directions. Shortly, he left and went to an adjoining county. The principal called me and asked if I would recommend the teacher for the position. I explained that I would not give him a positive recommendation. When he asked why I was withholding my recommendation, I explained that I had tried to help him improve and suggested he take some additional classes and he refused to follow through and that I was pleased when he left. The principal stated that he felt everybody deserved a second chance, so he hired him to coach football. He fired him before school started. Some people are just not cut out to teach school.

I have had teachers who came to me from other high schools and received a favorable recommendation from their past principal, yet, turned out to be terrible teachers and unwilling to accept positive criticism. That is one thing I will never do. If the person is not a teacher I would rehire, I will not recommend them to another principal just to get rid of them.

I had a principal who recommended a teacher who had left his school as a very good teacher. I hired the teacher only to find out shortly that that was not the case. When I confronted the principal about his recommendation, he said, "Oh, I never said that." Another administrator standing nearby spoke up and said, "Oh yes you did, I heard you." False recommendations have a way of coming back to haunt you.

Thomas Ledbetter,
Hendersonville, 4/13/2011

READING IS FUNDAMENTAL

Today, we give teachers so much more support than in the past where we had to get in there and dig it out on our own. One of the highlights of my career was when Fred Trantham chose me to be a part of our Reading Recovery program. The training I received taught me so much about reading and just changed my whole perspective. I still attribute that training to my belief and philosophy today about how children learn to read. And you, Dr. Hall, as Title 1 Director of Asheville City Schools, was instrumental in bringing the Reading Recovery program to Haywood County and several western North Carolina counties. I thank you for your help. I still don't know of a more successful reading program for teaching children to read.

Sandy Caldwell,
Waynesville, Haywood County, 11/11/10

HEAD UM UP MOVE UM OUT

knew this teacher back in 1970 who was a very strange bird to say the least. He was tall and skinny and always carried a black razor strap wrapped around his neck. Anytime a kid would get out of line, he would grab that strap and pop them on the butt. One day I was in my classroom teaching social studies and heard the most awful sound. Two boys came bursting through my door running for their lives with their teacher right behind them swinging his strap.

Dorland Winkler,
Malvern Hills, 8/12/11

GREAT TEACHERS I HAVE KNOWN

Over the years, for the most part, I have had really good teachers working with me as principal. Most have been highly qualified and would have been a success anywhere in the country. For instance, I worked with Hugh Hamilton. Hugh worked as my football coach, and he was also a great math teacher. He would ask to work with the lower kids in his math classes, not because he could have not succeeded with any student, but he felt by working with the lower students, maybe he could help them to succeed. He had graduated from Western Carolina and Peabody University and had worked as Asheville's coach before he came over to East Henderson High school with me. Several colleges had offered him a position as a coach, but he had no interest in leaving the high school. Earlier, he won the state championship.

I had this other teacher who would step up to the plate whenever the need called. I asked her to teach a science class for which she was not certified, but at that time if one was certified in health and P.E., they were also certified in science. She stated she had not taught science before, but she was willing to do it if I needed her. She said later that she had to study much harder than the students to stay ahead of them, but she succeeded.

Thomas Ledbetter,
Hendersonville, 4/13/2011

ROCK ON AT THE ORANGE PEEL

Back in my earlier days, I played in a rock and roll band called "Soulful Strut". In seventh grade, I had learned to play a musical instrument in the school band. I chose slide trombone because I could not afford to purchase reeds for the saxophone. I loved to play in the band. We began our own rock and roll band and started out playing music from the "Scat Cats." They were good and a leading band at that time. We played several places, one being the Orange Peel over on Biltmore Avenue here in Asheville. That was in the late 1960s when the Orange Peel was an all black club. Most folks don't realize that that club used to be an all black night club. It was during this time that I met Bill Flupp, who later became Assistant Principal at Asheville High School. His children played in our band. We backed up several big name entertainers back then and went on the road every weekend. My brother and I worked at a restaurant back then and when we got off work at ten o'clock, we would go to some club and play until the wee hours of the morning. We both had our hair done up in an Afro and wore our bell bottoms and ruffled shirts. As soon as we got off work, we were on our way. During the turmoil of integration in 1969-1970, they would play our songs over the speaker system during lunch at Asheville High School to calm the tense situation.

Ron Lytle,
Woodfin School, Oasis program, April 28, 2011

THE BUCK STOPS HERE

Although most of my teachers were wonderful, I did have a few who were a little short in some areas. I had this one teacher who taught drivers education; he was always late. Many times, he would not show up until ten minutes after his class should have started and the students were waiting. He wasn't on tenure yet and was working on a yearly contract. Finally I brought him into my office and said, "You will either resign at the end of the school year or I am going to fire you." He said, "I just didn't know you were that upset about it." "I have talked to you three times," I said, "and I don't have to get red in the face and cuss to fire you, but you are just not doing the job and you won't try, so I've had it." He turned in his resignation and I placed it on file until the end of the school year which was in about three weeks. The next weekend, he turned the drivers education car upside down and was found to be driving under the influence, (DUI). The superintendent called me first thing Monday morning and asked what I was going to do. I told him I already had his resignation in my desk and the superintendent decided to let it ride for the next two weeks. Of course, the teacher did not show up after the wreck.

Thomas Ledbetter,
Hendersonville, 4/13/2011

ARE YOU SURE HE WAS LATE?

I had one teacher who was always late. She was the type of person who carried about everything she owned with her and, wherever she went, she was always late getting there. She taught Music and English both, so she had to move between buildings and she would usually stop in the teachers' lounge to have a cup of coffee and chat before wandering into the classroom maybe five or ten minutes late. I had tried to encourage her to be on time for class several times, but to no avail. One day one of her students was late for her class and she had the nerve to bring him into my office for discipline. I know it was mean on my part, but I just couldn't resist. When she explained her reason for bringing the boy to my office, I put on a puzzled look and asked, "How do you know he was late?" She looked surprised, then took the boy by the arm and left my office. I never had a problem from her being late after that.

Thomas Ledbetter,
Hendersonville, 4/13/2011

I GREW UP ON THE OTHER SIDE OF THE TRACKS

I have had some really good teachers in my life. I would have to say my Daddy and my Mama were my best teachers. They really stayed on top of my twin brother and myself. Like they would tell us to stay in the yard and my brother and I would say, "Let's go down to the creek and play." When we got back, we would get a spanking, but we always knew they were doing it for our own good, just not right then.

While I was working at the Detention Center, I served as a councilor over one of the dorms. I lived with the kids and slept in the dorm. We were like a big family with thirty-six kids. We worked hard and put in long hours. Our day started at six in the morning and would go until about ten at night. The next morning at six we would start all over again. I would teach the kids manners, social skills and how to get along with their peers. I would take them to their activities during the day and sometimes I would even take them off-campus on field trips. I never had anyone run away from me on a field trip, but I did have two boys run away one day. They took off running and I was left with the other thirty-four kids so I could not chase after them. They were caught a couple weeks later.

I never really had a bad situation while living in the dorm with the kids. Although, one time a kid tried to hit me. I was quick back then and when I saw his fists clinch, I knew he was going to come at me. When he swung at me, I wrapped my arms around him and held him until the supervisor came. Like I said, I never had much of a problem with fights. I always tried to be professional and would bring in movies that could be earned by good behavior. Most of the kids respected me. One day a boy cussed me and, all of a sudden, another boy hit him in the nose and blood started to pour. The boy who did the hitting said, "That was wrong cussing Mr. Ron out." The other kid just walked away. They seemed to have a great respect for me because I treated them with respect.

When my supervisor saw that I could handle myself, they gave me a dorm where the more aggressive kids were housed. I was glad to take on the extra responsibility because those kids were totally out of control. I had an experience in my younger years which worked to my advantage in this situation. I had lived in the "projects" of Shiloh while I was a child after my parents had broken up. My mother was working and trying to keep food on the table at a department store when the unthinkable happened. This was in the 1960s and before black folks were accepted by white folks. My mother was a department manager at the store when a young "white" man who was her supervisor called out in an angry manner to an older black man who was working as a janitor. He said, "Hey Boy, get yourself over here and sweep this floor!" My mother stepped over, and speaking to the angry young man, said as kindly as she could, "Sir, you shouldn't speak to that man like that. You need to show him some respect since he is old enough to be your grandfather." The next day she was fired. They used the excuse that my mother had allowed a woman to pay for her two candy bars as one item instead of separating them and therefore being charged the extra penny in tax.

Now, we did not even have enough money to put food on the table. Friends would bring us enough food for us children to eat. I am sure many times my mother did without so her children could eat. It is hard to understand how hard it is to go from having whatever you needed to having nothing and really no place to go. One thing that sticks with me was the time when I realized that my mom had only three dimes to her name. I knew then that we were poor. In addition to having it hard financially, even our so called "friends" would have nothing to do with us or play with us any more because we were now just "poor project kids." I became very angry and had all kind of thoughts about hurting people to rob them to get something to eat. There were some times when my brother and I went for three days without anything to eat. Looking back, I can better understand why some kids act out against society, but that is not the answer.

After making the move to the projects, we realized it was not all that bad. We had many women who lived there and helped the children by providing activities to keep us out of trouble, but not a lot of men. My brother and I worked when we could and would take the younger kids down to the local store and buy them some candy or ice cream. The small children would call us Uncle Ron and Uncle Rodney because they looked up to us. There were very few positive male role models for us to look up to; there was this one man who lived next door to us and led the local drill team. He was a major positive influence in my brother and my lives. One year we took some of these kids to a carnival. These "project kids" had never been anywhere and going to the carnival was a great treat. My brother and I went around and asked several ladies if they would drive them, and we got some donations to pay their way. Even though this was before black folks were accepted, there were some white folks who gave donations for us to take them to the carnival.

When I came to Asheville in 1969 I attended a gathering about the racial issue. One of the white boys said the "N" word and one of the black boys hit him. We got the boy out of there, but that just goes to show how bad the racial tensions were at that time.

Around about that time, my brother and I decided to go to a gym and learn to box. One night, I had beaten the boy I was fighting and my brother had beaten his opponent and, as we left the ring, there were some white boys who drew knives on us. After that night, we stopped boxing here in Asheville and only did our boxing over at Warren Wilson on campus.

One time when I was a child my daddy and his family were going across Tennessee to see his brother. We were planning to stay with him a couple days. My daddy's car broke down in a small white neighborhood outside Kingsport, Tennessee and it was frightening for us because of the race issues.

When I was a kid of about eleven, I was allowed to attend camp one summer. We black kids got one week and the older ones and younger ones all went together, whereas the younger white kids were allowed to go for a week and the older kids were allowed a week. During our week, white folks hid in the woods and shot guns into the cabins and a cross was burned outside the cabin doors. That's hard growing up in a time like that with no way to defend yourself. During the night, when you had to go to the bathroom it was very dangerous to go outside the cabin. One boy was so scared he used the bathroom right in the cabin because he was too afraid to go outside.

Everything that happened at that time in my life was not bad. I had this one white friend by the name of David Bledsaw. He loved ping-pong and running track. My brother and I could beat him in ping-pong, but we could not beat him in track. That boy could run. His family was well off and he really became a close friend. He took my brother and I to our first concert in Knoxville, Tennessee when we were sixteen. We got to see James Brown and it was really something. This happened at a very hard time in our lives, just after my mom had lost her job. It meant the world to my brother and me.

When Christmas time came, some white people brought us food so we would have a good meal on Christmas. They told my mother she should sue the department store but she didn't. My mom was a strong person. She didn't want to accept things from others and she didn't want welfare. Her strength taught my brother and I a great lesson.

This is the main reason I am in this business of helping children who need a loving hand on their shoulder. I have been in that situation and can understand from where the child may be coming.

Based on my past experiences, I feel I was led into the field of social work where I could make a positive difference in the lives of young people. These children that we are serving in the Oasis program are special to me. We never know what's going on in their lives, whether they have missed meals or what they have to live with every day of their lives. I know in my life when I couldn't eat and didn't know what the next day held, I had anger in my mind and wanted to strike out at those around me. Many of the children I serve may be going through the same thing. I always keep this foremost in my mind and do my best to find what needs to be done to provide for this young person. I have found that when I help a child, we form a bond and build a sense of respect which will last throughout life.

Ron Lytle,
Woodfin School, Oasis program, April 28, 2011

STOP, OR I'LL SPRAY

I remember this one teacher who had this thing about germs. She was overly conscious about spreading germs and carried around a can of Lysol wherever she went. I'll call this teacher Mary Ann to protect the guilty. One day she came in my office and, of course, had her can of

Lysol ready. Mr. Johnson, the custodian, was on the telephone and as soon as he finished with his phone call, Mary Ann grabbed his arms and sprayed both of his hands before spraying the phone receiver. Mr. Johnson was so surprised he just stood there and did not say a word.

Dot Bryson,
Malvern Hills, Buncombe County, 1/12/11

SHE GAVE HER MOST VALUABLE TREASURE

There were so many outstanding teachers over the years, but one stands out as being the most unique. Ms. Rodgers as I will call her, was an unmarried elderly woman who wore very heavy make-up. She always used bright red lipstick that was applied very heavy and thick. She was a hoarder of materials and would not allow any other teacher to share her supplies even if the other teacher ran out. The last year she worked before she retired, she unexpectedly took a young teacher under her wing and asked the young teacher to come in her room as there was something she wanted to show her. Entering her supply room, she showed the teacher construction paper stacked to the ceiling and told her she had saved all this paper and, when she retired, she wanted the young teacher to have all the paper she had saved. The young teacher thanked her, realizing it was Ms. Rodgers' hidden treasure and was so very important to her. After Ms. Rodgers retired, the young teacher had to throw out all the construction paper because it was all faded from being an the shelf all those years. Ms. Rodgers had been at Vance for years when I came in as secretary and I recognized her as a teacher I had gone to school with in Glenville, NC years ago. When I reminded her of our school days in the mountain country school, she said she didn't go to that school. Maybe she was ashamed to admit she had attended a country school. Who knows?

Dot Bryson,
Malvern Hills, Buncombe County, 1/12/11

CHAPTER FIVE

INTERESTING EXPERIENCES

THE BOY COULDN'T FIND IT

School had been in session for about two months when a new five year old boy by the name of James entered kindergarten for his first day of school. His mother had brought him and enrolled him in Ms. Jones' class. James seemed to be a shy little boy and when his mother left, he started to cry. Ms. Jones got him settled down after a few minutes by getting him interested in playing with a truck. He and another boy, Jim, had played with the truck for about fifteen minutes when little James walked over to Ms. Jones and said he needed to go potty. Ms. Jones took James by the hand and led him to the classroom door and pointed to the restroom two doors down the hall. She told James to use the potty and come right back. James was gone only a few minutes when he came back to Ms. Jones with a puzzled look on his face and told her that he couldn't find it. Once again, she stepped to the door and watched little James enter the restroom door. In a short time, he once again enters the class and informs his teacher that he couldn't find it. A little frustrated, Ms. Jones asked Jim to take James to the restroom. Shortly, Jim came into the room and informed Ms. Jones that James couldn't find it. Now, Ms. Jones was puzzled and rather strongly said, "What do you mean he couldn't find it? I saw you take him through the door. Whereas, Jim said, "No, his mother put his underwear on him backwards and he can't find it."

J. Terry Hall,
Scott Mountain, Buncombe County, 3/3/11

CHILDREN ARE HONEST

I have always expected my teachers to love their children first and teach them second. One morning while I was Principal at Jones Elementary in Asheville, I was out front unloading the buses when little Dominique, a kindergarten student, came running up and grabbed me around the leg and said, "I love you Mr. Cutshall!" I said, "I love you too, Dominique." I can still see those little eyes looking up at me as he added, "Ooh, you need to blow your nose!" He then ran off down the hall.

Charles Cutshall,
Sodom Laurel, Madison County, 7/14/11

NEVER DISTURB A HUNGRY MAN'S LUNCH

Our custodian at Hill Street School went to the dumpster one afternoon to empty trash and found a homeless man sitting in there, eating discarded food with both hands. He seemed to be angry at the custodian for disturbing his lunch. It was hard to believe since we regularly put rat poison in the dumpster to help keep out the rats. I didn't know what to do so I called the police and we took the man over to his son's house which was not too far away. When we took the man up to his son's door and knocked, his son cussed us out for bringing him to his door.

Dorland Winkler,
Malvern Hills, 8/12/11

I SPEAK SEVERAL LANGUAGES

One day I was talking to some students and they were complaining about having to take a foreign language. I explained to them the need to learn other languages and told them I knew three languages. They asked what three languages I could speak and I said, "Some English, Pig Latin, and Profanity. They said, "You really know all those?"

Larry Liggett,
Skyland, Buncombe County, 7/21/11

I PUTTY CRACKS

When I became Principal at Asheville Junior High School, it was about the time boys started wearing their pants about half way across their butts. To this day, I still don't understand this fad. But anyway, I simply made it known to the boys that I putty any cracks I see. Well, needless to say, when I rounded a corner, you could see the sparks fly as they jerked up their pants.

Charles Cutshall,
Sodom Laurel,Madison County, 7/14/11

GRADUATION DAY

Graduation ceremonies in high school were always interesting. First of all, I had some parents who said they had been invited to go visit in another state during the time of graduation. They asked, "When can we schedule to have a graduation when we get back?" Another parent asked, when told her child had not completed his work and could not graduate, "But we have just bought him a new suit, why can't he graduate?"

When the graduates came across the stage, all kinds of things happened. One year we had comical dress. Kids tried to dress in the most bazaar dress possible. Another year many of the kids wore silly socks. Also, one year they decided to walk across the stage without any shoes on their feet. After we started requiring caps and gowns, so everyone would dress alike things were somewhat better. Although, one of the big ones was the coke bottle hand shake. The students would palm a bottle cap and when they shook hands with the Superintendent or Chairman of the Board, they would press the bottle cap into his or her hand. I quietly whispered to those waiting in line, "Anyone I catch with a bottle cap in their hand will be escorted out the back door." They said, "Would you do that?" I said, "Try me." That worked, so the next year they had pennies in their hands and you could hear all these pennies hitting the floor. One year, we had graduation on the football field so they could bring as many people as they wished. Everything went great until someone decided to turn on the sprinklers and water the football field. Another year, the parents got so unruly that I had to announce that if we did not maintain some sort of order, the graduation would end. They brought it down after that, but they had been yelling so loud no one could hear the name of the next person being called forward. So graduation was always interesting at Asheville High.

Larry Liggett,
Skyland, Buncombe County, 7/21/11

NATURE CALLS

During my first year teaching, I had a little girl named Mary in my room. Since I was the first male teacher she had ever had, she was somewhat intimidated and, instead of asking permission to go to the bathroom, she just sat there and peed on herself. I had no idea what had happened until the next day when her mother came to school and explained what had happened. After that, I made sure that all students knew to let me know if they needed to go to the bathroom during my class.

Fred Trantham,
Waynesville, Haywood County, 11/11/10

THE MAN WITH THE MOON

One day, I was standing behind the bleachers at Asheville High School looking up at the chemistry lab when I spotted a young man mooning me out the window. I rushed up the stairs and, of course, no on knew anything about it. I never did find the perpetrator.

Larry Liggett,Skyland,
Buncombe County, 7/21/11

FOR A GOOD TIME SEE ME

Traveling to conferences was always a great part of my career. As an Assistant Principal group, we were known for pulling pranks on each other. One particular conference I remember was in Charlotte. I checked in early and left a gag note at check-in for my friend Pat, who was checking in later. The note simply said, "for a good time come on up to room 302". Pat came in to register and the desk clerk said he had a message for her. What the desk clerk did not notice was that Pat had stepped to the side to fill out a hotel card, and this other woman that the clerk thought was Pat, came up and was handed the note. She opened it and said in a very irritated voice, "Well, obviously this was not meant for me!" Pat and I tried to dodge that woman throughout the conference.

Charles Cutshall,
Sodom Laurel,Madison County, 7/14/11

LOCK AND LOAD

During all my time at Asheville High School, I only confiscated two guns. My two secretaries chose to take shooting lessons at the ROTC shooting range in order to protect me if the time should ever come when it was necessary. Colonel Thomas and Sargent Fisher trained them. I don't think they even had a gun, but they had been trained.

Larry Liggett,
Skyland, Buncombe County, 7/21/11

IN DANGER OF BEING SUED

After I became Principal at Asheville High School, the track coach came and said he was going to have team practice, although the field was undergoing construction. I told him to go ahead but not to do any field events. A short time later, he came into my office with this girl. She had a towel wrapped around her head and was bleeding from her face. I quickly asked what had happened and he said they were throwing discus and one flew into the stands and hit her in the face. I was upset that he had proceeded with field events although I had instructed him not to do so. We took care of the girl and there was nothing more said about it, but we were lucky not to get sued.

Another time, we had a bus load of visitors from Hickory on campus and as the bus came around a bend in the field, some kids walked out into the road and a woman, standing up talking to the students on the bus, was thrown forward against the front of the bus. Shortly thereafter, we got word that they were suing us. O L Sherill, Co-Principal at the time said he was not going to be sued. He said, "If she wants to come in here and show me the bruises where she was hurt, I'll believe it." She had hit her butt. After his reply, we never heard any more about it.

Larry Liggett, Skyland,
Buncombe County, 7/21/11

CHANGE CAN BE SCARY

In 1969, integration came to Asheville City Schools and I was secretary at Vance Elementary School in West Asheville. It was an interesting and sometimes dangerous time to be working in the schools. Thank goodness we did not have any real racial problems at Vance Elementary, but at Asheville High School, there were marches and riots all over the campus. Police were called to the high school to control the situation and there were police stationed at the Jr. High School to put down any problems. We, in the elementary schools were not in the middle of the violent situation, but were very anxious, thinking that at any moment the violence could spill over to our campus. We did have several irate phone calls from African-American parents during those times.

Dot Bryson,
Malvern Hills, Buncombe County, 1/12/11

PICKY THIEVES

While I was Principal at Hill Street School, we had many breaking and entering. Every few nights I would receive a call from the police stating that someone had broken into the school and they needed me to come over and assess the damage. One night, they had broken in and stolen a computer. The following night, I was called once again and this time, there was the computer sitting next to my office door with a note which said it was not the kind they wanted.

Dorland Winkler,
Malvern Hills, 8/12/11

WILD—WILD ASHEVILLE

Back in the early 1970s, when we intergrated Asheville City Schools, we had some riots at Asheville High school. A new teacher was hired that year and other teachers could tell he was a little nervous, to say the least. One teacher jokingly told him to be sure to go by the office on his way out and pick up his gun. That afternoon the new teacher came into the principal's office and asked for a gun. The principal's mouth dropped open as he said, "What are you talking about!"

Larry Liggett,
Skyland, Buncombe County, 7/21/11

GERBILS FROM HELL

While a fifth grade teacher at Claxton Elementary in Asheville, two of my close friends, Pat and Ann, came in my room and said they had two gerbils they wanted to give me. They had them in an aquarium and were careful to assure me that they were both males. That should have been enough to tip me off, but I was naive. In a short time, my aquarium was running over with twenty-six gerbils. I ended up taking them home to keep them from getting out into the school. I placed them on my deck and my wife said, "I'm taking them to the mall and giving them to the pet shop." I said, "What if they don't take them?" She said, "If they don't take them I will sit them down and run." She did just that.

Charles Cutshall,
Sodom Laurel, Madison County, 7/14/11

LET ME TELL YOU A SECRET

While I was Principal at a Junior High, I had some wonderful assistant principals. One was short, bald and didn't smile a lot. One day, a student asked me why he never smiled. I told the boy that I would tell him in confidence but to never tell anyone else. I said, "He is constipated and that's why he looks like he does." A few days later, my assistant came up to me and said, "What have you been telling these students, especially the boys? They keep walking by, looking at me and smiling". Of course I told him nothing.

Charles Cutshall,
Sodom Laurel,Madison County,7/14/11

THE MOUNTAIN MAN'S DOG

When I was working in Madison County, I was told by Superintendent of Schools, Bob Edwards, "As an administrator in the mountains of North Carolina, you can mess around with anything you want, but don't mess around with a man's dog."

Larry Liggett,
Skyland, Buncombe County, 7/21/11

WHERE AM I ANYWAY?

I thought it was funny that sometime kids would get into such a big way of talking that they would forget if they were at school or at home. I have been called mother and I have been called father and other names and, there was always a look of shock on their face when they realized what they had said.

Larry Liggett,
Skyland, Buncombe County, 7/21/11

DO WE REALLY NEED THE MONEY?

When I was monitoring education programs, I spent a lot of time on the road. Nights became very boring so, I looked for anything to do to get me out of the motel room. In the metropolitan areas, that was not a problem but in rural areas, there just was little, if anything to do or see. I was in one rural mountain county looking for something to occupy my evening. I saw in the local newspaper there was a public meeting on an educational bond referendum that evening at one of the schools. I had nothing better to do and had never attended such a meeting, so I decided to attend. The night was cold and raining cats and dogs! I arrived at the school and saw a sign to enter the side door as loose bricks might fall from above the front entrance. I went around to the side door, was greeted, and directed to the meeting room. As I entered, there were several people already there, some holding cans to catch the water leaking through the roof. There were also several buckets positioned around the room. I had to admit, it bothered me to think any community would allow their children's school to get in this condition. Once the meeting began, community and school leaders spoke about the obvious need for this proposed school bond. Now it was time to hear from the public—imagine my amazement upon hearing these people stand up and argue that a bond was not needed to update their schools. One young man particularly sticks in my memory. He stood there, holding a can to catch the rain, telling everyone why this bond referendum was not necessary. I must admit that to this day I am still perplexed.

Don Carter,
Garner, May 24, 2011

You Were Blowing Where?

We were going to Pisgah Ranch one day for an end of the year celebrations with our Title I Teachers. Larry Liggett and I were riding together down the interstate with Larry driving and me riding shotgun. He and I had decided to pull a prank on one of the single women who had no boy friend at the time. As part of the prank, we had bought a male blown-up doll. Picture this, here we were going down Interstate 40 with me trying to blow up this male doll. It just so happened that the tube into which I had to blow was in the butt of the doll. As I continued to blow, we were laughing and I was getting hot from blowing. I rolled down the window and out popped an arm that hit Larry in the head. Then a leg flew out the window and there I sat blowing into the butt of the doll. People were laughing their heads off as they passed us on the interstate and at the traffic light that we had to stop. It was a good thing the police didn't pass us or we would have been put in jail.

Charles Cutshall,
Sodom Laurel, Madison County, 7/14/11

WOULD YOU ZIP ME UP, PLEASE?

I decided I would take part in some of our classes at Asheville High School so I went into the Home Economics Department. That happened to be the day they were learning how to install a zipper. They gave me a pair of pants and I was to install the zipper. Thinking I had done a good job, I turned in my work to find that I had put the zipper in backwards and upside down and I would have had to reach down inside my pants to use the zipper. I decided this was not working for me.

Larry Liggett,
Skyland, Buncombe County, 7/21/11

READ DIRECTIONS CAREFULLY

I had this boy who drove the school bus for me while I was at Pisgah High School in Canton. He was not the sharpest knife in the drawer, but he was a good boy and was a good bus driver. One morning, he parked his bus at school and came into my office. He said, "Doc," everybody always called me Doc, "I've got to go back home. I'm sick. I'm sick as a dog." "What's wrong with you son?" I said. "I've got diarrhea in the worst way," he groaned. "I've just got to go back home. I've had it for about a week and I'm so weak I can hardly make it." Feeling his pain, I said, "Why don't you go to the doctor?" Looking pitiful, he said, "I went to the doctor last Saturday." "What did he do?" I asked. "He gave me some big old horse pills and I've been taking them every since but I'm not a bit better than I was. I think he called them suppositories or something."

Thomas Ledbetter,
Hendersonville, 4/13/2011

THE PLOT

We had a tradition of not celebrating our friends birthdays on their actual birthdays, but to set them up at a time they least expected it. One year, we had arranged for two of our high school teacher friends to stage an argument in a restaurant. We were to meet at Shoney's Restaurant to celebrate Pat's birthday. We thought the Shoney's at Enka/Candler would be like the one on Tunnel Road and have sliding doors where we would have some privacy. When we got to the restaurant, there were no sliding doors and it was wide open to the public. By the time we found this out, it was too late to let the two high school teachers know.

The plot was for the couple to be sitting in a booth next to us when the woman would get into a verbal fight with the man about him two-timing her. She would then jump up to leave and accuse Pat as being the woman with which he was cheating. She was standing there shouting accusations at Pat while Pat was saying, "Mam, I don't know your husband! I really don't know your husband!" Well, needless to say we entertained that entire restaurant.

Charles Cutshall,
Sodom Laurel, Madison County, 7/14/11

THE NIGHT I TUCKED HER IN

When I was President of the Association of School Curriculum Development, I attended a conference with the former past president of ASCD and the president before him, who happened to be a woman. The woman drank a little too much and by the time we were to leave, she could not walk on her own. My friend and I both took her by the arms and carried her back to her hotel. Picture this, here we were two men about two o'clock in the morning literally carrying a very drunk woman back into her hotel and asking the desk clerk for her room number so we could take her to bed. We managed to get her in the room and in bed and then we left. On these ASCD trips, I was always the bartender and the designated driver and this time the one to put them to bed.

Larry Liggett,
Skyland, Buncombe County, 7/21/11

Spare The Rod

Working with small groups of children as I did, I did not have many discipline problems. Although, one day I had this child who just would not behave. He was so out of control that I could not conduct my class. After several warnings, I paddled him. I felt so bad; I am sure it hurt me more than it hurt him and I never ever gave another child a spanking. Not long after that, they banned corporal punishment and I was glad.

Anonymous,
Western North Carolina, 5/6/2011

Walking On KKK Turf

One time, Francine Delaney and I were going to a conference down state and went through the town of Smithfield. Francine was probably in her fifties at the time and an African-American. I grew up in Ohio. We stopped at this nice restruant to eat lunch when the waiter showed me to a table. I pulled out a chair for Francine and the waiter took my arm and said, "Stop! She cannot sit here; she will have to sit at a table in the back room." I looked at Francine in shock and said, "This isn't the place for us." Then we walked out the door. I did not realize until later that Smithfield, North Carolina was the home of the Klu-Klex-Klan. Welcome to the south, Yankee!

Larry Liggett,
Skyland, Buncombe County, 7/21/11

SPIT SHINE

We had a custodian one time who was, to put it kindly, not the sharpest knife in the drawer. He failed to clean the restroom in a proper manner. The principal told me as assistant principal, that if things did not improve, he was going to fire the custodian I spoke with the man and informed him that the principal was going to fire him if he did not clean the restroom much better. He took me at my word and spit cleaned the restroom until everything glistened. The principal, who was a scholarly individual, took the custodian and went in to inspect the restroom. Upon completing an inspection like a military general and seeing everything in such a clean condition he said, "Its Immaculate! Its Immaculate!" The custodian took his keys off his key ring and throwing them on the floor, said, "If you think you can do it any damn better you can do it yourself!"

Dorland Winkler,
Malvern Hills, 8/12/11

THE WRONG PLACE AT THE WRONG TIME

After I retired from Asheville City Schools, I took a job as secretary at the Asheville Pre-School up the street in West Asheville. One morning, I walked into the office getting ready to start work and a parent was already there talking to a teacher. She was seemingly upset and just as

I came through the door, the parent turned to me and pointing a finger shouted "See!" and walked out the door. I guess that was a case of just being in the wrong place at the wrong time.

Dot Bryson,
Malvern Hills, Buncombe County, 1/12/11

THE PREACHER OF BOURBON STREET

A good friend of mine from Madison County, Owen Fish, and I took a trip to New Orleans years ago. Owen was a very religious man and a teetotaler when it came to drinking alcohol. All Owen could talk about as we flew to New Orleans was that while we were there, he wanted to meet the Preacher of Bourbon Street. Well, we went down to Bourbon Street and in a few minutes, we missed Owen. We found him in the house where the nearly nude woman swings out over the street. He was asking if they knew where he could find the Preacher of Bourbon Street. A little later he entered a bar and asked customers if they had seen the Preacher of Bourbon Street. He never did find that preacher, but he did visit several bars.

Larry Liggett,
Skyland, Buncombe County, 7/21/11

DON'T STEP ON A FROG

One day, we were studying frogs and toads. I had brought some frogs to school and we were going to look at and actually feel the skin of a frog. Well, I learned very quickly that if you are going to bring frogs to school, you should keep a lid on the jar. Those frogs got out and started jumping all over the classroom. Have you ever seen frogs jumping around in the middle of one hundred children? I was running around trying to catch the frogs while the girls were screaming and crying and I was yelling, "Don't step on them!" It was chaos.

Jan Lunsford,
Averys Creek, Buncombe County, 12/2/10

SHOW ME YOURS AND I WILL SHOW YOU MINE

One day, I had stepped out into the hall to speak with a teacher who had a class across the hall from me. While we were talking, there was the biggest commotion and noise coming from his room that you ever heard. He rushed back in his room and, later, I asked him what had happened. He said he had this one eighth grade girl who was kind of frisky and she had asked the boy sitting behind her to show her his penis, and he did. Of course the entire class went wild.

Charlie McConnell,
Sylva, 6/17/11

LET NATURE TAKE IT'S COURSE

One time, while I was Principal at Asheville High School I had this boy and girl who thought they were in love. In the middle of Asheville High, there is a great big rotunda, so this boy and girl decided they did not want to be separated and took a chain and chained themselves together in the middle of the rotunda and refused to leave. When I was told they were doing this, I went and asked them to leave. They refused. I thought, I could have them picked up and carried out or I could leave them alone. Walking away I said, "If that is what you want, that's fine with me, just stay there." After a couple hours, she told him she had to go to the bathroom and they unlocked the chain and went on to class. We passed up a lot of problems by doing it that way because there were several students standing around wondering what we were going to do. The way we handled it was to let nature take it's course.

Larry Liggett,
Skyland, Buncombe County, 7/21/11

To Our Friends Across The Pond

When I was at Hill Street School, we had a couple of exchange teachers and one of them was from Ireland. The Irish teacher and his wife lived in a house on Cumberland Avenue and they were walking to the Asheville Mall, a distance of about four miles, through a part of Asheville that is known to be unsafe. They thought nothing of it since they were used to walking great distances back home in Ireland. They had no problem with safety, but as they passed a store with a sign which said One Hour Martinizing, a cleaner, they went in and ordered martinis.

Another time, I was showing an Irish exchange teacher around town and when I slowed down for a speed bump in a shopping center, he looked at me and asked, "So you are also getting bombed here in Asheville?" I asked him what he meant and he explained that the speed bumps in Belfast were to discourage bombers from making a fast getaway.

Dorland Winkler,
Malvern Hills, 8/12/11

Three Times Zero Equals What?

I was employed with the West Virginia Department of Education as the Program Coordinator for Reading, Language Arts, and Social Studies.

One of my friends, Beth taught reading at a college in West Virginia. She invited me to her college to discuss the new learning outcomes in West Virginia schools. After our discussion ended, we were discussing our former students, and she mentioned one of her students who got "into some hot water" with a parent the first year of teaching.

The teacher, Miss Williams was teaching third grade in a public school in an affluent community. One day, she along and the class were working on their multiplication tables, and as Miss Williams would say 3 x 0, the sum of which equals 0 and the children would repeat. The class continued until they completed tables 3 and 4. Well, that night Miss Williams received a strange call from her principal advising her to be in his office the next morning before school opened to discuss a matter. The tone of his voice indicated that something was really wrong. He wouldn't tell her what it was.

Being a new teacher, she had no clue why he wanted to visit with her before school. With no sleep, the Miss Williams promptly goes to the principal's office the next Morning. As she walks through the door of the office, Miss Williams recognizes the mother of one of her students. Miss Williams greets the parent, but the parent just glares at her. About that time, the principal walks out of his office and invites the parent and Miss Williams to come in and have a seat. Miss Williams was shaking in her shoes. It was very evident that the parent was extremely upset. The principal advised Miss Williams that the parent complained about the language she was using in the classroom. Miss Williams responds, "What do you mean?" The parent shouts "My son was working on his multiplication tables last night at the kitchen table. He was saying out loud 3 x 0 the son of a bitch equals 0 and so on. I was absolutely horrified. He told me that that is what you and the class were doing with the multiplication tables. I believe that that language is inappropriate for young children."

Miss Willliams said, "Oh, we were practicing our multiplication tables out loud, but we were saying 3 x 0 the sum of which equals zero." The parent still didn't smile. The principal asked her to return to her classroom as the children were beginning to arrive at school. Meanwhile, the parent still was not satisfied. Being a highly educated lady, the parent said, "Well, I don't know who taught Miss Williams how to teach math, because there is no sum in multiplication. With these words, she stormed out of the school.

Dr. Judy Pierce,
Winston Salem, 6/15/11

THIS KID NEEDED ATTENTION

I had this boy, Michael, come into my office and said, "I was just in the rest room and there were some black boys in there and they beat me up." I told him I would check it out. I then assigned one of my assistant principals to monitor the rest room. A couple days passed and nothing happened. Then Michael came back to my office and said the black boys had once again beat him up. I asked him where they had hit him and he pointed to his face. I looked at his face and there were no marks at all. I once again told him I would monitor the situation. A few days passed when a teacher brought Michael into my office and he had red hand prints on both sides of his face. The teacher said, "I was walking down the hall and heard this noise going on in the rest room. I entered the rest room to find Michael slapping and hitting himself in the head as hard as he could. Later, Michael was sent to the Juvenile Evaluation Center and his father killed himself shortly thereafter. The student had a rough road ahead of him.

Larry Liggett,
Skyland, Buncombe County, 7/21/11

Big Bubba Drives a Bus

I remember one afternoon we were loading the school buses in front of the building at Hill Street School when all the students started screaming and running off the bus in terror. I climbed onto the bus to see what was going on to find a wharf rat as big as a grown cat sitting on the back seat. The big old burly bus driver walked to the back of the bus, reached down, grabbed the rat by the neck, carried it out of the bus, slammed it against the side of the bus, and then stepped over and dropped it in the dumpster. Needless to say he never had any trouble with discipline on his bus.

Dorland Winkler,
Malvern Hills, 8/12/11

Look Out! The Monitor Is Here

While an educator in N.C., I became a monitor of federal funds. My job was to ensure these funds were used as intended by the federal and state governments. Of course, there were many times the county or school became creative in the spending of these funds. Here are a few of those cases:

When the federal reading program was first funded (I believe this was part of President Johnson's "War on Poverty"), funds were allocated to set up reading programs for low income children. These funds were sent to the state, then to the LEA (local education agency) and, finally to the school level to establish these reading programs. In the early years, what the federal government intended and what the school level saw as a good reading program were often very different. On my site visits, one of the first real problems I ran into was a school that used the funds to buy band uniforms. There was no question that the band needed uniforms but I did not think that was the best "reading program" for low income children. The principal felt differently and argued for about an hour before I went to the finance officer to make arrangements for the money to be returned to the state. In the end, however, it all worked out as the reading program was established and the principal got his uniforms through other means.

The next case did not work out as well as the uniforms. The superintendent in this county used the federal funds to build a school cafeteria. His argument was that good nutrition was fundamental to good learning and reading. I could not disagree but this was about how the funds were intended to be spent and not where the children were eating nor if they were eating. At the time, the lunches were brought from another school and the children ate in their classroom, a practice still in use to this day. I took exception to the expenditure of these funds. The superintendent replied, "Come get your cafeteria." To make a long story short, I lost that one!

The next two incidents took place in the same county. During a monitoring visit, a principal told me he was using his federal reading funds to buy playground equipment. We went round and round until we wound up in his superintendent's office. We both explained our sides and the superintendent handled it in an interesting way. He told the principal "I'm going to let you buy this playground equipment." I was thinking, "No, you're not" but kept my mouth shut. The superintendent added, "I want you to know you're making a career decision here." After about two minutes of thought and not a word from the superintendent, the principal said "I'll set up reading programs." These funds were used to set up a great reading program for low income children who were reading two to three years behind their peers.

On another monitoring visit to this county, I gave the local director a list of the schools I wanted to monitor. She told me I was going to another school not on the list. I knew immediately there was a problem at this school and she needed help. After just a few minutes in the school, it became clear the principal was using the federal reading funds to reduce class size and not set up a reading program. I explained why he could not do that and he said this was his school and he would "do what he damn well-pleased!" I called the superintendent. She was in a meeting so I requested the finance officer. I explained the situation and added that from right now, this county no longer had an approved application and could not spend any federal funds until we came to an understanding. He requested that I remain at the school until I heard back from him. I waited in the principal's office with a "not so arrogant now" principal. The phone rang, the principal answered, said "yes sir, yes sir," hung up, turned to me and said "will you help me get this straight?" I said I would be glad to and turned to leave. The principal added that the superintendent requested I call. He had one question, "Is everything straight?" I said "yes sir." He told me to have a good day. That superintendent was a good administrator.

I agreed to do an outside review of an Indian Education program for an LEA. I did not work with Indian Education, but they required outside reviews. This was quite an eye opener for me. I had worked in several state and federal programs such as Exceptional Children, Migrant Education, Chapter I, Title I, Homeless, and Neglected/ Delinquent. Unlike these programs, I learned that Indian Education was run by the parents of the children. They set up a counsel that designed the program and approved the expenditures. I questioned whether parents were the most appropriate to design an education program but was interested to see what they created for their children. First, I reviewed the needs of the Indian children in the school; on an average, they were far behind their counterparts in reading and math. There were many programs that might bring these children up to grade level. So, of course I was looking forward to see how the parents spent these funds and what programs they implemented that would best address their children's needs. However, they used the funds to send parents, mostly the council members (about 25), to the National Powwow. I did my best to further explain their children's needs and how these funds could help with their remedial needs. They replied that they approved all expenditures. They thanked me for my wonderful report and made their plans for the National Powwow. As far as I know they are still enjoying the National Powwow.

Don Carter,
Garner, May 24, 2011

What In The Crap Does He Mean?

We had an epidemic of someone pooping in the restroom sinks, and were doing everything we could think of to find the pooper, and without success. The principal, being a very proper person, walked up to a big tall seventh grade boy by the name of Eric and asked in such a dignified manner, "Son, do you have any knowledge as to whom has been passing feces in the lavatories?" The boy stood there with his mouth opened and giving him a blank stare. I leaned over close to Eric's ear and whispered. "He wants to know who's crapping in the sink?" Eric said, "Jerome."

Dorland Winkler,
Malvern Hills, 8/12/11

Could You Do Me A Favor

While I was Transportation Director for Asheville City Schools, the superintendent asked me to chair a mediation committee between a disgruntled parent and bus transportation. The issue involved a mother who stated she was not always at home the same time each day and if she was not at home when the bus arrived, she demanded that the bus driver drive around the neighborhood until he saw her car in the driveway before letting her daughter off the school bus.

Dorland Winkler,
Malvern Hills, 8/12/11

Blowing Off Steam

One event which took place in my classroom was both funny and scary. I had the best room in the building during the winter. I had an old steam radiator on my outside wall. Every teacher in the school was jealous because their rooms were always very cold during the cold winter days. Teachers would stop in my room often just to get warm. One day I had three little kids in my class and all of a sudden, that steam radiator blew up. Steam was exploding from the blow off valve and the room was quickly filling up with steam. I was trying to protect my kids the best I could by huddling them toward the opposite wall. It wasn't funny at the time, it really freaked me out. The fire alarm was sounding and the assistant principal came running down the hall as we exited the room. Of course, everyone had to go outside the building and wait until the fire department gave us permission to reenter the building. Once we had the children safe, I was worried about my purse and my lesson plan book. Evidently, they were my most prized possessions and I felt I needed them. The assistant principal climbed into my room on his hands and knees and retrieved my purse and plan book. After that, they took out my radiator.

Anonymous,
Western North Carolina, 5/6/2011

It Was Not Fair

In high school in the early 1960s in the eastern part of N.C., I was attending a rural school with first through twelfth grades. A new high school building was in the process of being built and the gym was located between this new building and the other school buildings. My gym class teacher had to leave for a few minutes and told us all just to relax and behave until her return. As an avid reader, I immediately grabbed a book and tuned out everything else. The rest of the girls drifted to the open windows (no air conditioning in the 1960's) to watch the new school. Of course, there were young men working there and they started making cat calls at the female students—and the students, surprise, surprise, responded. I totally missed what was happening as I was in my own "book world." The other girls kept calling me to come look but I ignored them; finally two of them grabbed me by the hands and pulled me over to the windows. Of course, the gym teacher walked in at that exact moment and, even though the other students told her they had "forced" me over to the windows, she reprimanded us and then insisted we all had to write a thousand word theme on proper behavior for a young lady. The other girls told me they wrote the first and last pages but with past homework/class work papers in between and that I should, as well. I, of course, wrote the whole theme and the gym teacher shredded them in front of us without reading any of them.

Beth Carter,
Garner, 5/1/2011

Pass it Around

One hot day in late spring, I led my sixth grade students to lunch. Usually, I sit with my students in order to more closely monitor their behavior and build a better relationship with individual students, although on this particular day, I was fairly stressed out and elected to sit at the teachers' table at the front of the room, facing my students. After all, I could see them from there as well as at the students' table and I felt they needed some time away from me where they could talk quietly to each other. On this particular day, I noticed some unusual activity going on at the tables but, still, the students were orderly and relatively quiet so I did not go back and check on them as I continued to monitor their behavior.

After twenty minutes, lunchtime was over and we were ready to return to class and resume afternoon classes. We lined up, went down the opposite long hall to the restroom then returned to the classroom on our hall. As usual, I stood at the door as each child entered the classroom. About ten children had entered the room and taken their seats when one little girl, as she entered the room whispered to me: "Mrs. Hutchens, Mable had a beer for lunch." Someone always tells! I said, "Thank you. Please have a seat."

When Mable, who was near the end of the line, came to the door, I asked her to wait in the hall and told the other students to get busy. I said, "Mable, what did you have with your lunch today?" Mable, who happened to be taller than I, looks down at me and said, "I had a soda, Mrs. Hutchens."

I said, "Mable, what did you do with the soda can?"

Hearing this question she started wiggling and twisting like she was in a nest of bees, "I threw it in the trash can with all the garbage, Mrs. Hutchens."

I softly, but sternly, said, "Go get the soda can and bring it to me."

She said, "It's in the garbage can with all that mess!"

I replied, "That is OK. Go get the can!" By this time, she was almost dancing with nerves. "Mable, go, get the can so I may see it." "Now!"

She grunted and groaned, twisted and turned, and finally, said, "I had a beer, Mrs. Hutchens."

"Did you drink the whole beer Mable?" I asked.

"No, Mrs. Hutchens, I shared it with everyone."

My brain, by this time, was screaming. This kid has just caused me to lose my job, I thought to myself. The parents in this neighborhood will not tolerate sixth graders drinking beer for lunch at school. I grabbed Mable and we headed to the principal's office. The story was repeated and the principal told me to return to class while he handled the problem. Mable did not return to class that day! The principal later told me he called her daddy, told him what had happened, and that he had to take her home for the rest of the day. When Daddy entered the office his first and only words were, "What did you mean bringing one of my beers to school, Girl?"

Of course, that night I did not sleep and the next morning, I expected the office to be filled with parents demanding that I be fired. I didn't have a quiet, calm day that day, either, always expecting someone to come to my door to escort me out of the school.

Would you believe? I never heard another word about this from anyone! Could it be that not one child told anyone! Remember every single child had at least tasted that beer, and right from the one can!

Ollie Hutchens,
Elkin, 2/27/11

SNOW SNOW GO AWAY COME AGAIN ANOTHER DAY

During my tenure as Transportation Director for Asheville City Schools, I received a phone call from some woman who had just moved to Asheville from somewhere where evidently it did not snow. She asked me to provide her with the snow days for the coming winter. Shocked, I asked her to explain what she meant. She continued by explaining that it would help if she knew in advance of the days in order to plan her schedule. Playing along, I asked her if she had any preference for what days we would have snow days and I said that I would pick some days and then she could pick some days. I added that I personally would like a couple Fridays in late February because my wife is a avid skier and she would like those days to go skiing. She agreed that those would be acceptable.

Dorland Winkler,
Malvern Hills, 8/12/11

LOVE WILL FIND A WAY

The story is told in my family (this would have been before the 1920's) of my Great-Grandfather who kept a tight rein on all of his children, but especially his daughters. He did not want these girls to marry nor to leave home. One of his daughters, Ila, finished school at sixteen and so much wanted freedom that she accepted a teaching position in a one-room schoolhouse near High Point, N.C., unbeknownst to her Father. She loved teaching and was soon being courted by a young man in the area. Meanwhile, her Father was looking for her and finally got wind of her location. He immediately left for High Point, kidnapped Ila, and started the journey home. Her beau followed, intercepted them en route and a grand fight ensued. The young couple prevailed and returned to High Point to marry and start a family. I guess they all reconciled because there are many pictures of Great-Grandfather and his children and grandchildren, including Ila. The story continues with Great-Grandfather still ruling with an iron fist, but it is recorded that his other daughters had an easier time of leaving home.

Beth Carter,
Garner, May 24, 2011

I Have My Tires Rotated

One time, while I was serving as principal at Claxton Elementary School, we had this one set of parents who drove me crazy. They were always bringing their son Moses to school a couple hours late or picking him up a couple hours early. They would call in the middle of the school day with something trivial and attempt to keep me on the phone for an hour or more. Well, one morning Moses came to school about three hours late carrying a note which said, "Moses is late this morning because we had to take him to the doctor to get his bowels rotated."

Dorland Winkler,
Malvern Hills, 8/12/11

Watch Your Head!

One summer while I was principal, I decided to make some shelves for my teachers so they could use them for their reading groups. I called the lumber company and found out they had the lumber I wanted. I then called to the central office to get a truck since I did not have a truck at that time. They didn't have a truck available, but they let me use the van. I went to the lumber company and loaded twenty-five pieces of that slick eleven inch shelving board. I loaded the boards into the van and when I got within a mile of my school, the highway department was working on a ditch. The flagman motioned me on by, but just as I came even with him, he jumped back out in front of my van and started waving his flag. I hit my brakes and that slick lumber came flying through the van with the first board hitting me just behind the ear. The boards knocked out the front window and flew all the way out in the road. I reloaded the boards and took them to the school before driving the windowless van back to the central office which was six or seven miles. It was a hot day with bugs everywhere and when I got back to the central office, I had bugs all over my face. Just my luck everyone was there when I got to the central office and I had a hard time living that down.

Charlie McConnell,
Sylva, 6/17/11

How Students Know When a Teacher is Old

While serving as assistant principal in an inner city elementary school which was known for low test scores and "bad" students, I walked the halls during the day and sometimes, I would go into the classrooms. On this particular day, I went by our special education class of ten boys when they were having a break. I went into their room and sat down with them and their teacher just to visit. We were all talking and all of a sudden, one of the students asked, "Mrs. Hutchens, How old are you?" Now remember, this was my thirty-third year in education.

I replied, "Don't you know you don't ask a lady how old she is?"

Another student said, "Oh, Mrs. Hutchens, you're the same age as Mrs. Young." I turned and told him he would receive an "A." Now, Mrs. Young was a beautiful young teacher probably in her thirties.

Another student said, "No, Mrs. Hutchens, you're the same age as Mr. Rondavest." Mr. Rondavest, their teacher, was only twenty-nine years old.

As several of the students continued trying to guess my age, this one little "rascal" that I knew well and who was quietly sitting beside me, staring up to me, spoke up at this point and said, "Uh-Nuh, you're o-l-d, Mrs Hutchens. Do you know how I know you are old Mrs. Hutchens?" Before I could answer, he continued, "I know you are old because you have a black hair growing out of your chin and only old people have black hairs growing out of their chins." What could I do but laugh along with their teacher! What do you think I did as soon as I left that room? Yep,went straight to the lounge to check my chin and sure enough there was one long black hair growing out of it. Thereafter, each morning this chin was thoroughly inspected!

Ollie Hutchens,
Elkin, 2/27/11

FROM THE MOUTH OF A CHILD

Another experience I had in the classroom was banking. I went down to Wachovia Bank in Biltmore and explained what I was getting ready to do with my children. They gave me enough checkbooks so that every child could have their own. The children received play money to place in their checkbooks for their good behavior or when they did something extra. That was the way they built up their bank balance. This one boy Jim, had built up a good amount of money in his bank account and I said, "What in the world are you planning to do with all that money?" He looked up at me with the eyes of a child and said, "I was going to buy you a watch." You never know what is going to come out of their mouths.

Billie Lewis,
Enka, Buncombe County, 11/15/10

And Now for The News

I remember after lunch each day, we would set the room up for a news report. Students would take turns sitting at the news desk and give the news of the day. They enjoyed doing that and it was also good for them to get the experience of speaking in public. One day WLOS-TV came and recorded our news broadcast and played it on the local news. This was a special day for my children.

Billie Lewis,
Enka, Buncombe County, 11/15/10

What Is A Budget Mommie?

I remember teaching writing and trying to get them to only begin the word with a capital letter and then use small case letters and they would say, "That's not the way my mommy does it." It was funny that before long parents would say when they would help their child that the child would say, "That is not the way my teacher does it." I believe teaching kindergarten was the best job I have ever had including the one I currently have because they are so open and just say everything.

I had a little boy by the name of John who was crying at lunch time and when I asked him what was wrong, he said he was poor. Well, I told him everybody was poor in some way and asked him why he thought he was poor?. He said he heard his mother and daddy talking about money last night and they said they were poor. I explained that they were most likely just talking about their budget. He was OK with that.

Sandy Caldwell,
Waynesville, Haywood County, 11/11/10

A Teachable Moment

During the year of the Olympics, we would give medals for doing certain things like good behavior, doing extra work and helping others. (That was a good thing that we did, there were so many things over the years.)

Billie Lewis,
Enka, Buncombe County, 11/15/10

Before There Were School Nurses

I was teaching fifth grade in a fifth/sixth intermediate school in Winston-Salem, North Carolina. The school district had just gone through desegregation and some students were required to ride a school bus twenty miles to attend school. I had a very bright young student in my class who suffered from a severe case of asthma. His mother came to my class the first day of school and advised me of the situation and what to do if he had an attack. I made it through the year until April came and all of the pollens. One day, walking back to the classroom, he had a serious asthma attack. I was able to get him into the teacher's lounge so he could lie down. I asked a trusted student to get one of the other fifth grade teachers to watch my class and to search for his inhaler. The young man began to turn blue. The students in my class finally found his inhaler. It saved the day. We called his mother and made her aware of the situation. Shortly afterwards, she drove twenty miles to pick him up and take him to the doctor.

Dr. Judy Pierce,
Winston Salem, 6/15/11

THE SECRETARY ADDED FIRE TO AN EXPLOSIVE SITUATION

One day, we had a fire in a ceiling fan. The fire truck had been called and every teacher was trying to keep their children calm. Well, one of the school secretaries, not my mother-in-law who was a school secretary, came running down the hall shouting, "Emergency! Emergency! Fire! Fire! Everybody clear the building! Everybody was excited and the children were running every which way with the teachers trying their best to keep them together and exit the building in an orderly fashion, but the secretary's excitement did not help.

Jan Lunsford, Averys
Creek, Buncombe County, 12/2/10

CALL FOR BACK UP

A couple weeks after I had been appointed assistant principal, we had this fight break out in the front yard of the school between two girls. They ripped each others' clothing, pulled hair and knocked each other from one end of the school yard to the other. I suspended both girls for three days according to school policy. In a couple days, I was informed that their parents had filed a formal protest with the superintendent against me for suspending their girls. I thought the world was coming to an end with me being an assistant principal for only two weeks. Mr. Griffin, School Superintendent, came down to the school to talk with me about it and said, "Don't worry about it, I am going to appoint a central office administrator to come over and chair the hearing and he is going to listen to both sides carefully and then he is going to rule in favor of you." I really appreciate Mr. Griffin because he knew the situation and he supported his administrators and had their backs.

Dorland Winkler,
Malvern Hills, 8/12/11

THERE IS A TIME FOR EVERYTHING UNDER THE SUN

When they tore down the old school at Fairview Elementary, it was a sad occasion. We realized it was needed but it was a very important part of the local community. They sold bricks from the old building to raise money for the Parent Teacher Organization. I hated to see it come down but it was time.

Jan Lunsford,
Averys Creek, Buncombe County, 12/2/10

WE INTERRUPT THIS PROGRAM FOR A SPECIAL ANNOUNCEMENT

While I was Superintendent in Haywood County, the TV was calling for heavy snow to fall early in the day, but it was not snowing at the time.

All the snow spotters went out to their destinations and had reported in that there was no snow at that time. The spotters called and asked what to tell the drivers. I had them wait for fifteen more minutes and called back and wanted to know what to tell the drivers. I told them to go. All ninety-six buses pulled out around six o'clock. Well, they got out there and the snow flakes started falling and they were about the size of quarters. I radioed back and said, "Have the drivers go straight to the school and don't let the kids get off the bus. Have the drivers gas up their buses and take them back home. We had to gas up each time we made a run because the buses only got about five miles per gallon. We finally got them all back home around eight o'clock. Now the local radio station had a live call in program. A boy called in and live on the air said, "My mama said that that Superintendent of Haywood County is full of shit."

Charlie McConnell,
Sylva, 6/17/11

Hitch Up Them Britches

I don't know if you ever had problems with "saggy" pants. Well, I did, and anytime I saw a boy with his britches below his butt, I told him to pull those britches up because I did not want to see his underwear. This particular morning, I was walking down the first grade hall and there was this little boy walking slowly to class. Every few steps he would hop, as he tried not to step on the legs of his britches. These britches had to have been his daddy's because this child would have fitted into one half of one pant leg! Suddenly, he realized that somebody was behind him. He looked around, saw me, and speeded up, hopping, hesitating, and pulling up his pants as he went. All of a sudden, those britches fell to the floor, and guess what, he did not have any underwear on.

He stopped without looking back, bent over, pulled up those britches with both hands and made a dash into the classroom. I continued down the hall.

Ollie Hutchens,
Elkin, 2/27/11

FAD DAY

One year, we decided to have a "Fad Day" where students could dress up any way they liked. Most of them dressed up in white shirts with their collars turned up to look like we did in the fifties. Although Johnny came to school wearing a dress. We wondered why a boy would wear a dress, but allowed it because after all it was "Fad Day." Later in the day, we received a phone call from Johnny's grandmother and she was very upset. She said, "I just don't understand what this world is coming to when a school who is supposed to be teaching children values and good citizenship and moral behavior would go out of their way and sponsor "FAG DAY".

Dorland Winkler,
Malvern Hills, 8/12/11

THE PREGNANT BOY

While teaching fifth grade at Vance Elementary in Asheville, I decided to take a course in first aid at the local Red Cross. Well, I found I loved that sort of work where I could help someone if the need arose and still continue with my teaching. Before long, I had become an Emergency Medical Technician. I would spend my days teaching and each night and week-end on call for the local rescue squad.

One day, I had given my class a restroom break and I stayed in the room while my ten year olds used the rest room three doors down the hall. When most of my students had returned, Tommy came running into the room and told me that Mac had taken some pills while in the restroom. My EMT training kicked in as I rushed to the rescue. I grabbed Mac and, noticing a medicine bottle on the floor, I picked it up and rushed to the office to call poison control. As soon as poison control answered, I identified myself as an EMT and proceeded to tell the technician on duty my situation. He asked if there was a medicine bottle available and I hurriedly read the scientific name listed on the bottle. When I had finished, he started laughing. Shocked, I said, "What are you laughing at? This boy has been poisoned!" He calmed down enough to say, "I guarantee this boy will never get pregnant; these were his mother's birth control pills." After I stopped laughing, I said, "Well, I had some Epicete that I was going to give him to make him vomit." He instructed me to go ahead and give it to him and it might teach him a lesson. I did.

J. Terry Hall,
Scott Mountain, Buncombe County, 3/3/11

TEACHING IN THE RED LIGHT DISTRICT

My friend Beth, shared a story of a first year teacher teaching kindergarten in a brand new school built in the red light district of Charleston. There had been several cases of a stomach virus circulating throughout the school and many students had been absent due to the virus. One morning, the kindergarten teacher called her students to come to the carpet. She told the children, "Boys and girls, Miss Karen doesn't feel well today. So, I want you to be on your best behavior." A little boy in the last row was about to fall over from waving his raised hand. Finally, Miss Karen called on Johnny.

Johnny said, "Miss Karen, if you don't feel well, why don't you get yourself a prostitute and go home?"

Dr. Judy Pierce,
Winston Salem, 6/15/11

SUCK UP AND PUCKER UP

I was asked to come and speak to a local school board and suggest how they could consolidate one county school district and three city school districts. During the presentation, they asked me how I dealt with county commissioners? I told them I could sum it up in four words, suck up and pucker up. They liked that and thought that was real honest. I then went on and elaborated about what I meant.

Charlie McConnell,
Sylva, 6/17/11

GIVE ME FLOWERS WHILE I AM LIVING

I had a brilliant student one year who attended the North Carolina School for Math and Science. This school is supposed to be the top school in the state, but, after one year, he returned. I asked him why he had not stayed and he said, "It's a very good school, but it is no better than what I can get here. In fact, some of the classes here are better than they have at the School of Math and Science." I really believe we had a great school with a bunch of great teachers.

Thomas Ledbetter,
Hendersonville, 4/13/2011

OH DEER ME

When I moved back to Asheville from Virginia, I taught at Pleasant Gardens Elementary. One day in the middle of a class, a deer came crashing through the window. This, of course, caused a great amount of disruption, to say the least, as children were running every which way and screaming at the top of their voices.

Julia Clark,
Biltmore Lake, June 2, 2011

A COMPLEMENT PAID

I always tried to be strict in my discipline, yet fair. I believe I was able to pull that off throughout the years. I have seen several teachers who try to be a buddy to their students in order to be their friends. This does not work. First of all, a teacher must have the respect of her students. In order to maintain that respect, a teacher must have high expectations of her students. Most students will live up to your expectations if you treat them in a fair and structured manner. A teacher must let her students know what will happen if they choose to not follow the rules, and always follow through with whatever you say will happen if they make the wrong choice.

I had this one teacher at Vance Elementary come to me and ask me how I was able to keep my class so well behaved. This is difficult to explain. It has a lot to do with who you are as a person, your personality and experiences you have had in the past. I shared some of the things I attempted to do in my class and suggested she try some of those techniques. I felt that was a compliment to have someone seek help from me because they admired the way I taught.

Julia Clark,
Biltmore Lake, June 2, 2011

CHANGE CAN BE GOOD

During the period of integration in Asheville City Schools, I had this one black girl walk by me and reach up and touch my hair. She had never been close to a white woman's hair and was just curious as to how it felt. There was confusion and uncertainty all around. It was a very trying time.

Billie Lewis,
Enka, Buncombe County, 11/15/10

THE RIGHT PUNISHMENT FOR A BULLY

While serving as an elementary school assistant principal, I saw many students, mostly boys, for just about any reason or excuse you could name. One year, I got to know Leroy, a fifth grader, extremely well. He came to see me—at the request of his teachers—for just about everything, especially bullying other students. I also got to know Leroy and his family because Leroy just could not behave himself on the school bus. Let me pause here to say, that in this school system, it was against school board policy to spank and suspending an elementary student from school was highly frowned upon, as well! I was, however, known for calling, in dire situations, usually a grandma—most of our students lived with a single mother, grandmother, or in some cases a great grandmother, and explaining the situation to her. Grandmas, as a rule, frowned upon misbehavior and usually were most willing to spank if I would take a student home and then return him to school.

I finally did this with Leroy, but it still did not help improve his conduct. One morning when I went outside for bus duty, what should I see but one of the buses had arrived early and there was Leroy standing outside the bus! Also standing there was this young, extremely angry, black man. He had Leroy backed up against the side of the bus, holding him by his shirt collar, and screaming at him! I thought he was going to hit him or at least wipe the dirt off the bus with him! I stepped up to the man and asked him what was happening. He informed me that Leroy had been "picking on his younger brother who was in the first grade and he was there to beat his black a—." By this time, Leroy had gotten around behind me and I was facing this young man. Here was my brave, "afraid of nothing" Leroy hiding behind me! I told the man who I was and that I had heard nothing about these incidents. I emphasized that we would handle the situation. He refused to do as I asked and once again, I invited him to the office or I was going to call the police and take out a warrant on him. I told him that "no one was coming on the school ground and threaten one of my young'uns." By that time, two men working in the school heard the commotion and came outside. I asked them to escort this young man to the office.

Believe it or not, this was the right punishment for Leroy! I did not see him in my office after this! Sometimes a little fear can go a long way, or, just maybe, this was the first time Leroy had ever had an adult defend him.

Ollie Hutchens,
Elkin, 2/27/11

WHAT ARE YOU TALKING ABOUT?

Back a few years ago, school systems were allowed to waive two school days due to missing school because of snow and Earl Hopper, Superintendent of Jackson County, had just waived two days. Well, Lowell Crisp, Superintendent of Graham County, Earl Hopper Superintendent of Jackson County and I were going to Southern Pines, North Carolina for a meeting with State Superintendent, Craig Phillips. Lowell asked, "What did you think about Craig's memo?" I followed up and said, "I just don't think it's fair and I don't see how he can do that." Earl asked what we were talking about and said he didn't get the memo. I explained that Craig Phillips said that the local school system would have to pick up the pay for all the teachers for the two days waived. Earl was very upset, and the further down the road we went, the madder he became because Jackson County had just waived two days. We thought that this was just too good to let it go and then we forgot about it. We went on to the meeting and, as was Craig's practice, after he finished what he had to say, he would have his secretaries move around the crowd with microphones in order for the audience to ask questions. Earl stood up, and, taking the mike said, "Craig, I just don't think it's fair the way you are making the local school systems pick up the pay of teachers for the two waived days. There is just no way my local district can pay those teachers." Craig, looking puzzled said, "Earl, I have no idea what you are talking about." Earl looked over there and Lowll and I were doubled over laughing, and Earl said, "Never mind."

Charlie McConnell,
Sylva, 6/17/11

THIS CLASS IS NOT "BURGER KING"

Shortly after our school system was integrated back in the seventies, I was assigned to over-see the curriculum program in two schools—three days a week at one and two days at the other. The discipline at the second school where I was for two days was terrible. I didn't know that students behaved this way ever and I had already taught sixth graders for thirteen years. I was absolutely horrified by the students behavior!

My room happened to be next door to a special education class of fifth and sixth grade boys and girls. I heard all kinds of "racket" coming from this room—loud voices, furniture movement, slamming of the door, and etc. One day, after hearing a crash, I heard someone crying hysterically. Not having a class at the time, I rushed out in the hall and saw the young teacher rushing out of the room and entering the nearby lounge with a towel over her face, crying. Not a sound was coming from the class at this time. I checked on the students, saw that they were busy and went to check on the teacher. She had just realized that she could not manage that class and walked out of the building and resigned.

A substitute teacher was hired for a few days and then one morning, to the surprise of the students, when they walked into the room, there was this big, black lady in the room who introduced herself as Miss Smith, their new teacher. She informed the students that she had been told about their behavior in the past and she was not leaving because she was being paid to be there and if anybody was going to leave, it would be one of them. She said, "I am going to draw my paycheck every month." She proceeded to take the next two hours to lay down the procedures and rules of conduct for this class. In explaining her expectations for them, she often said, "This is not Burger King and you are not going to have it your way!" They were in "her" classroom and they would do things "her" way!

Of course, there is always one student who does not believe the teacher! And one day, not knowing that Miss Smith had been told about him, the ring-leading trouble maker, Daron, confronted Miss Smith. Before he knew what was happening, she had grabbed his arm, pulled him across a desk and was sitting on him. He wiggled and twisted but could not budge the teacher. He gave up with Miss. Smith still sitting on him, talking to the other students. Finally, Daron whimpered, "Please, Miss Smith let me up." She looked down at him and asked, "Do you understand that you must obey me in this classroom, that it is not Burger king and you are not going to have it your way?" "Yes Ma-am" he timidly replied. That was the end to the discipline problems in this classroom for the remainder of the school year. All Miss Smith ever had to say if there was ever a hint of trouble was, "This is Not Burger King!"

This lady became one of my best friends and I worked with her many years in other situations. The students came to love and respect her.

Ollie Hutchens,
Elkin, 2/27/11

YES JESUS

Mrs. Sims, a kindergarten teacher, had a class one year where she did not dare leave the room for a moment because of Sammy, an unruly five year old who would get out of his seat and run around the classroom in circles. Although, one morning Mrs. Sims needed to go four doors down the hall to the office in order to check her mail box. Now, this was before we had teaching assistants and she had left the class alone for a short time. Upon arriving at the office and knowing Sammy would already be up running, she stepped to the intercom and pressed the button for her room. Speaking in a stern voice she said, "Sammy, get back in your seat!" Then listening, she hear this small timid voice say, "Yes, Jesus."

J. Terry Hall,
Scott Mountain, Buncombe County, 3/3/11

Offering A Kid A Bribe

While I was Principal at Robinsville High School, we always took attendance at the beginning of each class. One day a teacher came into my office and told me Johnny had skipped class. About thirty minutes later, I saw this boy going down the hall and I walked up behind him and led him into my office. I said, "Johnny, you skipped class." Johnny looked surprised and said, "No, Mr Crisp, I didn't." I said, "Yes you did, now put your hands on the desk here." He did and I took out my paddle. I asked them to place their hands on my desk as a sign that they were confessing. I paddled him and he walked out of my office and went on his way. About thirty minutes later, I thought that wasn't Johnny, that was Nick! I thought, man, I have paddled an innocent kid. I ran down Nick and apologized. I said, "I am so sorry, take this five bucks." Nick looked at me and said with a smile, "That's OK Mr. Crisp, you can paddle me anytime!" This was in the early seventies and five dollars was a lot of money.

Lowell Crisp, Robinsville,
Graham County, 6/15/11

My Secretary Deserved A Bonus

My secretary really helped me out one time. We had a school bus that turned over. We had a high school boy driving the bus and he was going very slow. A school board member and a teacher were following him and as he turned a corner, the bus just leaned and rolled over on its side. No one was hurt and all students were taken to the hospital to be checked out. Everybody was driving by and looking at the overturned bus and my secretary called me aside and suggested I go out there and be on site. A little while later, the radio station called and asked me some questions and I could answer because I had been to the site.

Lowell Crisp,
Robinsville, Graham County, 6/15/11

PASS THE HAM BISCUITS PLEASE

We were at a superintendent's meeting in Polk County one time and they had breakfast for us. There was this big platter of ham biscuits in the middle of the table. We look over and Susan Lenord, Assistant Superintendent of Poke County, at that time, had left her purse on her chair while she had gone out of the room for something. Charlie McConnell, Superintendent of Haywood county and I filled up her purse with ham biscuits. We thought she would open her purse to get her car keys as she started home and would find the ham biscuits. To our surprise, when she returned to the table she placed her purse on the table to get something out of it. Biscuits came rolling out of her handbag and onto the table in front of everyone. This embarrassed her to death. She started saying, "You-all, now I tell you-all, I didn't put those in my purse! You-all know I'm not stealing those biscuits!" We just sat there and didn't say a word. Finally, someone said, "You must have been awfully hungry."

Lowell Crisp,
Robinsville, Graham County, 6/15/11

LITTLE JOHN AND THE WITCH

During my time as Assistant Principal at Vance Elementary, I was walking the halls supervising when I had an interesting experience. It was Halloween and several of the teachers were giving their children a Halloween party. Mrs. Harris, a kindergarten teacher, was in the middle of her party when I walked by her room and stopped to look in her door. Now, each year Mrs. Harris' mother would dress up like a witch with a long black robe and a pointed hat and visit the classroom. She usually left the window of the first floor classroom open and came to the window and climbed through into the classroom. Well, Lttle John, happened to be sitting with his back to the window that "the witch" was going to enter. As I watched the event unfolding from the doorway, I saw "the witch" peeping through the window. Little John, having his back to the window, of course, did not see "the witch" approaching and just as she placed a foot through the window, little John slowly turned around and seeing "the witch," let out a scream and came running across the floor toward where I was standing at the door. About five feet from where I stood he, leaped and ended up with his arms and feet wrapped around my body. Little John continued to grow and not only ended up being Asheville's best football player, but following graduation from college he was drafted into the NFL.

J. Terry Hall,
Scott Mountain, Buncombe County, 3/3/11

WHAT IF IT GETS YOU FIRST

This story is of a more personal nature. It involves my son Ben, and my grandson, Dakota. When Dakota was around three years old, he was sleeping in his own bedroom when it started to thunder and lightning during the night. Soon, it became a horrific thunderstorm and just after a big streak of lightning and an earth shattering clap of thunder, Dakota came running into his dad's bedroom, screaming that the thunder was going to get him. Taking him into his bed, his dad hugged him and told him the thunder and lightning would not hurt him because his dad was there and he would take care of him. Dakota looked up at his dad and asked a very serious question. He said, "What if it gets you first?"

J. Terry Hall,
Scott Mountain, Buncombe County, 3/3/11

THE TRUTH OF A CHILD

This story is also personal and involves my grandson Anthony, his dad Ben and myself. Anthony was about seven years old when he began to notice that his dad, and especially his granddad, were not as young as they once were. He was wanting to do something or the other that took considerable effort and was bugging his dad to take the time to do it with him. Ben told him that he just didn't feel like doing whatever it was at the time and Anthony looked at his dad with a puzzling look in his eye and said, "I guess you and Paw-Paw are just falling apart."

J. Terry Hall,
Scott Mountain, Buncombe County, 3/3/11

I PUT RANCH ON MY CABBAGE

I heard this story from a parent. It seems that their child's third grade class was studying plants and their teacher had given each child a cabbage plant in a paper cup to take home and watch it grow into a healthy cabbage. Billy was very excited about being able to grow his very own cabbage plant and handled the plant like it was gold. That afternoon, Billy carried the precious cargo with both hands in order to protect it as he got on the school bus to go home.

One of the older boys on the bus asked him what he was carrying and Billy explained about being able to grow his very own cabbage plant. The older boy said, "I usually put Ranch Dressing on my cabbage." According to Billy's dad, about an hour after Billy arrived home, his dad entered the kitchen to find the cabbage plant in the cup half covered with Ranch Dressing.

J. Terry Hall,
Scott Mountain, Buncombe County, 3/3/11

What Did He say?

Another time, it began to snow and the streets were getting slick. Our aristocratic principal came on the intercom and announced, "The Superintendent called and has deemed it necessary to suspend the remaining academic portion of our studies for the remainder of the instructional day due to the precipitation beginning to solidify." Teachers were sticking their heads out of the classroom doors saying, "What's he saying?"

Dorland Winkler,
Malvern Hills, 8/12/11

Covering All The Bases

A fourth grade boy by the name of Nick came up to my desk one Friday afternoon and proceeded to tell me he was going to be baptized the next day at the Baptist Church. I smiled and congratulated him. Nick stood for a few seconds looking at the floor before looking up at me, in deep thought, and said, "There are four people I would like to meet before I die." Shocked, and expecting some serious revelation, I asked, "Who would that be Nick?" He replied and in a very serious tone, "God, Jesus, Willie Nelson and Larry the Cable Guy."

J. Terry Hall,
Scott Mountain, Buncombe County, 3/3/11

A COUNTRY BOY TEACHES CITY KIDS

When I began teaching fifth grade in Asheville in 1970, I was shocked at how little these city children knew about farm life. I had grown up on a farm in Kentucky and had raised all kinds of livestock and had taken it for granted that children knew at least some things about farm animals. Now, this was before the state Standard Course of Study and each teacher had the discretion of teaching whatever they thought the children needed and I was convinced that these city children needed to know at least something about farm animals. I developed a curriculum where we covered several different farm animals and the correct name for the male and female of each.

I asked questions like where does milk come from and got the answer that milk came from the local grocery store. The same type of answer was received when I inquired about beef, pork, chicken and lamb. Now, these were ten year old children who had grown up in downtown Asheville. Finally, I mentioned that a bull was the name of a male cow; a boy said he visited his uncle's farm one day and rode a bull. Being a little skeptical, I asked the boy to come up to my desk and show me a picture of the type of bull he had ridden. He looked over the several pictures presented and chose the one he had ridden. It was a mule.

J. Terry Hall,
Scott Mountain, Buncombe County, 3/3/11

WHATEVER IT TAKES

Nancy came to school with such a bad body odor that the other children could not stand to be around her. One day, I asked her to come out in the hall to help me do something. I took her down to the teachers' lounge and gave her a paper towel and some hot water and told her to wash herself. I never heard anything about it from her parents. Maybe her parents were trying to get her to do it also.

Billie Lewis,
Enka, Buncombe County, 11/15/10

SELF ESTEEM AT ITS BEST

After I retired from North Carolina and moved back to Kentucky to serve as an administrator, I met the sweetest little girl. Her name was Megan and she was in preschool when I first saw her. I had been around children for over thirty years and had never had the opportunity to meet a child like Megan. She was a chubby little girl with big brown eyes that would melt the toughest heart. She was unique in that her mother allowed her to dress in the manner of her choosing. For some unknown reason, Megan loved to dress in a long formal gown with white cowgirl boots. The day I met Megan, I was making my rounds through the school, supervising as was my custom, when I came to the door of the preschool room. The teacher had placed a full length mirror in the room and when I approached the room, I noticed Megan. She was standing in front of the mirror turning around and around looking at herself in the mirror. I was captivated and just stood there and stared. After a couple more turns, Megan noticed me watching but continued turning. She had her name tag on so I could see her name was Megan so I said, "Megan, you are so beautiful!" Without stopping her graceful turns she replied, "Yes, I am."

J. Terry Hall,
Scott Mountain, Buncombe County, 3/3/11

POPPING A WHEELY

While serving as an Assistant Principal at Vance Elementary, I was asked to obtain my bus driving license in order to become a substitute bus driver in case we were short a driver. I attended classes and succeeded in obtaining my license, but there were a couple things I remember well about that class. The instructor gave his students a hypothetical situation where the driver had a bus full of children and as he was driving down the road, a big dog runs across the road just in front of the bus. He asked if everyone could picture the situation. When we nodded that we did, he continued to ask us what kind of dog was it that ran across the road. The students looked at each other, giving a puzzled look as the instructor said, "A dead dog. Don't ever try to miss an animal and place the lives of your children at risk." I never had to face that situation, but I knew what to do if it occurred.

Toward the end of the course, I was required to do a drivers test. The instructor took me out in an old straight shift bus and had me start up this big hill. About half way up the hill, he asked me to stop. Following his directions, I stopped just as an old station wagon pulled up behind the bus almost touching my back bumper. The instructor told me to proceed.

I looked at the vehicle behind me and said, "Hold on!" As I floored the accelerator and let out my clutch, I am sure the old bus's front wheels left the ground as I literally popped a wheelie on a school bus. But, I never allowed the bus to roll back even an inch.

J. Terry Hall,
Scott Mountain, Buncombe County, 3/3/11

DON'T GET SMART WITH ME

I had a lady from Fines Creek call my office one day and said, "You let that bus driver haul her kid around and her kid is not in school. That ain't right and I want to be able to ride the school bus from my house to my work in Waynesville every day." I said, "That will be fine, just give me your name and address and I will ask the driver to come over there and pick you up every morning." She said, "Don't you get smart with me!" She started cussing and threatening me. I told her that I really would have them pick her up and she said, "Don't you be a smart ass with me. I am going to report you to Raleigh. what is that number?" I made up some 919 number and gave it to her. She again said she was going to call Raleigh, but then said, "You are Mr. Stephens ain't you?" I said, "Yes Ma-am."

Charlie McConnell,
Sylva, 6/17/11

HE MEANT WELL

Around the time I received my Doctor's Degree and was moved to the Central Office, a new Principal was placed at the school. It was his first principalship and he was trying hard to show his concern for all teachers. As Assistant Principal, it was my duty to take the new

Principal around and introduce him the his staff during a work day. As we made our way around the building from room to room, he was accepted warmly by all the teachers. As we approached this one room the teacher happened to be standing on a chair screwing a screw into the bulletin board. Being the helpful person that he was, he said, "May I help?" She told him she could manage, to which he replied with all innocence, "I'm really good at screwing." As he stood there, with his mouth open, not believing what he had just said, I started on up the hall laughing under my breath. I never let him forget his first day at the school.

J. Terry Hall,
Scott Mountain, Buncombe County, 3/3/11

USING TECHNOLOGY TO DISCIPLINE A CHILD

Another personal story, I would like to share had to do with my grandson, Anthony when he was around five years old. He was staying at our house one night and he was really wound up; he was talking almost nonstop and I could not hear the program I was attempting to watch on TV. I reached for the remote and muted the TV. Then, turning to Anthony, I punched the remote and said I am going to mute you, Anthony. He starting talking and I acted like I could not hear him. I asked my wife where Anthony went that I can not hear him. She played along and said she could not hear him either. After a couple minutes, he walked up to me with a sad look on his face and said, "Unmute me Paw-Paw."

J. Terry Hall,
Scott Mountain, Buncombe County, 3/3/11

WHO RUNS THIS PLACE ANYWAY?

I had this boy once who was sent to the office for something or the other. He was trying to get mad but didn't know what to say. He looked at me, slightly trembling, with hate in his eyes and he said, "You think you run this school, don't you!" "Yes," I said, "I'm pretty sure I do, that's what they pay me for and that's what I am trying to do. I just want you to behave yourself."

Thomas Ledbetter,
Hendersonville, 4/13/2011

NEVER TEASE A PEACEFUL BEAR

I had this girl one time who came from a pretty rough background and was brought to my office for misbehavior. Speaking in a gentle voice, I said, "You are a good girl, and I will help you, but you are going have to behave and everything will be all right." Thinking all was settled, I dismissed her and she went back to class. A couple days later, she was walking down the hall when another girl walked up behind her, pushed her and called her a name. The girl said, "Leave me alone, you know I can whip you but I don't want to fight you; if I do Doc, "the name they always called me," will kick me out of school and I can't play basketball. I promised him I'm not going to fight." Well, she started walking off, according to the other kids, and the other girl walked up, pushed her again and called her another name. Once again she said, "Just leave me alone. I don't want to get in trouble. Just don't bother me." She started walking off again when the girl walked around in front of her, slapped her and called her something. The girl came up with a right straight to the nose and broke it in three places. All the other students told the same story.

Later, the parents of the girl with the broken nose wanted me to kick the other girl out of school but I said, "I'm not going to do anything about it. She asked for it and she got what she asked for. I hope she has learned that if you push a person far enough, you are just going to get whipped."

Thomas Ledbetter,
Hendersonville, 4/13/2011

Be Careful For What You Ask

I had one boy who must have gotten up on the wrong side of the bed. He came to school looking for a fight. He picked on two or three boys first thing in the morning and, when he went to P.E., he jumped on another boy's back and started choking him. The boy being chocked turned around and knocked out three front teeth of the boy doing the choking. The next day the boy's father came in my office and demanded that the school system was going to have to pay for fixing his son's teeth. I explained the situation and told the father that his son had asked for what he got and I hoped he had learned a lesson.

Thomas Ledbetter,
Hendersonville, 4/13/2011

Times Like This Makes It All Worthwhile

I had this boy, who drove a school bus for me, come into my office and say, "Doc, my old car has run out of gas and I need some money to get home; Would you loan me twenty dollars?" I felt sorry for him and knew that he and his family were having a hard time making ends meet, so I gave him the twenty dollars, never expecting to get it back. In line with my expectations, he never returned to pay the money and I soon forgot about it. Three years later, the boy had graduated, and enlisted in the army. One night, I heard a knock on my door at home. It was the boy in an army uniform. He extended his hand and said,, "I believe I owe you this," and handed me the twenty dollars. Times like that make this business all worthwhile.

Thomas Ledbetter,
Hendersonville, 4/13/2011

Computer Savvy Children

When I was serving as Director of Title 1 for Asheville City Schools, I had a part in purchasing and setting up a computer lab at one of our elementary schools. It was a state-of—the arts lab with a very successful program and several surrounding school systems sent personnel to preview the lab and computer program. I had one such visit from Dr. Owen Fish, Title 1 Director of Madison County. Upon visiting the lab while it was being used by a kindergarten class and learning about the new program, I noticed there was one computer not in use so I suggested that Dr. Fish sit down at the computer and try out the program. He did so and after a couple minutes stood up and walked to the center of the room. I noticed one of the kindergarten students get up from his computer, walk up behind Dr. Fish, yank on his pant leg and say, "Hey mister, you forgot to log off." From the mouth of babes.

J. Terry Hall,
Scott Mountain, Buncombe County, 3/3/11

DODGING THE BULLET

I had one little fellow Joe who was a hand full. One time we were outside playing dodge ball and he decided he was going to change it and do it his way. I got mad and I had my pocketbook in my hand, so I swung it and hit him in the back. Immediately I said, "Uh-Oh, I better go tell the principal what I had done." So I did and he said, "Oh, don't worry we are always having trouble with that child." I will never forget that day, I tell you that. They called me out of the classroom after that and said they had an opening at another school and asked if I would like to try for it. I said, "Oh yes." I didn't like down there anyway so I was sent to Vance Elementary. That was the old building that was built in 1922 before they tore it down and built the new one. I thought the old building was beautiful.

Billie Lewis,
Enka, Buncombe County, 11/15/10

THIS WAS MY BUILDING

My favorite student that first year was Peter, who later became a policeman for the city of Asheville. I told my Principal that I loved it at Vance Elementary School and would like to stay for the rest of my teaching career, and that is exactly what I did. When they tore the building down twenty-nine years later was when I retired. I never taught in the new Vance School building; I don't think I would have liked it.

Billie Lewis,
Enka, Buncombe County, 11/15/10

The Old Lady Of The Mountains

One of the most fun memories of all was when I had Heritage Week in my room. I had a little log cabin built in my room with a rocking chair on the front porch. I had to get permission to wear a long dress because they were afraid for me to go up and down all those steps since we were on the third floor. They finally gave me the OK and I became the old lady who lived in the log cabin. If we had a good morning I always read to them after lunch. I would sit in the rocking chair on the front porch and read to them. They would gather around me and we would have popcorn and I would read to them. The children always looked forward to that time of the day. I always felt so pretty when I was dressed up in my long dress and bonnet.

Billie Lewis Enka,
Buncombe County, 11/15/10

CHAPTER SIX

TALES FROM LONG AGO

A Kentucky Colonel

Elizabeth attended a one room school down on Mill Creek in Monroe County Kentucky, from 1921 until 1928. During these eight years, her only teacher was Miss Alice Patterson, an old maid school teacher that everyone called Miss Alice. For the first two years Elizabeth was in school, Miss Alice did not have a teaching certificate, but obtained one during her third year.

According to Elizabeth, the Mill Creek School was a white weatherboard building consisting of one large room with individual student desks and one large teacher's desk at the front of the room. Each wooden student desk had iron legs and a round hole on the right side of the desk top to place an ink bottle. Desks were placed around the room in small groups with each group representing a grade. All eight grades were located in different sections of the room. In the center of the room was a large pot bellied stove that glowed red hot in the winter. Older boys were given the responsibility of keeping the fire going in the stove throughout the day.

There was no toilet in the building and students had to go outside to use the toilet. There was not even an outhouse until she was in the fourth grade and children had to go out in the woods. She took me to the old school building when I was young and showed me where they had to go to use the toilet. The boys went over behind an old oak tree over the hill on the right side of the schoolhouse while the girls went behind a tree on the left side of the schoolhouse. She explained that there was a crooked root under the tree where the girls could sit while they took care of business.

Elizabeth and her family lived about two miles down Mill Creek up on the side of a hill. She was the oldest of eight children of which three girls died either as infants or as small children. Elizabeth, being the oldest had the responsibility of seeing that her brothers made it to school. Her daddy provided her with a horse and tied a pillow behind the saddle. Elizabeth would ride on the saddle and her two brothers would ride on the pillows. She told me how she loved to ride horses. In order to get to school, she would have to ride for about one half mile down Mill Creek, and in the winter Miss Alice, as everybody called her, had to come out and pour water over Elizabeth's stirrups in order to get her feet out where they had frozen from water splashing up from the creek.

After attending Mill Creek for eight years, passing her test for graduation and receiving her Monroe County Grade School Certificate, Elizabeth's mother had her go about eight miles into the small town of Tompkinsville to attend school where her uncle, Eston White, taught school. Attending school in the "town" also allowed her to graduate from the Monroe County City Schools which was considered a little higher up on the educational ladder

Elizabeth R. Hall,
Tompkinsville, Monroe County, 5/24/1999

GROWING UP A COUNTRY BOY

Frank attended a one room schoolhouse called Mount Zion in Monroe County, Kentucky between 1921 and 1928. Mount Zion was located about one half mile as the crow flies, from where he and his family lived. Frank and his brother, Leroy, would walk across the pasture fields to reach school each day. Mount Zion was a one room white weather boarded building sitting about two feet off the ground on big flat rocks. There was no underpinning under the building and it provided a nice cool place for the small boys and girls to play on hot days. Like all one room schoolhouses of the day, it consisted of one large room with wooden student desks scattered around the room to represent the different grades. Grades one through eight were grouped together according to grade levels. Since there was only one teacher and eight grades, the teacher assigned older children who had already learned simple reading and arithmetic to work with younger children.

Frank enjoyed school, but he enjoyed playing baseball more than anything else. Each summer day would find Frank playing shortstop out in the ball field. His teacher, Mr. Glenn Wax, was a wonderful teacher, according to Frank, and loved baseball as much as he did. Mr. Wax would challenge neighboring schools to play baseball and Mount Zion was often the county champions.

Before Mr. Wax came to the school, Frank had a lady teacher. She was small in stature and felt she had to act tough in order to keep the older and many times bigger boys in line. One story Frank told me was when a neighbor boy, who today would have most likely been classified mentally handicapped, was accused by the teacher of some misbehavior. Frank always claimed that the boy was not guilty. The teacher, in order to prove to the class that she was boss, told the boy, who was a big rawboned country boy and much bigger than the teacher, that he was going to get a whipping. The boy decided that was not going to happen and started walking home. The teacher sent two older boys to go get him and bring him back to take his medicine. After running a good ways and realizing he was going to be caught, the boy stopped and filled his pockets with rocks. His persuaders caught and carried him back to the schoolhouse and was instructed by their teacher to hold him down on the front bench while she took a big stick and whipped the daylights out of him. Frank said he felt so sorry for him as he yelled and screamed and the rocks came falling out of his pockets and on to the floor.

Another story Frank told me was one that always got a laugh. He explained that two outhouses were out at the back of the schoolhouse. The boys' was on the right and the girls' was all the way across the yard on the left. One day the boys were talking about what was going on over in the girl's outhouse and some brave boy decided he would go find out. To the snickers of the other boys, he told them he was going to go over to the girls' outhouse, lay down on his back and slide under the outhouse to have a look. All the boys urged him on as he left on his mission. Just as he made it under the outhouse, he started kicking and squirming and trying to get out. It seems that one of the girls peed in his eye.

William Frank Hall,
Tompkinsville, Monroe County, 10/30/1999

A GIRL FROM BEELOG

I grew up in the Beelog community of Yancey County, North Carolina in the 1920s and 1930s. I was the youngest of 11 children of which only one sister, Elva, and myself are left. My mother died when I was small and my older sister Reba more or less raised me. Reba, being the oldest girl still at home at the time, took the responsibility of the house and of trying to keep me in line. I came to look upon her as a substitute mother because of the manner in which she looked after me.

Yancey county is one of the most mountainous counties in North Carolina and back when I was growing up, it was a very isolated place to live. Even today, folks high up in the mountains have their own particular ways because it has always been that way.

Back in the day, I attended Beelog School. My brothers, sisters and myself attended this one room school just down the road and across the creek from where we lived in the "Tom House." I never knew why they called it the "Tom House," except a man by the name of Tom might have built it. It was about a mile from the school and we would walk to and from school each day.

I don't remember many things about those days, but I do remember some things like they happened yesterday. One thing that keeps playing in my mind happened shortly after I started school. Of course, I don't remember the name, but there was this little girl in my class who always wore the most beautiful dresses that I had ever seen. Her parents must have had money to have bought her those beautiful store bought clothes, but with me being from a very poor family, I had never seen such wonderful dresses.

I clearly remember one day when my sister and I were walking to school. It was winter time and was still dark as we walked along the mountain path. As we ran around a curve in the path, I caught my foot on a tree root and fell forward over a cliff. I fell several feet before hitting the ground. When I finally crashed into the hard mountain soil, I bounced against an old pine tree before beginning to roll. I thought I would never stop rolling as I tumbled faster and faster down the steep mountainside. Finally, I stopped rolling when I crashed into the side of a mountain cabin down in the valley. I could hear my sister screaming for me, but I was too hurt and scared to speak. The family living in the cabin and hearing the sound, came running to me and helped me into the house about the time my sister arrived. They cleaned me up and took me back home.

There was one thing I never understood that took place while I attended Beelog School. My teacher, Mr. McIntosh, was my daddy's brother, and his house was next to the schoolhouse. When it was time for lunch, some of the children would be taken over to Mr. McIntosh's kitchen and be allowed to eat their lunch. I, along with a few more of the children would not be allowed to go over there and eat. We had to bring our lunch from home. I never did understand why it was that way, but that is the way I remember it. You know, it wasn't right for him to not let me eat, and he was kinfolks too.

A funny thing happened one day while I was at school. Mr. McIntosh was teaching the children about the Civil War in the Yancey County mountains of North Carolina. As he was in a big way of telling his story, some mischievous boys climbed upon the schoolhouse roof and began throwing firecrackers off over the schoolhouse door. Mr. McIntosh suddenly jumped behind his big old desk and held his hands over his head. After the explosions stopped, he waited a minute and walked slowly toward the door. Reaching the door, he peeped around the door frame with caution, not knowing what he was going to encounter. Some of us children knew about the prank and were falling over laughing. I believe Mr. McIntosh thought the War of Northern Aggression had once again come to his door.

As I became a teenager, my sister Reba's job of watching over me became a greater burden. I may be an old woman now, but there was a time when I was young and full of spirit. I remember one time, Jim, a neighbor boy had bought a motorcycle and would go tearing up and down the mountain road. You could hear Jim coming a mile away as his motorcycle disturbed every living creature on the mountain. An old man I knew once called the motorcycle a "farting filly," because of the pop-pop-pop noise it made.

One afternoon, Jim came up the old dirt road in a cloud of dust and stopped in front of my house. He asked me if I wanted to go for a ride with him. I knew Reba would have a fit if she knew I was about to hop on the back of a motorcycle with some boy, but, like I said, I was full of spirit. I jumped on the back of the motorcycle and off we went up the mountain. It was a wonderful feeling to feel the wind blowing through my hair as we flew up the dirt road. When we reached the end of the road, Jim said he would only take me back home if I would promise to marry him. I took my fists and started hitting him on the back. He started laughing and took me back home. I never did tell Reba, but it was a lot of fun.

Eulala McCraw,
Bee Log, Yancey County, 4/26/2006

PUBLIC EDUCATION HAS COME A LONG WAY SINCE 1800

The nineteenth century marked a revolution in teaching—the concept of universal education was embraced and legislated. Schools were in place and staffed. Most, however, had no maps, slates, pencils, pens or globes. Classroom equipment and instructional devices were almost unknown to schoolmasters in 1800—the blackboard invented in 1809, was not in common use until 1820. But by 1830, the country had an organized system of state schools that were open to all, or almost all. For the first time, the education of girls was given official credence, although the education of Native Americans and slaves, were mandated in theory, it was not part of public policy. The proliferation of public schools during this period increased the demand for teachers and opened the door a bit wider for women. Based on the assumption that females could not maintain discipline, the profession stayed all male until the mid-1800s, when dividing students into different grades allowed the older most obstreperous boys to be taught by men and the youmger children to be taught by women.

The "feminization" of teaching advanced rapidly when schoolmasters returned from the Civil War battlefields and found their position occupied by females. Women had not only preformed adequately in their absence, but at a much lower rate of pay (about 40-60% of men's salaries.) For the first time, women teachers outnumbered men. Due to the historic disparity between men and women's salaries that exists to this day, the exodus of men from teaching accounts for salary rates being kept at a uniformly low rate over compensation. Wages are lower than they would have been had a larger proportion of males stayed in the profession.

Normal, or teacher training, schools were founded in great number after the Civil War to meet the increased demand for teachers. Most of these were absorbed into the state school system by the turn of the century. Teacher certification policies and regulations had varied from state to state and were confusing and often inadequate; the establishment of normal schools tended to raise standards and thus attract more qualified candidates.

Although school teaching is one of the few professions into which women made early inroads, the fact that school boards demanded unmarried women as teachers necessarily made teaching something of a temporary job on the road to matrimony for many. As late as the 1930s, 77% of school systems employed no married women as new teachers and 62% required teachers to resign if they married. (Moviegoers in the 1930s saw nothing unusual about Little Rascals' teacher Miss McGillicuddy who had to resign in order to get married.) Before world War I, teachers in many small communities dared not to go the the theater. Card playing and dancing were also forbidden. As late as 1929, a Kansas Board of Education fired eleven high school teachers for going to a local country club dance. The breakdown of social controls that followed both World Wars granted teachers an amount of freedom in their personal habits that formerly would have been decried.

Although far from adequate, a degree of support and respect accorded today's educators is an enormous improvement over the past. A teacher's private life has always been open to public scrutiny. Perhaps because a good part of teaching consists of being a role model for students, teachers are often expected to adhere to the standards of the most pious members of a varied community, and are sometimes targets of various pressure groups with a myriad of causes and restrictions to debate.

The twofold task of the teaching profession set forth by Willard Elsbree in his 1939 classic, "The American Teacher," has changed little in fifty years: "First, to elevate the position of the American schoolteacher through high standards of training and scholarship and, second to educate the public in respect to the importance of freedom in teaching." Only if teachers are allowed to lead free and normal lives will individuals who value freedom—and who are able to teach a love of freedom—stay in the teaching profession.

www.riverofwords.org/educators/education_history.html

1905 TEACHING CONTRACT FOR STORY COUNTY, IOWA

Teachers are expected to live in the community in which they are employed and to take residence with local citizens for room and board. (Many teachers lived with the students and their parents going from one house to another.)

Teachers will be required to spend weekends in the community unless permission is granted by the Chairman of the Board.

It is understood that teachers will attend church each Sunday and take an active part, particularly in choir and Sunday School work.

Dancing, card playing and the theater are works of the Devil and lead to gambling, immoral climate, and influence and will not be tolerated.

Community plays are given annually. Teachers are expected to participate.

When laundering petticoats and unmentionables, it is best to dry them in a flour sack or pillow case. (So no one sees them hanging on the line to dry.)

Any teacher who smokes cigarettes, uses liquor in any form, frequents a pool or public hall, or (for men) gets shaved in a barber shop, (or for women) bobs (cuts) her hair, has dyed hair, wears short skirts (could not be any shorter than two inches above the ankles) and has undue use of cosmetics will not be tolerated under any circumstances.

Teachers will not marry or keep company with a man friend during the week except as an escort to church services. (The only man a teacher could be seen with was her father or her brother.)

Loitering in ice cream parlors, drug stores, etc., is prohibited.

Purchasing or reading the Sunday Supplement on the Sabbath will not be tolerated.

Discussing political views or party choice is not advisable.

Men teachers may take one evening each week for courting purposes or two evenings if they go to church regularly.

After ten hours in school, the teacher should spend the remaining time reading the Bible or other good books.

Women teachers who marry or engage in other unseemly conduct will be dismissed.

Every teacher should lay aside from his pay a goodly sum for his declining years so he will not become a burden on society.

Teachers will each day fill lamps and clean chimneys.

Each teacher will bring a bucket of water and a shuttle of coal for the day's session.

Each teacher who performs his labors faithfully and without fault for five years will be given an increase of twenty-five cents a week in his pay providing the Board of Education approves.

www.ameshistoricalsociety.org/contract.htm

W.E.B. DU BOIS' (EXCERPTS FROM A NEGRO SCHOOLMASTER IN THE SOUTH)

W.E.B. Du Bois' A Negro Schoolmaster in the South was first published as an article in the "Atlantic Magazine" in 1899, then included in the "Souls of Black Folk" in 1902 with the title, "Of the Meaning of Progress." It is a fictional narrative of Du Bois' experiences as a schoolmaster in a rural black community in Tennessee during two summers when he was an undergraduate student at Fisk University.

Because education is such a pervasive theme in "The Souls of Black Folks", I have included an excerpt from Chapter XIII, "Of the Coming of John," the only short story in the book. The story revolves around John, who leaves his rural Georgia town to attend college, then returns to become the schoolmaster in the town's black school.

"Once upon a time I taught school in the hills of Tennessee, where the broad dark vial of the Mississippi begins to roll and crumple to greet the Alleghenies. I was a Fisk student then, and all Fisk men think that Tennessee—beyond the vial—is theirs alone, and in vacation time they sally forth in lusty bands to meet the county school commissioners. Young and happy, I too went, and I shall not soon forget that summer."

"First, there was a teachers' institute at the county-seat; and there distinguished guests of the superintendent taught the teachers fractions and spelling and other mysteries,—white teachers in the morning, Negroes at night. A picnic now and then, and a supper, and the rough world was softened by laughter and song."

There came a day when all teachers left the institute, and began to hunt for schools. So, I walked on and on,—horses were too expensive,—until I had wandered beyond railways, beyond stage lines, to a land of "varmints" and rattlesnakes, where the coming of a stranger was an event, and men lived and died in the shadow of one blue hill.

Sprinkled over hill and dale lay cabins and farmhouses, shut out from the world by the forests and the rolling hills toward the east. There I found at last a little school. Josie told me of it; she was a thin, homely girl of twenty, with a dark brown face and thick, hard hair. I had crossed the stream at Water Town, and rested under the great willows; then I had gone to the little cabin in the lot where Josie was resting on her way to town. The grunt farmer made me welcome, and Josie, hearing my errand to find a school, told me anxiously that they wanted a school over the hill; that but once since the war had a teacher been there; that she herself wanted to learn,—and thus she ran on, talking fast out loud, with much earnestness and energy.

"Next morning I crossed the tall round hill, lingered to look at the blue and yellow mountains stretching toward the Carolinas; then I plunged into the wood, and came out at Josie's home. It was a dull frame cottage with four rooms, perched just below the brow of the hill, amid peach trees. The father was a quite, simple soul, calmly ignorant, with no touch of vulgarity. The mother was different,—strong, bustling, and energetic, with a quick, restless tongue, and an ambition to live "like folks." There was a crowd of children. Two boys had gone away. There remained two growing girls; a shy midget of eight; John, tall, awkward, and eighteen; Jim, younger, quicker, and better looking; and two babies of indefinite age. Then there was Josie herself. She seemed to be the center of the family; always busy at service or at home, or berry—picking; a little nervous and inclined to scold, like her mother, yet faithful, too, like her father. She had about her a certain fineness, the shadow of an unconscious moral heroism that would willingly give all of life to make life broader, deeper, and fuller for her and hers. I saw much of this family afterwards, and grew to love them for their honest efforts to be decent and comfortable, and for the knowledge of their own ignorance. There was with them no affectation. The mother would scold the father for being so "easy," Josie would roundly rate the boys for carelessness; and all knew that it was a hard thing to dig a living out of a rocky side hill."

"The schoolhouse was a long hut, where Colonel Wheeler used to shelter his corn. It sit in a lot behind a rail fence and thorn bushes, near the sweetness of springs. There was an entrance where a door once was, and within, a massive rickety fireplace; great chinks between the logs served as windows. Furniture was scarce. A pale blackboard crouched in the corner. My desk was made of three boards, reinforced at critical points, and my chair, borrowed from the landlady, had to be returned every night. Seats for the children,—these puzzled me very much. I was haunted by a New England vision of neat little desks and chairs, but, alas, the reality was rough plank benches without backs, and at times without legs. They had the one virtue of making naps dangerous,—possible fatal, for the floor was not to be trusted."

"It was a hot morning in late July when the school opened. I trembled when I heard the patter of little feet down the dusty road, and saw the growing row of dark solemn faces and bright eager eyes facing me. First came Josie and her brothers and sisters. The longing to know, to be a student in the great school at Nashville, hovered like a star above this child woman amid her work and worry, and she studied doggedly. There were the Dowells from their farm over toward Alexander: Fanny, with her smooth black face and wondering eyes; Martha, brown and dull; the pretty girl wife of a brother, and the younger brood. There were the Burkes, two brown and yellow lads, and a tiny haughty-eyed girl. Fat Reuben's little chubby girl came, with golden face and old goal hair, faithful and solemn. Thenie was on hand early,—a jolly, ugly, good-hearted girl, who shyly dipped snuff and looked after her little bow-legged brother. When her mother could spare her, Tildy came,—a midnight beauty, with starry eyes and tapering limbs; and her brother, correspondingly homely. And then the big boys: the hulking Lawrences; the lazy Neills, unfathered sons of mother and daughter; Hickman, with a stoop in his shoulders; and the rest."

"There they sit, nearly thirty of them, on the rough benches, their faces shading from a pale cream to a deep brown, the little feet bare and swinging, the eyes full of expectation, with here and there a twinkle of mischief, and the hands grasping Webster's blue-backed spelling book. I loved my school, and the fine faith the children had in the wisdom of their teacher was truly marvelous. We read and spelled together, wrote a little, picked flowers, sang, and listened to stories of a world beyond the hill. At times the school would dwindle away, and I would start out. I would visit Mun Eddings, who lived in two very dirty rooms, and ask why little Lugene, who's flaming face seemed ever ablazed with the dark red hair uncombed, was absent all last week, or why I missed so often the inimitable rags of Mack and Ed. Then the father, who worked Colonel Wheeler's farm on shares, would tell me how the crops needed the boys; and the thin, slovenly mother, whose face was pretty when washed, assured me that Lugene must mind the baby. "But we'll start them again next week." When the Lawrences stopped I knew that the doubts of the old folks about book-learning had conquered again, and so, toiling up the hill and getting as far into the cabin as possible, I put Cicero pro Archia in the simplest English with local applications, and usually convinced them—for a week or so."

"On Friday nights I often went home with some of the children; sometimes to Doc Burke's farm. He was a great, loud, thin, Black, ever working, and trying to buy the seventy-five acres of hill and dale where he lived; but people said that he would surely fail, and the "white folks would get it all." His wife was a magnificent Amazon, with saffron face and shining hair, uncorseted and barefooted, and the children were strong and beautiful. They lived in a one-and-a-half-room cabin in the hollow of the farm, near the spring. The front room was full of great fat white beds, scrupulously neat; and there were bad chromos on the walls, and a tired center-table. In the tiny back kitchen I was often invited to "take out and help" myself to fried chicken and wheat biscuit, "meat" and corn pone, string beans and berries. At first I used to be a little alarmed at the approach of bed-time in the one lone bedroom, but embarrassment was very daftly avoided. First, all the children nodded and slept, and were stowed away in one great pile of goose feathers; next, the mother and father discreetly slipped away to the kitchen while I went to bed, then blowing out the dim light, they retired in the dark. In the morning all were up and away before I thought of awaking. Across the road, where fat Reuben lived, they all went outdoors while the teacher retired, because they did not boast the luxury of a kitchen."

"I liked to stay with the Dowells, for they had four rooms and plenty of good fare. Uncle Bird had a small, rough farm, all woods and hills, miles from the big road; but he was full of tales,—he preached now and then,—and with his children, berries, horses, and wheat he was happy and prosperous. Often, to keep the peace, I must go where life was less lovely; for instance, Tildy's mother was incorrigibly dirty, Reuben's larder was limited seriously, and herds of untamed bedbugs wandered over the Eddingses' beds. Best of all I loved to go to Josie's, and sit on the porch, eating peaches, while the mother bustled and talked; how Josie had bought the sewing-machine; how Josie worked at service in winter, but that four dollars a month was "mighty little" wages; how Josie longed to go away to school, but that it "looked like" they never could get far enough ahead to let her; how the crops failed and the well as yet unfinished; and finally, how "mean" some of the white folks were."

W.E.B. Du Dois', A Negro Schoolmaster
In The South, Atlantic Magazine, 1899
"Souls Of Black Folks", "Of The Meaning Of Progress", 1902

CHAPTER SEVEN

FEARFUL EXPERIENCES

The Day I Thought My Time Had Come

When I was Assistant Principal at Vance Elementary, if the Principal was out of the building at a meeting or whatever, they would hire a substitute to handle my class and allow me to work out of the Principal's office. There was this one time when I was working out of the office and I received a phone call. It was the mother of a boy I had suspended from the bus due to fighting. When I answered the phone, she began cussing and even called me some things which I had never heard. I tried to calm her down to no avail. She kept escalating until she wasn't even making sense with some of her vulgarity. I raised my voice and said over her shouting, "If you calm down, I will speak with you, but I will not listen to this vulgarity." She did not even pause and I hung up the phone. The phone rang once again and she continued where she had left off, calling me all matter of names. This time I slammed down the receiver and waited for it to rang again. It did not and I felt a sigh of relief. Twenty minutes passed and I heard the front door slam down the hall from the office. It was a very cold day in mid winter and around the corner and into the office came a big, fat, woman. As I said, it was cold and she had on a long black coat with a big purse hanging from a strap around her shoulder. As she entered the office, she suddenly reached into the purse as if to grab something. I literally felt the hair on my head rise as my hands began to shake. I had no doubt in the world that I was going to die right there, sitting with my back against the wall and no where to run. As she approached my desk spewing profanity, she withdrew her hand from the purse and brought out a cigarette lighter and lit up a cigarette. I was not about to tell her it was a no smoking zone. I was never so glad to see a person smoke in my life. She continued to cuss me for a good five minutes, although it seemed like thirty. When she finally stopped to take a breath, I calmly said,

217

"Would you like for me to tell you what your child did to cause me to suspend him?" She took a deep breath and said, "Go ahead and tell me what happened." I explained the best I could, under the circumstances, what had transpired. When I finished, she said, "Well, that's not the story he told me. You just wait until I get home; I am going to beat his butt till he can't sit down." She got up, reached across my desk and shook my hand, saying, "Thank you, I will take care of the situation." I never heard any more about it, but that is one reason why my hair is white.

J. Terry Hall,
Scott Mountain,Buncombe County, 3/3/11

CALL THE LAW!

One of my most frightening days as a Principal came when I was Principal at our Junior High. One day a student came into my office and said, "Mr. C," they always called me Mr. C., "Jack has a loaded gun in his locker." I doubted that there really was a gun, but decided I had better go check out the locker. When I opened the locker, I found a loaded automatic pistol. To say that my knees went to cheese was putting it mildly.

Charles Cutshall,
Sodom Laurel, Madison County, 7/14/11

I WAS NOT TRAINED FOR THIS

I was teaching fifth grade in a renovated high school in Lewisville, North Carolina. My classroom was located at the end of a long hall on the second floor. The first day of school for teachers, a very nice lady knocked on my door. I invited her in along with the cutest red headed, freckled faced, blue-eyed young man. He was to be in my class the coming year. I noticed that half of his head contained a metal plate. The mother proceeded to tell me about her son. He had been in an automobile accident and had a serious brain injury. The only way to save him was to place the metal plate to his head. The mother went on to tell me that her son had epilepsy. She asked, "Have you ever had a child who was epileptic?" I said, "No." The mother then proceeded to show me how to keep her son from swallowing his tongue should he have an epileptic seizure. She also advised me that he was on medication for epilepsy and it made some sleepy. If that wasn't enough, the mother also told me that if anything hit the metal plate on her son's head, it could cause death. Therefore, he could not walk down the hall with the children to the bathroom or down the steps to the cafeteria. She would pick him up after school and bring him to school in the morning.

During the year, I took him to the bathroom after my class returned and walked with him hand- in-hand down and up two flights of steps to the cafeteria. We ability-grouped children in math and reading; however, I kept this young man with me. He sat close to my desk in the classroom away from other students. I was afraid that someone might hit him. At the end of each day, I breathed a sigh of relief—I had made it through another day.

Dr. Judy Pierce,
Winston Salem, 6/15/11

BE CAREFUL—IT IS DANGEROUS OUT THERE

I remember well the day of the Columbine shootings in Colorado. On that day, teaching changed for me. No more did I consider myself working in a protected cocoon. I realized from that day forward, anytime a person is working with the public, whether it be in a hostile environment or in the safe confines of a school house, there are people out there that for different reasons or no reason at all can place your life in danger. Ever since that dreadful day, I have been more aware of potential danger. At the time of the shooting, my wife was at home with a new baby. After that day, she realized like me the danger faced every time I left home and walked into a school. I try not to dwell on it, but it is always in the back of my mind. It made me think of how we deal with students who have been bullied or have been marginalized and live their lives on the fringes of society. We need to always be aware of the fact that at any moment bad things can happen to good people because they just happen to be in the wrong place at the time when a person with a problem explodes. I attempt to always be aware of the very quite student and reach out to him or her and try to let them know that I care.

Darren Barkett,
Canton, Haywood County, 1/23/11

A Very Sad Day

One of the saddest events that ever happened in my career was when a sweet little girl who lived in a foster home, missed her bus. Her class was scheduled to go on a field trip that day and she wished very much to attend. She decided to run all the way to school rather than to miss the field trip. She made it to within a few blocks of the school when she ran across the road and was hit by a car and killed.

Charles Cutshall,
Sodom Laurel, Madison County, 7/14/11

Kids Need A hug

There were kids who really got good at pushing my buttons and could really get me upset. If I was not careful, I would fall into a power struggle with them, although, that doesn't happen as much as it once did. I have learned some strategies of taking myself away from the situation by giving kids difference choices to get out of the power struggle and the fight. I have also developed some predictive skills and am able to predict what is coming and cut it off before it reaches the point of no return. I believe that most all teachers fear getting fired up and saying something that they will regret. One time, I was talking in the lunch line after I had told the kids not to talk in line. When they all looked at me, I said, "Sorry kids I screwed up," just as the principal walked by. You would have thought I had dropped the F-Bomb or something. These kids hear worse than that all the time on TV and at home. But it is scary that I might say something that could end up in a law suit, or I am going to walk out of the room when some kid is going to poke another kid in the eye with a pencil and I am going to have a neglect case on my hands. My mom, as a school nurse, had some charges filed against her. One year at summer camp one child was poking another kid and mom kind of did it back to the kid and said, "How do you like it?" There was a law suit brought against my mother. It is really scary that someone may bring a law suit against me. I want to be able to give my kids a hug and put my hands on their shoulder as a reminder to calm down or refocus, but I am always afraid that some kid will take it the wrong way.

Elizabeth Middleton,
Candler, Buncombe County, 10/21/10

Boys Will Be Boys

One of the scariest things that ever happened to me in a classroom was when I was in Jacksonville, Florida, where they did report cards different than we did in Asheville. The children brought their own report cards and gave them to us at grading time to let the teacher put the grade on them. We were sitting in the class and I was sitting at my desk when this one boy, Leroy, placed his card on my desk with the others. When I opened it, he had one of those rubber bands and a paper clip in there and that thing went off and it scared the life out of me. I didn't know what to do. I asked Leroy, "What do you think I aught to do?" He said, "I guess you better give me an F." I said, "Oh no, that was too much fun," so I let him get off with that one, but that was one of the funniest things.

Billie Lewis,
Enka, Buncombe County, 11/15/10

The Wrong Place At The Wrong Time

A very sad event took place while I was Principal at Claxton Elementary School. I had this little third grade girl in school by the name of Keisha who lived in the projects across town. While playing out in her front yard, she was shot between the eyes in a drug deal that had gone bad and she was caught in the crossfire, a beautiful life snuffed out by just being in the wrong place at the wrong time. Dealing with that and being with her family at the funeral just tugged at my heart and still does to this day. The first guy at the scene of her death had been a Marine and he completely lost it when he saw her. He said she was lying there with her lunch box on one side of her and some cookies wrapped in a bag on the other. Why she had to die I will never understand.

Dorland Winkler,
Malvern Hills, 8/12/11

UNCERTAIN DAYS

I remember the year 1970 when we first integrated Asheville City Schools. My Principal, Steve Mitchell's, hair turned white during that time. There was so much stress across the entire city. There were riots at Asheville High School and we were afraid it would spill over to the Jr. High and even the elementary schools. My room was on the second floor and directly across from the flag pole. It was my children's responsibility to raise and lower the flag each day. One day, during the year of integration, I received a call on the intercom asking me if everything was all right in my classroom. I told them it was as far as I knew and they asked me to look out the window at the flag. My children, by mistake, had hung the flag upside down which was a sign of distress and, a neighbor from across the street had called the school and asked if there was a major disturbance taking place at Vance School. Those were uncertain days.

Billie Lewis,
Enka, Buncombe County, 11/15/10

A GOOD TEACHERS ALSO CRIES

One of the saddest events I can recall happening during my entire career in the field of Education was when one of my students and his brother died in a house fire at their home over the Christmas break.

This was supposed to be a time for families to be together and for love to grow. It was supposed to be a time when children ran to the Christmas tree to find out what Santa brought them the night before, but on this Christmas, death came calling. My heart just broke when I visited the family and attended the graveside service. My Principal and friend, Steve Mitchell showed up to be there for the family and to help provide the strength to see me through this tragic ordeal.

Sue Harris,
Hominy Valley, April 26, 2011

DON'T MESS WITH MOUNTAIN BOYS

One school which I served was a grades one through twelve school and the room they gave me was a corner of the typing room. The room had a padlock on the door where I could keep my supplies. One day my door had been unlocked by the janitor and as I entered the room, I observed a boy of about sixteen destroying a typewriter. I went to the office and reported the incident to the principal. Following his meeting with the school principal, the boy and his friends proceeded to take a knife and slice the tires on my car. The principal reported this to the superintendent and he came out to the school and spoke to the entire school of about one hundred students. He said, "You students have no idea how lucky you are to have a person such as this to serve as your teacher." He then read them their rights and nothing like that ever happened again. But, I never felt completely safe at that school. I worried what would happen if I was out on the road by myself and had car trouble.

Anonymous,
Western North Carolina, 5/6/2011

QUIET WORDS CALM THE STORM

While serving as Principal at Hall Fletcher Middle School, I had an experience which caused me some concern. A father came bursting into my office with a cigarette hanging from his lips and hatred in his eyes. He was wearing a white t-shirt with a cigarette pack rolled up in the sleeve. I was standing behind my desk as he rushed forward and backing me into a corner, he proceeded to cuss me in a very loud and vulgar voice. Swinging his arms toward my face, I was afraid he was going to hit me, but I managed to speak in a calm voice and he slowly began to calm down. I failed to tell him that he was in a no smoking area.

Sue Harris,
Hominy Valley, April 26, 2011

KEEP IT BETWEEN THE DITCHES

There were times, especially during my first year of teaching, when I was really scared. Just driving those mountain roads alone from school to school was extremely dangerous. It was more frightening because I was a lone teacher traveling through the mountain wilderness. Where other teachers only served one school and formed a network with teachers teaching similar classes, I was the only traveling teacher in the county, and although other teachers were supportive, I lacked the network due to my unique teaching area.

Anonymous,
Western North Carolina, 5/6/2011

NEVER FORGET THE CHILD

During my first few years, parents were somewhat intimating. Many parents were older than I and I had not developed the confidence needed to hold my own. As intimating as they were, my greatest fear, even to this day, is not meeting the needs of those children with which I come into contact that most likely have no chance of success if someone does not reach out and give them a hands up and assistance. Some children just do not have the support of home and it falls to the teacher to supply the support necessary for success. I am always afraid that I may miss that one child who may need my help. We teachers need to understand that some children live in such an environment where they do not have time or a place to do homework, or their environment is so dysfunctional that they are always in fear or cannot get a good nights sleep. Maybe they just need someone to care.

Sandy Caldwell,
Waynesville, Haywood County, 11/11/10

THIS SITUATION TURNED UGLY

A part of my responsibility, during summer school, was to take some students home in my own car. On one of these trips, I was taking three students home. One was an elementary student, one was a middle school student and the other one was a high school student of about seventeen. On the way home, the seventeen year old suggested that I take the elementary and middle school student home first and then take him home since he lived further up in the mountains and I was not familiar with the mountain roads. Being a young twenty-one year old woman, I should have, but did not, even consider the danger. As we proceeded deeper along the mountainous road, I began to feel uneasy. As I looked forward, I noticed that the road ended up ahead. Turning to the boy I said, "Where do you live? The road ends up ahead." Smiling, he said, "I know," as he grabbed for my keys. I remained calm, although very frightened, and proceeded to tell him the trouble he would be in if he did anything stupid. When grabbing for my keys, he tore my clothes. I was able to regain my keys (and my composure) and turned the car around. As we approached his house, he jumped out of the car and ran in. I rapidly drove home and told my husband what had happened. He started to run out the door and go after the boy, but I managed to convince him to let me handle it the next morning. Reluctantly, he agreed and I called the school superintendent and reported the incident. The next morning, the superintendent met with the boy's parents as I waited in an office next door. The kid came in crying and telling them that I was trying to seduce him. The police were not called in and my husband didn't shoot him like he wanted to; so I left after that first year because of the long driving distance and the fact that I was scared. In my opinion, many folks in that area just don't take to outsiders.

Anonymous,
Western North Carolina, 5/6/2011

STICK UM UP

There were a couple of situations that could have been very dangerous. There was this third grade boy, I will call him Jack, who came into his classroom with a loaded gun. He walked up behind his teacher, poked the gun against her back and said, "Stick um up!" Thinking that he was playing around, she said rather harshly, "Jack! Get in your seat right this minute!" A little girl on the front row quietly said, "Ms. Lewis, it's really a gun." Turning, she quickly realized the situation and talked Jack into handing her the gun. Jack was very, very angry and decided to bring a gun to school. It was a sad situation. When Jack turned sixteen, he shot and killed someone.

Anonymous,
Western North Carolina, 5/6/2011

A THREATENING RESPONSE

After I retired from Asheville City Schools and moved to Kentucky to take a position as an administrator in an elementary school, I had an experience which caused me to experience some fear. There was this one family who had a reputation for taking the law into their own hands and we had one of their sons in sixth grade at the school where I worked. One morning, I was making my rounds through the building when I heard a commotion coming from the sixth grade restroom. I stepped around the corner to see a boy swinging like a monkey from one of the support beams. I walked over, and with both hands, grabbed him around the waist and jerked him down. He hit the floor on his feet and came up as if to fight. I grabbed him and shoved him against the bathroom door and then took him to the office and called his mother.

When his mother arrived at school, she was irritated and ready for battle. She started off shouting that she was going to the Superintendent's office I explained that she would probably have better luck parking if she went in the back door, just to let her know that I could care less about her going to the Superintendent. She then threatened to take me to court for child abuse and I explained she had that right. I then explained that I was suspending her son for three days; for him not to come to school during that time or I would have the police bring him home. She got up and she and her son stormed out of my office.

It was only about an hour until school was to be dismissed and she went out to the parking lot and moved her car straight across from where I stood, each afternoon, directing traffic during dismissal. She sat in her car, staring at my office window, during the last hour of school. I told the secretary to watch the situation and, if she tried to run over me, to call the police. When the bell rang for dismissal, I went about my regular duties, but kept an eye over my shoulder at the car parked right behind me with the wild-eyed woman at the wheel. She took her child out of the school system and I never heard from her again.

J. Terry Hall,
Scott Mountain, Buncombe County, 3/3/11

I REMEMBER THE DAY

I remember the day President Kennedy got shot. We were working with paper mache and had all the goo on our hands when they came on the intercom and told us the president had been killed. That was such a shock. Everything in the room just stopped and became real quiet. That was a bad time.

Billie Lewis,
Enka, Buncombe County, 11/15/10

DON'T MESS WITH THAT FAMILY

When I first worked in the Kentucky school system back in the 1960s, I taught sixth, seventh and eighth grade science and social studies in Barren County. Barren County was a country school system with mostly farming families. Most folks were friendly and always willing to help their neighbor. There was one exception.

I was setting up an old sixteen millimeter projector to show a science film for the first class of the day while my eighth grade students were coming into the room and chatting before the beginning of class. My classroom was located on the second floor of the school building and some boys had walked over to the window before going to their seats. As I worked with my back to the students, I heard a thump, and turning around, I saw one of my boys standing in the middle of the room with his hand over his mouth and blood oozing between his fingers. Standing next to the injured boy was this big tall skinny boy with an eight inch steel pipe in his right hand. I grabbed the injured boy and took him immediately to the Principal's office. I then returned to find the perpetrator standing in my room still holding the steel pipe. The boy was larger than I and he was armed so I politely asked him to come to the office with me. He returned with me still holding the pipe. The Principal called the County Sheriff and the injured boy's father, who were there in about ten minutes. The Sheriff asked the injured boy's father if he wanted to press charges and the father said, "No, if I press charges his family would come and burn me out during the night." Turning to the Principal, the Sheriff asked if he wanted to press charges for trespassing on school property and the Principal just shook his head no. The boy walked out of the office, still holding the steel pipe.

It seems that the boy had dropped out of school a few months before and was just walking across the school grounds when, according to him, the injured boy spit out the window and it hit him. Following his families' law, it was his right to do what he did and there was no one who had the nerve to stop it.

J. Terry Hall,
Scott Mountain, Buncombe County, 3/3/11

Desperate Housewife

In another case, a parent came into the school with a knife and chased a spouse through a classroom. He saw her approaching and ran out the back door with her in close pursuit. Our fearless leader diffused that situation.

Anonymous,
Western North Carolina, 5/6/2011

CHAPTER EIGHT

FIGHTS AND DISCIPLINE

CULTURE IS IMPORTANT

I had this little black girl, Zella, who was not following directions so I took her out in the hall and had her stand against the wall. I then placed my finger under her chin and tilted her head so she would look up at me. When she got home the story, was that I shoved her head against the wall. When her parents called, they were somewhat upset. They explained that in the black culture a child is taught to look down to show respect to an adult.

Billie Lewis,
Enka, Buncombe County, 11/15/10

THE RIGHT WAY TO HANDLE A TENSE SITUATION

During the turbulent times of integration, we were scheduled to have a pep rally at Asheville High School. Word got out that some white boys were planning to wear white jackets with a Rebel flag on the back, and a group of African-American students were going to challenge their right to wear the flag. While I considered cancelling the pep rally some white students came in my office and asked me to let them handle the situation. On the night of the pep rally, as a student wearing the Rebel flag entered the area, they were immediately taken away and their jackets removed. We had a great pep rally and there were no racial problems.

Larry Liggett,
Skyland, Buncombe County, 7/21/11

AND YOU WERE SAYING?

I had suspended this boy while I was serving as Principal at Hill Street School and, the next day, his father came into my office and began to cuss me out for suspending his son. He was sitting on one of those flimsy plastic chairs and, as he ranted and raved and pointed his finger in my face, the legs slipped out from under his chair and he landed butt first on the floor. Talking about taking the wind out of his sails, it did. He got up, turned and walked out of my office.

Dorland Winkler,
Malvern Hills, 8/12/11

HE SAID WHAT?

I remember little Bill. He came from the same area of Mt. Stirling where I was raised and he cussed like a sailor. At that time, we were in a K-6 school and our principal, Dr. Leatherwood came down to work on him for cussing on the bus. Dr. Leatherwood was around six foot four and Bill was about as high as my knee and Dr. Leatherwood got down on his level and, pointing his finger in his face, said, "You are just going to have to stop using this bad language on the bus!" He continued telling him that he couldn't do this and this while Bill just kept looking bewildered at the Principal. After a while Dr. Leatherwood looked confused since he didn't seem to be getting through to Bill. I leaned down and whispered in his ear, "Bill, he means you need to stop cussing." Bill said, "Oh, OK." Dr. Leatherwood just walked off, shaking his head.

Then there was little Allen who went home one day and told his mother that his class had won the "damn God art award." The mother was surprised, to say the least, and came to school the next day to see what we were teaching her child. Come to find out what had happened, as the class was coming back down the hall from art class, little Bill had said, "Well, we won the GD art award." Little Allen had gotten it backwards.

Sandy Caldwell,
Waynesville, Haywood County, 11/11/10

BEAM ME OUT HORACE

Two sixth-grade girls got into a fight at Hill Street School one day. I had much rather see boys fight where they throw a couple punches and it is over. With girls, they pull hair, rip clothes, bite and scratch. These two girls were really getting it on when I arrived. There were about fifty people gathered around the fight by the time I arrived and I waded in, pushing my way through the crowd. Horace Medford, a big, tall, strong, gym teacher started looking around and could not find me in the crowd. He pushed through the crowd to find me and pull me out of harms way.

Dorland Winkler,
Malvern Hills, 8/12/11

A LESSON WELL LEARNED

I had this teacher, he was probably around sixty-five years old and a former NFL player, who was in very good physical shape for his age. He asked a student to stop driving around the school campus, in a nice manner, but the student continued his circling and called the custodian a name. The custodian proceeded to pull his car across the road so the student had to stop. He then walked up to the window and confronted the boy, who was showing an attitude and cussed the custodian. The custodian quickly reached through the car window, grabbed the boy, and started pulling him out the window. The boy got back into his car and left the school grounds. He then proceeded to call me and complain about one of my teachers. I explained to him that he was doing his job and if he came back again, he most likely would get even worse. I heard no more from the boy.

Thomas Ledbetter,
Hendersonville, 4/13/2011

PLAYING TOUGH

I was a Reading Coordinator and Assistant Principal in a fifth/sixth intermediate school in Winston-Salem, North Carolina. One day a fight started between two students at the bus stop. Both boarded the school bus. When the bus reached school, one student got off the bus and told me that a boy had been stabbed. He was lying on a seat in the back of the bus. I quickly summoned the Principal. We were able to remove the young man from the school bus and the Principal carried him to the hospital.

One day, in the same school, the Principal and the Assistant Principal were attending a meeting.

In the afternoon, I was called to the second floor of the building to break up a fight between two special education students. One student called the other student's mother a honkey. Well, everything finally was settled and the students went home. Shortly after the last bus left, I saw a large group of fifty parents walking down the street towards the school. One lady, leading the group, was carrying a heavy chain and the group was shouting up a storm about the student who called her a honkey. I had to face the group. I told the secretary that I was going to the edge of the school property to try to talk to this group of angry parents, and advised her to watch the situation carefully and, if after five minutes, the group hadn't dispersed, to call the police. Thankfully, the group calmed down after I told them that if they put one step on school property, I would have them all arrested. They left. Wow!

Dr. Judy Pierce,
Winston Salem, 6/15/11

A DAY IN KINDERGARTEN

During my years teaching, I have had some pretty good tantrum throwers. Susie was a spoiled little girl. She got really upset when things had to be picked up and put away. She always felt like she had to finish something before she would put it away. She would throw herself on the floor, scream and cry at the top of her lungs and throw her shoes across the room. Of course, this was very disruptive. We had a hard time that year.

Another kid, Joey seemed like the only word he knew was NO! One day, he was a little bit wild and looking for some attention. He would go over to a poster on the door, reach up, rip it down, and throw it on the floor. He would then pick it up and put it back on the door. One day he climbed up on the rectangular table, ran down the table and jumped off while screaming at the top of his lungs. He was the same kid who, when I started asking my kids to say yes-mam to me, would shout NO! I told him NO was not welcome in this class and the only word he was allowed to say was Yes-mam. He learned after a while. There are so many kids who have seen more than they should have seen in this world or don't understand what they have seen and don't understand why they should not be saying it.

Elizabeth Middleton,
Candler, Buncombe County, 10/21/10

A Quiet Voice Turns Away Wrath

When I was teaching third grade, I had this cute little boy who got upset over something or the other and drew back to hit me. I leaned down and looked him straight in the eyes and said, in a very kind voice, "You need to think about what you are about to do." I then took him by the hand and led him out in the hall. The rest of the class were just sitting, with their mouths open. When we reached the hall, I said, "You need to get yourself under control." He turned and rammed his fist against the wall as hard as he could. I know it must have hurt him, but he was so mad, he didn't act like he even felt it. I don't remember the situation which caused him to lose control, but it was something minor. I figure it was something that had happened on the bus on his way to school. Many times things would happen on the bus that would affect them for the rest of the day.

Julia Clark,
Biltmore Lake, June 2, 2011

Discipline To fit The Crime

I remember one day Tommy came to school and brought some firecrackers. When I found them, I asked him what he thought I should do with them. He said he didn't know so I asked him to stay right there while I went out in the hall and filled a quart jar with water. When I returned, I told him to drop his firecrackers in the jar of water. For years after that, I would see Tommy from time to time and he would always remember me having him place his firecrackers in the jar of water.

Billie Lewis,
Enka, Buncombe County, 11/15/10

Don't Mess With My Sister

While teaching at Vance Elementary School in Asheville, I had the task, I would not say pleasure, of dealing with two twin racial girls. The twins were eleven years old, about five feet ten inches tall and weighed around one hundred fifty pounds. They were, to put it lightly, "Big old gals." In addition to being big for their age, they were as mean as uncle Josh's old Jersey bull. They had rather fight than eat when they were hungry and could cuss like a sailor.

There were many stories that could be told concerning these girls, but I will only relate two that happened while they were in my fifth grade class. Actually, Wanita was in my room and her sister Bonetia was in the other fifth grade teacher's class.

Both fifth grade classes had lunch at the same time each day which placed both girls in the lunchroom at the same time. One day, things had been going fairly calm with the two girls until lunch. It happened to be a day when, of all things, we had spaghetti with meat sauce. My class was seated on the left side of the lunchroom and the other fifth grade teacher had her class all the way across the large room on the right. Wanita was sitting with her left foot sticking out in the aisle as another student walked by and accidentally tripped over her foot. Wanita jumped up, grabbed her full plate of spaghetti and dumped it over the head of the other girl. The fight was on! Bonetia, seeing her sister in a fight, ran across the room and literally dived into the fray. Fists were flying, feet were kicking, hair was being yanked out and spaghetti was being thrown over everyone on that side of the lunchroom. Assessing the situation, I, ran and jumping into the middle of the fight, attempted to disentangle the combatants. Order was restored and lunch continued.

Another situation, involving the twins, was a time when we were coming back from the lunchroom. Procedure was for the other fifth grade teacher to bring her class back from the basement lunchroom up to their third floor classroom first, stop and allow her class to take a restroom break before going back to the classroom. I then would bring my class up and follow the same procedure.

On this particular day, things had been somewhat unruly all morning, and, as I was bringing my students up the stairs, I heard a commotion taking place outside the restroom. As I rushed forward and came around the corner, I saw Bonetia strike another girl in the mouth. Moving swiftly, I grabbed Bonetia around the waist and threw her against the wall. Keep in mind, these girls were almost as big as their teachers. Just as I had gotten control of Bonetia, I heard this blood curdling scream as Wanita came running and jumped on my back. She had both legs wrapped around my waist and was banging on my head with both fists. The other teacher, seeing what was happening, grabbed Wanita around the waist and threw her against the opposite wall.

These girls were so big and wild that later their mother was reported to the Department of Social Services for hitting Wanita on the side of her head with a two-by-four DSS would not press charges because the situation constituted self defense.

J. Terry Hall,
Scott Mountain, Buncombe County, 3/3/11

Just Another Day On The Job

There were so many times in my career, especially in high school, when I had to get in the middle of a fighting situation. Back then, we did not have School Resource Officers in the schools like we do now and, some times, we would be in a fearful situation. We really needed School Resource Officers, even back then, but that time had not yet come. One time two school boys got in a fight in a flower garden between two buildings. I had to wade into the flowers and pull them apart. Another time, one boy was chasing another boy across campus with the intention of doing bodily harm. I ended up chasing the boy that was chasing the other boy. Most of the time, students would realize their error after they had calmed down and would willingly agree to take whatever punishment was due.

Fred Trantham,
Waynesville, Haywood County, 11/11/10

HERE COMES FIVE-O

One time, I had taken my fifth grade class on a field trip to Winston Salem and we were returning back up Old Fort Mountain. When we stopped at a rest area, Hilton, one of my students, called 911, and, of course, another child told me. I was so upset. We had had a wonderful trip and then he had to go and do something like that. The next morning after I had read him the "riot act," the police came to my door, and we had to take Hilton and all the boys who encouraged him to do it to the auditorium to talk to the police about why that was inappropriate.

Julia Clark,
Biltmore Lake, June 2, 2011

WATCH OUT—HERE COMES JOHNNY

I had one kid, Johnny, who just for attention, would attack other kids. For no reason, he would grab them or choke them and throw things around the room. It is not fun when you have to put yourself between two five year olds to protect them by trying to restrain them or get them out of the room. Yet, when there was something Johnny wanted to be engaged in, like when I brought my pet snake to the room, he would act like a little angel and control himself. But if he was not totally engaged, he was just out of control.

Elizabeth Middleton,
Candler, Buncombe County, 10/21/10

INDIVIDUALIZATION

There was one little boy, Ricky who was a hand full. He would get in trouble almost every day by just pestering other children. He seemed to really enjoy getting other children angry. After trying several things to keep him from bothering other children, I finally placed his desk next to mine so I could always reach out and touch him if he was getting out of control. I had to do a lot of hands on with him that year.

Billie Lewis,
Enka, Buncombe County, 11/15/10

THE CHOICE IS YOURS

I had this one boy who was a dropout who started coming back on campus and driving his car around and around in front of the school, probably trying to impress the girls. I went out and explained to him that he should leave the school grounds. He stated he was just driving around, and continued. I stepped into the office and called the police. They were there in about five minutes and he, seeing them approach pulled his car into the small grocery store next to the school. I explained to the officer that he had refused to leave when asked and told him that he was in the car at the store next door. The officer went up and brought the boy back to where I was waiting. He said to the boy, "Are you going to stop coming on the school grounds or am

I going to have to take you to jail?" The boy began to see the light and left. I had no further trouble out of him. For the most part I never had much of a problem with people.

Thomas Ledbetter,
Hendersonville, 4/13/2011

LEARN TO READ BETWEEN THE LINES

One time, I was writing notes to parents at the end of the day, describing what had happened during the day. The next day, I got a note back from one parent who was upset by the way I had worded the note. I called her and explained I was writing twenty notes in the last fifteen minutes of the day and it was difficult to go into detail in each note. After I explained the situation, she said she didn't really realize what had happened and she was sorry. Most parent issues I have had, I have been able to handle diplomatically.

Elizabeth Middleton,
Candler, Buncombe County, 10/21/10

TAKE IT LIKE A MAN

I had this old country boy, when I was principal, who got into something or the other and I called him into my office. I said, "Son, you know you messed up and I'm going to have to spank you or everyone else will think they can get away with whatever and nothing will happen." He gave me a sheepish smile and said, "I know I done wrong and let's just get it over with." I popped him on his behind three times, and, shaking his head he said, "I deserved it, and you won't have any more trouble from me." As he walked out of my office, there were five or six parents there to see me and the boy looked at them and, rubbing his butt, said, "Boy, did he whip my ass!"

Charlie McConnell,
Sylva, 6/17/11

CAN YOU BELIEVE IT?

During my years of teaching, I never really had a fight in my classroom. I had my rule written on the wall, "Do unto others as you would have them do unto you." I guess that made a difference. I can honestly say that during my twenty-nine years of teaching, I never spanked a child.

Billie Lewis,
Enka, Buncombe County, 11/15/10

BEWARE OF THE GIRLS

I never had many fights at school, but I had always rather have a fight between boys than I had with girls. Boys, when they fight will punch each other a few times and stop. Girls, on the other hand, will carry a grudge for months once they get mad.

Thomas Ledbetter,
Hendersonville, 4/13/2011

OUR NOTORIOUS ALUMNI

A short time before I retired from Asheville City Schools, I was asked to go over to the Middle School to serve as Assistant Principal. I was not very pleased with the request and was approaching retirement anyway so I was not very enthusiastic about the transfer.

One day, we had some dignitaries from Washington DC come to the school and I was assigned to show them around the building. For some reason someone had placed four wanted posters, like the ones at the post office, on the wall of the hallway (probably hoping someone would turn in someone from their community.) As I proceeded down the hall, I motioned in a nonchalant manner to the posters and said, "These are some of our former alumni." I kept walking as the visitors looked at each other.

Another event that took place at Asheville Middle School during my time there was rather funny. I was making my way down the hall when I heard yelling and screaming coming from around the corner. This was not unusual for the Middle School, although it usually indicated a fight. Walking around the corner, I saw a group of students gathered around two racial boys fighting. I shoved my way through the students to find two boys punching each other with abandonment. Both boys were wearing their pants loose and low as was the custom of the time and one of the boy's pants had fallen down around his ankles and he was standing there fighting in his white briefs. I was laughing so hard I just stood there and let them fight.

J. Terry Hall,
Scott Mountain, Buncombe County, 3/3/11

Sticks and Stones May Break Your Bones, But Words Will Never Hurt You While

I was a principal, I had this seventeen year old come to my office and tell me that his daddy said for him to leave school at one o'clock that afternoon. I asked him if his daddy had sent a note and he said he didn't. I refused to allow him to leave school, and, after a while, his daddy called me and gave me one of the worst cussings I had ever received. I had a psychology course one time and they had told me to just let them keep on cussing and they would get it out of their system. Well, he went on, and on, and on.

Lowell Crisp,
Robinsville, Graham County, 6/15/11

BE SURE YOU'VE HUNG UP THE PHONE

One day, this woman called very upset about something or the other and started calling me names. After running on for awhile, she turned to her husband and said, "That—hung up on me!" A short time later, the husband rushed into my office in an irate state and demanded to know why I hung up on his wife. I explained that I had not hung up on her and repeated the words she had used when she had told her husband. Realizing he had been sent on a fool's mission, he turned around and left, never saying another word.

Thomas Ledbetter,
Hendersonville, 4/13/2011

IF SWEET TALKING DON'T WORK

We had this man, one time, while I was Principal at Stecoah who had been drinking and he tried to ride a horse into the gym. We had a retired law officer working security that night, who was about seventy years old, but a very big man. He managed to get the man off the horse and was explaining to him that he could not ride the horse through the gym.

Well, the drunk was cussing the retired officer and calling him every name in the book and some that wasn't. The retired officer kept saying, "Don't do this, hush, hush." But the drunk just kept on cussing. I was standing next to them and, all of a sudden, the retired officer reached way down toward the floor with his right hand and, coming up, he slapped that man so hard that he literally fell backward. You talk about sobering a guy up-that sobered him up right on the spot!

Lowell Crisp,
Robinsville, Graham County, 6/15/11

GIRLS JUST DON'T FIGHT FAIR

One day, when I was teaching at Erwin Middle school in Buncombe County, I was in the lunchroom when two girls staring at each other across the room, suddenly jumped up and started toward each other, getting ready to fight. As they threw their first punches, I heard this sound like icicles hitting the floor. As soon as the fight stopped, I looked for the origin of the noise and found it to have been their false plastic fingernails breaking off and falling to the floor. I learned early on that I didn't want to be in the middle of two girls when they are fighting. They are much worse than boys and more dangerous.

Darren Barkett,
Canton, Haywood County, 1/23/11

BACK WHEN I WAS YOUNG

I had this seventh grader one day who had gotten into trouble fighting and refused to go to my office. I said, "You are going to have to go to the office with me." He refused and said, loud enough for everybody in the class to hear, "If you touch me, my daddy will sue you!" I said, "I am not going to touch you." I was in pretty good shape back then so I squatted down in front of his desk, wrapped my arms around his desk and carried him and his desk out of the room and into my office with his feet dangling in front of his classmates.

Charlie McConnell,
Sylva, 6/17/11

WORKING IN THE WAR ZONE

While serving as Assistant Principal at Vance Elementary School, I had the responsibility of bus duty each morning and afternoon. One cloudy cold winter afternoon, I was supervising the loading of the buses when a fight broke out between two girls. I had ten times rather attempt to break up a fight between boys than girls. Where boys usually fight with fists, girls will slap, pull hair and bite. When girls fight there are no holds barred. In this particular case, these two girls were getting it on pretty good by the time I reached the fight. As I said, it was cold with high wind and both girls had on heavy coats. Arriving, I grabbed hold of one of the combatant's coats just as she lunged for another punch at the other girl. My finger got tangled up in the material of the coat and, as she landed her punch, she jerked my finger and broke it. She didn't mean any harm to me but I was the one who was injured. As soon as they realized they had injured the Assistant Principal, they stopped fighting and I, holding my finger, walked back into the building. I stopped by the secretary's office and told her I had broken my finger. She suggested I go to the doctor and when I did, I was told it had torn the cartilage and I needed surgery in order to keep from losing the use of my finger. I went in the hospital the next day and had surgery, but to this day, I still cannot bend my ring finger.

J. Terry Hall,
Scott Mountain, Buncombe County, 3/3/11

WE DO THE BEST WE CAN

Public school teachers normally do not receive the training necessary to deal with emotionally disturbed and violent children. One time I encountered such a child. This child was only in second grade, but she was big for her age. She was a totally disturbed child, but I had not been informed of her condition. As events began to unfold, I soon realized she had a severe problem and called Joe Weinberger, our School Psychologist, to provide suggestions for working with the girl. I tried everything Joe suggested but to no avail. She seemed to be happy one minute and, the next minute, she would be screaming and throwing things. I just did not have the necessary training to help her; she needed more help than could be provided in a public school.

Sue Harris,
Hominy Valley, April 26, 2011

TAKE TIME TO KNOW YOUR STUDENTS

I have had some kids over the years who might be deemed a discipline problem, but the very last thing they needed was punishment, because you may not know from where they came. I found out years ago, that I needed to find out as much as possible about from where these kids are coming, instead of all of a sudden, deciding we are going to end the world with you or whatever.

One day, this six foot senior boy came to school seemingly wanting to fight. He was sent to the office for discipline and I asked him to take a seat. I said, "What happened to you this morning?" Looking up, with a tear oozing from his red eyes, he said, "Doc, I don't know if I can tell you or not." Swallowing back the tears, he said, "Well, all right, I'll tell you what's going on. My dad is a long distance truck driver and he came home last night and told my mom that he was leaving and didn't ever want to see her or me again." He sat there with great big tears running down his face, and he didn't need anyone to get after him right then; it was the last thing he needed.

I have always tried to realize that I need to attempt to find out something about these kids in order to at least understand where they are coming from; you can never tolerate it if they are going to hurt somebody or something like that, but many times, they just need an arm around their shoulder, even if they are bigger than you, they are still high school students.

One day I overheard two boys talking in the hall and one said, "Don't ever let Doc hear you cussing and don't ever tell him a lie." Most students realized I would be fair if they were up front with me.

Thomas Ledbetter,
Hendersonville, 4/13/2011

RAMBO

Another experience involved a Behaviorally Educationally Handicapped (BEH) child when I was Principal at Hall Fletcher Middle School. A tall drug using boy attacked another boy in the school cafeteria. He had a fork in his right hand and was going for the other boy's throat and eyes. Coming up from behind, and, not being able to reach his arm which held the fork, I literally climbed up his back and reached over his shoulder and grabbed the fork. The other boy was able to leave the scene and the tension was defused before the police took the boy into custody.

Sue Harris,
Hominy Valley, April 26, 2011

I Am Prejudiced Against Certain Things

Many schools in western North Carolina have very few minority students. Mainly, because the minority population is very small in the area, and second, because those who are in the area choose to live in the city schools attendance areas. One year when I was at a principals' conference down state, I was asked how many minority students I had in high school. I said, "We have three." "Three percent?" he said. I said, "No, three students." He then asked, "What is the population of your school?" "About nine hundred." I replied.

I will point out that most all of my minority students over the years have been wonderful. Although, one time I had this minority mom who had left her teenage children to survive on their own and went to Florida with some man for three months. During that time, one of her boys got caught stealing from a grocery store in order to have food for himself and his brothers. After she had returned, she became upset over some incident and came into my office claiming that I was prejudiced. Standing up from my desk, I said, "You are right! I am prejudiced! I am prejudiced against mothers who fail to take care of their children and provide for them." She stood up and stormed out of my office.

Thomas Ledbetter,
Hendersonville, 4/13/2011

BUT HE PROMISED

While I was serving as principal, I observed these two sixth grade girls beating the fire out of Harvey. I separated them and asked why they were beating on Harvey. One of the girls said, "Harvey asked me to show him my Coo-Coo this morning and, after I did, he went and told everybody about it.

Charlie McConnell,
Sylva, 6/17/11

CHAPTER NINE

REWARDING EXPERIENCES

WE ALL NEED A THANK YOU EVER
NOW AND THEN

I have had several parents who were glad I had their child for the second time in a different grade. This has been very rewarding. At the beginning of the year, I met a dad who said, "I am so glad you left second grade so now my kid can have you for another year. "That was such a good feeling to know that, even in the community, I have developed a positive reputation.

Sometimes I play with my kids about leaving the school and they shout "No! No!" One day, I explained that I was going on a trip and would be gone for a week. Some kids began to cry. I said, "It's all right, I will be back in a few days." That was such a nice feeling. It is always a good feeling when a sibling comes up to me and asks if they can have me the next year. Teaching has it's rewards.

There is always progress in the life of a child whether it be developmental progress, academic progress or emotional progress; they all go through change during the ten months of the school year. It is very exciting to see this change. At the beginning of the year, especially in kindergarten I may think these kids don't know anything, but, by the end of the year I can really see progress.

Elizabeth Middleton,
Candler, Buncombe County, 10/21/10

257

A HELPING HAND

I had a teacher who had a substance abuse problem and I worked with her and her husband to help her get clean. She was successful and has remained clean for the past twenty-five years.

Dorland Winkler,
Malvern Hills, 8/12/11

"THANK YOU, MAKES IT ALL WORTHWHILE"

There was this one student who, would have most likely become a success, with or without me, but he helped me realize the great impact a teacher can have on a young person's life. I had him in eighth grade at Enka middle School in Buncombe County. Five years later, when he was a senior in high school and I had moved to another school, I happened to run into him while my family and I were getting some ice cream. He turned around and said, "Mr. Barkett! It is so good to see you". I knew his face but I told him I could not recall his name. He told me his name and said, "There was something you said when I had you as a teacher in eighth grade about the connections a person makes in their lives. How that interacting with people-it is those connections we make that will help us throughout life. That was something that has stuck with me and has really made a difference in my life."

Another student met me one afternoon and told me he really enjoyed being in my class and that I helped him so much and made him want to be a better person. It is stories like these that make it worthwhile to be a teacher.

Darren Barkett,
Canton, Haywood County, 1/23/11

I Feel I Made A Difference

I feel over the years that I have made a difference in the lives of a great many students. I also had the privilege to serve as Faculty Chairperson while at Vance Elementary. It was very interesting to go to the Principal and express the concerns of the faculty. Another personal success story was when I was selected by the faculty at Vance Elementary as Teacher of the Year. This was a huge honor.

Julia Clark,
Biltmore Lake, June 2, 2011

Eyes Are A Gateway To The Soul

Being in the school business, I can remember several success stories which were more the result of the teacher than it was of me. One particular story, that I remember, involved a family who had several children in our school and system. Most of them were in the special class for behavior problems. In meeting this child for the first time, I immediately noticed something very peculiar. I had heard that a person's eyes were the gateway to their soul. One thing that I immediately noticed was that this particular student had no "soul" reflection in his eyes. No matter how hard we worked, there was never a spark in his eyes until his fourth grade teacher. This teacher, in one year, through her delicate strokes of her paint brush, created a whole new student with purpose. I can still remember him saying to me one day, "I made it . . . I'm a star." What he was referring to was his passing scores on his end-of—grade tests. I could see then as I looked into his eyes that there was a soul there. That was an example of the difference a great teacher can make in the life of a child.

Charles Cutshall,
Sodom Laurel, Madison County, 7/14/11

Children Always Came First With Me

I have had many wonderful, rewarding experiences during my career, but the most rewarding was the Arts Center at Asheville High School. It is an outstanding center for theater, for dance, for music, for pottery and the center has won many awards for achievement. It is a fantastic center.

I am also proud to say I have always attempted to know each student on a personal basis. During graduation I would be sitting with the superintendent or a board member and I would whisper, "This kid did so and so, or this one has made wonderful progress."

Since I retired, I am still part of the Buncombe County Caring for Children Association, a group I helped start. We help many children and many of these are Buncombe County children. We provide homes where they can stay or shelters where they can go to be safe when they are mad or have run away from home. From all our homes, we always take the children back to their home school and a lot of those children are from Asheville High for various reasons.

Larry Liggett,
Skyland, Buncombe County, 7/21/11

To Teach A Child

One of the most rewarding experiences was with a little Indian boy after I moved to Asheville. His name was Navarro. At the end of the school year, he was not ready to go on, so I kept him back and he didn't like that so I asked him to stay in my room for the next year. He did and we got along all right. Other people kept telling me not to spend much time with him because he would never learn to read but I was always patient with him and helped him all I could. I gave him books that fit his interest and kept on encouraging him to read. The following year, after he had moved on to fifth grade, my Principal, Mr Harwood came in and said, "You know who I saw today?" I said, "Heavens no, who did you see?" He said, "I went to the West Asheville Library and, coming out of the library, was Navarro; he had checked out some books." That made me feel real good.

Billie Lewis,
Enka, Buncombe County, 11/15/10

It Was The Right Thing To Do

I had this girl who had MS and could hardly make it from one floor to another of our three story building. I assigned her a locker on each floor and gave her an open hall pass so she could manage without carrying her book bag up and down the stairs. For years after she left the school, her father would see me and thank me for giving her the extra help. It was just the right thing to do.

Dorland Winkler,
Malvern Hills, 8/12/11

Good Times

I had some very good times during my teaching experience and wouldn't give it a second thought to return to teaching, if I were younger.

Billie Lewis,
Enka, Buncombe County, 11/15/10

I AM PROUD OF MY CHILDREN AND TEACHERS

After I left Asheville City Schools I went back to my home area in Madison County and became Principal at Laurel Elementary, where I had attended school many years before. At this point it was a K-5 school with only ninety-four students and a high percentage of free and reduced lunch students. A highlight that I will always remember happened during my last year at Laurel. We had 100% of our third, fourth and fifth grade students pass the end-of-grade assessment in reading, math and science. This had come about due to hard work by our staff and great support from our parents. As a result we were the only public school in North Carolina named as a National Blue Ribbon School in 2010.

Charles Cutshall,
Sodom Laurel, Madison County, 7/14/11

GIVE ME FLOWERS WHILE I LIVE

I have kept in touch with some of my former students over the years and have been given thanks for making a positive difference in their lives. One of my former students, in particular, who is now serving as Superintendent in a North Carolina county gives me some credit for his success.

Another child who was a twin was in my class in the early years and I recognized he had a problem and recommended that he be tested. They found out he had dyslexia and provided the help he needed. He went on to college and became a success in life. He later came back to school and gave me credit for finding out what was wrong with him and for helping him succeed.

Julia Clark,
Biltmore Lake, June 2, 2011

It Makes It All Worthwhile

As a traveling teacher in public schools, I have worked with many children over the years. One of the most rewarding things that happened to me was to have several former students who are now parents themselves come up to me and say, "I had you as a teacher when I was in school and now I have a child in school. I would like very much if you could be his teacher."

Anonymous,
Western North Carolina, 5/6/2011

A Nice Way To Start The Day

Kids in my class always looked forward to me playing on the piano I had in my room. They looked forward to me playing and singing. When I would get to school in the morning, I would go in and sit down and start playing. I thoroughly enjoyed playing and singing. The children seemed to enjoy it also.

Billie Lewis,
Enka, Buncombe County, 11/15/10

DIFFERENT STROKES FOR DIFFERENT FOLKS

David was one funny little character when it came time to read-he would take his book and crawl under my desk to read his library book. This was his special area and he felt comfortable reading under my desk. I thought that he was doing what I had asked him to do and he was enjoying himself so I figured that was where he needed to be.

Billie Lewis,
Enka, Buncombe County, 11/15/10

REACH OUT AND TOUCH A CHILD

During my second year of teaching in Virginia, I had this little tow-headed boy in my first grade class who was having a problem learning. I felt he was able to learn what was required, but he was having a problem. As it turned out, I found out he was almost blind. I was able to get him some glasses and he did just fine. I later learned that his family were poor and could not afford to buy him the glasses he needed. His parents were appreciative and I always felt like I made a big difference in his life.

Julia Clark,
Biltmore Lake, June 2, 2011

THANKS FOR A JOB WELL DONE

One of the nicest things that happened to me was when I retired. All of us teachers went up to the governors residence on Beaucatcher Mountain here in Asheville and had a retirement party. There was a song out at that time called, "I Heard It Through The Grapevine," and

Carol Goins and some others dressed up like big grapes and danced to the song. Julia Clark did a wonderful job singing a solo. It was so nice. I really appreciated it.

Billie Lewis,
Enka, Buncombe County, 11/15/10

RAISE THE BAR

Because of my strict discipline, I was sometimes seen as being a mean teacher. I would always tell my students, at the beginning of the school year, that they may have heard how mean I am, but I would ask them to wait awhile and make up their own minds whether I am mean or not. Many of them later would say, "You were not mean Mrs. Clark, you just had high expectations for your students." I have found over the years that most students will live up to high expectations.

Julia Clark,
Biltmore Lake, June 2, 2011

GET YOUR PRIORITIES IN ORDER

I was assigned as a mentor to a teacher who had taught before and had moved into Asheville City Schools. She felt, since she had previously taught, that she did not need a mentor, but, in time, she came to me and asked how I managed to seem to always be prepared for my class and never take work home with me. I explained that I always tried to never take work home. I would stay as late as needed to complete my work, but when I went home, it was a time for me to be with my children and my husband. I never allowed school work to get between me and my family. She seemed to appreciate my suggestion.

Julia Clark,
Biltmore Lake, June 2, 2011

A WORK THAT WILL PASS ON THROUGH THE YEARS

A few years before I retired, Roy Harwood, our Principal, decided to do a woodcarving of Zeb Vance's birthplace which is located just north of Asheville. He took several pictures of the cabins, the rail fence and the mountains and asked for volunteers from teachers to help him with the wood carving. Only Terry Hall and myself agreed to help, even though neither of us had ever done any wood carving. It took us several months, working after school, to finish the large wood carving. Upon completion, the large wood carving was placed at the entrance of the new Vance School building. Mr. Harwood submitted the work to the North Carolina Museum in Raleigh and received a letter that, when the new Vance School is torn down, it will be placed in the state museum. It is beautiful if I do say so myself. Terry Hall was asked after, it was completed, if he did the wood carving and he said, "Roy Harwood is the wood carver; Billie Lewis and I were only the wood peckers."

Billie Lewis,
Enka, Buncombe County, 11/15/10

MASTER TEACHER

I had three different principals who wrote in my evaluation that I was a "Master Teacher." That meant so very much to me. One day, Charles

Cutshall, my Principal at Vance Elementary, came in my room after I had had a very stressful day the day before, and brought me a beautiful picture of a sunset and said, "I just thought you might need this." That was just the kind of person Charles was, when he observed that you had a problem, he was always there to make your day brighter.

Julia Clark,
Biltmore Lake, June 2, 2011

EACH CHILD IS DIFFERENT

One child I remember had an unusual problem. I was teaching handwriting and Patricia came up and said when she started writing, that she would start a one point, and, as she wrote, her handwriting would run up the page. I worked with her for a while with no success and decided to take her to the special education teacher for help. After providing some techniques for her to use, she was able to succeed in keeping her handwriting straight.

Billie Lewis,
Enka, Buncombe County, 11/15/10

GIVE SOMEONE A HELPING HAND

I own a cabin I received from my grandmother in the Mt Sterling area where I grew up, and the family who lived right above me, at the top of the mountain, sent their daughter, Nita to school in Waynesville. She would have to get on the bus at the crack of dawn in order to come to school and they would keep pillows on the bus so she could sleep on her way to school. Nita was a very bright little girl and is very dear to my heart. When she finished high school, I really wanted her to have the opportunity to attend college. I would keep her on week-ends every once in awhile, since she lived so far away, in order for her go to go a dance or a basketball game. If she had gone home, there was no way she was going to be able to attend school functions. I always tried to do things with her and I figured her parents couldn't afford to send her to college, so I started looking at Berea College in Berea, Kentucky. I talked to her mom and she agreed to go with Nita and I to Berea in order to check it out. Nita and her mom both just fell in love with the college. They gave us a tour and made us feel welcome. Her mom was very much excited about the prospect but her father was a little bit leery about it. He did, eventually, agreed to allow her to attend and she went to Berea and graduated with a nursing degree. She has just recently completed her Masters Degree and is currently teaching nursing at Asheville-Buncombe Technical Institute in Asheville. I couldn't be more happy for her; she now has two little kids of her own and is a very special and bright young woman. I am very proud of her.

Sandy Caldwell,
Waynesville, Haywood County, 11/11/10

PATRICIA REALLY TOUCHED MY HEART

Patricia was a beautiful little five year old girl. I had her brother in my fifth grade class a couple years before and had become acquainted with their family's situation. They were very poor, and their mother, being the sole provider, worked very hard to provide for her four children. There was never enough money to last to her next paycheck.

I felt sorry for the family and went out of my way to see that Robert, her brother in my class, knew someone really cared for him. When Patricia enrolled in kindergarten, I would stop by her classroom and check up on her. One year, Christmas was coming and I knew she would not receive much, if anything under the tree, so I went to K-Mart in search of a doll for Patricia. I found this wonderful doll that looked like a princess in a beautiful gown. It was placed in a clear plastic dome case and was hanging from a hook on the rack. I thought, this is the doll for Patricia. I bought the doll and had it Christmas wrapped. The following day was the last day of school before Christmas break and I took the doll and placed it around the corner from her classroom. I stepped through the door and asked her teacher to send Patricia out in the hall. She came out with her big beautiful eyes flashing with wonder as I knelt down so I could look her in the eyes. I said, "Patricia, I was out in the parking lot a few minutes ago when I met this old man wearing a red suit. He had a long white beard, a fat belly, and he was saying "Ho-Ho-Ho." Her eyes widened and brightened even more than they were as she exclaimed, "Santa Claus!" I looked puzzled for a few seconds before I agreed that must be who it was. I then reached around the corner and explained that he had asked me to give her this present. She squaealed with glee as she tore into her present. When she saw the doll, she literally jumped up and down. I let her go back in her room with a smile on her face as big as a slice of watermelon. I watched her grow over the years and met her one day after she had moved on to middle school. I told her I was glad she was doing well in school and she told me she still had her Christmas doll hanging from the ceiling just above her bed.

J. Terry Hall,
Scott Mountain, Buncombe County, 3/3/11

READING RECOVERY PROGRAM

One project stands heads and shoulders above all others when it comes to my feelings of achievement over the course of my career in the field of education. Upon receiving my Doctor of Education degree, I was promoted to the central office in Asheville City Schools and placed as

Director of the Elementary Curriculum and Asheville's Title 1 Program. For those not familiar with Title 1, it is part of the ESEA, (Elementary/ Secondary Education Act) and is therefore funded by the federal government. The purpose of the program is to provide extra assistance to low income children and attempt to close the gap between those children of low income and those with higher income. When I was asked to take on this responsibility in 1988, the first thing was to familiarize myself with the situation as it existed and to formulate a plan to help those from low income families succeed.

Following the investigation, I discovered that Title 1 funds were being spread throughout the entire spectrum of the schools and were being used in kindergarten through grade twelve. I am and have always been convinced that it is much better to prevent a problem than it is to attempt to fix it later. Therefore, my philosophy was to concentrate available funding on earlier grades in hopes of preventing the reading and math problems before they had a chance to become major. In my opinion, the school system was spending far too many funds in troubleshooting the problems in the upper grades, whereas they could be far more successful concentrating funding in preschool through grade five. Based upon my recommendation, Asheville City Schools revamped their federal funding.

Since reading was obviously the area most needing reconstruction, I established a committee of teachers to recommend a researched reading program that would be the most likely in producing success. After visiting several school systems, and listening to and visiting reading program demonstrations around the country, the committee recommended the Reading Recovery program. This program is a one-on-one tutoring reading program, where a teacher who has been trained specifically works with one first grade child at a time, actually diagnosing and treating his or her specific reading problem. It can be viewed as a clinical reading program.

Obviously, such a program would have a much higher start-up cost than the regular program which allowed one teacher to work with several children at a time. Although, if my philosophy was correct and the problem needed to be addressed before it mushroomed, then the higher cost could be justified by not having to provide remediation later on.

My task then was to convince my superordinates to follow my recommendation. After convincing our Superintendent, my next step was to address the Board of Education and seek their approval. During my presentation, I suggested that I conduct a longitudinal study over a three year time frame and compare reading achievement scores with a control group of similar children. Following discussion, I was granted permission to proceed with administration of the Reading Recovery program to Title 1 students.

Over the next three years, and beyond children who had been administered Reading Recovery not only scored as well but better than the control group and, when the North Carolina Standard Course of Study was administrated in third grade, they scored significantly better than the overall average third grade student and far exceeded expectations.

The resulting success also brought additional benefits. Ten surrounding school systems, seeing Asheville's success hired our Reading Recovery Teacher Trainers to train teachers in the Reading Recovery process and become certified Reading Recovery teachers for their school systems. In addition, I applied for and received a grant from the state of North Carolina for serving other school systems through the state Title 1 monies. One other perk was when word got out about our success, I was invited to speak at several national conventions, discussing and showing the results of our longitudinal studies. Don Carter, my state consultant and friend, and I traveled to several national conferences including two in California and presented our data on the Reading Recovery program.

J. Terry Hall,
Scott Mountain, Buncombe County, 3/3/11

LISTEN TO YOUR PEOPLE

When I came to Haywood County, there was a real war going on between the County Commissioners and the School Board. Also, the teachers had been very unhappy with their former Superintendent. I was able to handle both situations in a short time. The Chairman of the School Board said he had call, after call, after call, before I came on board, but in my first three months he had no problem calls at all. I spent a lot of time out in the schools talking and listening to the teachers and they respected me for being there.

It took a little longer to solve the problem with the Commissioners, but it turned out that the daughter of the Chairman of the Board of Commissioners was a friend of mine in college and that helped. We went from the Commissioners fighting every issue of the school board to the Chairman of the Commissioners implementing the first supplement for teachers in Haywood county.

Charlie McConnell,
Sylva, 6/17/11

MY GREATEST SUCCESS

As Superintendent of Jackson County, my greatest success was The New Century Scholarship Program. Fifty-five students from Jackson

County were chosen for a scholarship to Southwestern Technical Community College. If the students succeeded there, Western Carolina University picked them up for the next two years. It was funded through initial gifts from local businesses placed in escrow to support the scholarship. The award was not only academic, but was based on whether the student put forth effort and his/her attitude. The students were chosen in sixth grade and followed throughout high school. They had to honor a contract throughout the program.

Charlie McConnell,
Sylva, 6/17/11

In Some Small Way I Touched Their Lives

I looked back through my school yearbooks and thought about all the children I have taught over the years. They are now doctors, lawyers, members of congress, political leaders, bankers, teachers, and other professionals. It may be in a small way, but I have touched their lives over the years and just may have helped them along the way.

Jan Lunsford,
Averys Creek, Buncombe County, 12/2/10

A Great Challenge

Graham County passed a bond to build a new high school. We went through all the steps with consultants to decide where to build the school. So, we finally decided where we were going to build and the board approved the plans. We realized that there was a possibility that there may be some water problems, but we were told that it could be fixed. Well, I had some of my worst problems over that building. Looking forward, it turned out to be a beautiful building and was a great success, but it caused me many sleepless nights to get it finished.

Lowell Crisp,
Robinsville, Graham County, 6/15/11

SOMETIMES WE WIN ONE

One of my dearest success stories was Milagoa, a little miniority girl, who I had a few years ago. She was so pitiful, all her teeth were rotten and she had a white color around her eyes that I understand was a sign of malnutrition due to not being able to eat because of the condition of her teeth. We spent the first part of the school year calling everybody trying to get her help. We knew that until we met her medical needs there was no way she could learn. She wanted to learn and did everything we asked her, but she was just not able. Finally in February, she went into the hospital and had all those teeth removed. After a while she came back a new girl. She looked good and seemed to feel wonderful. We worked with her individually and she blossomed. Once she started, there was no stopping her; she went from a level zero in reading up to the level where she needed to be. Her mother thanked us and hugged us and cried at the end of the year because she was so happy because of the change in her daughter. She has now moved to South Carolina and I pray she will continue to grow.

Jan Lunsford,
Averys Creek, Buncombe County, 12/2/10

CHAPTER TEN

OFFICE POLITICS

THE PAPER CHASE

In 1985, I undertook the longest paper chase of my career. I decided to pursue a Doctor of Education degree from the University of North Carolina in Greensboro. It was going to prove to be a long hard road. I had previously decided I could not get an Ed. D. because I would need to quit my job and attend college as a full time college student due to the school being several miles from where I lived. Later, the college decided to offer classes at the University of North Carolina in Asheville for two years and then allow the students to drive the one hundred eighty miles to campus on the weekends to meet the residency requirement. After completing the required courses, I began the most challenging part of obtaining an Ed. D., that of writing and defending a dissertation. Completing my work in around six months, I felt it was ready for defending. I submitted it to my dissertation committee and was told by three members of the four person committee that it was ready, but the fourth member would not agree. This continued for five months with me making all the changes required by the one committee member but to no avail. After all this time and stress, I learned that the dissenting member was appointed acting Dean of the College and the Chairperson on my Committee was on the search committee for a permanent Dean and would not choose the person on my committee. For him to sign off on my dissertation would have been a feather in the cap of the Chairman of my Committee and he was not going to allow that to happen. I had become a pawn in a game in which I had no control. After six months of this hassle, I was informed I could change the make-up of my committee. I did so and received my degree within a week. So much for office politics.

J. Terry Hall,
Scott Mountain, Buncombe County, 3/3/11

OFFICE POLITICS STINKS

The further I moved up the administrator ladder, the more I was amazed at the politics involved. I would go to the Superintendent to address an issue and he would say he agreed with me but the Board would not go along with the idea. I would then go to two Board member friends of mine and address the same issue and would be told they agreed but the Superintendent would not budge on the issue. It is enough to make a person become very cynical.

Dorland Winkler,
Malvern Hills, 8/12/11

COVER YOUR ASS

After retirement from Asheville City Schools and moving out of state to serve as an administrative assistant, I encountered a situation where office politics played a part. Serving in a situation where I had the responsibility of signing off on financial matters caused me to make a decision that was not popular with the local Financial Director. The situation involved federal monies and to sign off on a particular issue would make me liable for prosecution under federal law and therefore was something I was not willing to do.

In this particular case, I checked the monthly financial statement to find a line item stating that federal monies were used to pay the salary of a person who was not fulfilling the duties required under federal guidelines. I immediately consulted the Financial Director and pointed out the error. I was told that she was the Director of Finance and this is the way she was planning to spend the federal monies. Realizing the futility of argument, I went back to my office and typed out a letter and sent a copy of it to the Financial Director by placing it in her mail box. The letter was as follows:

Dear Ma'am: On ___ date I brought it to the attention of ____, Financial Director of _____ county schools and stated that the following expenditure was not allowed under federal guidelines. I was told at that time that she was Financial Director and she was going to spend the monies in the manner she thought fit. I then signed the letter and placed the copy in the Financial Director's mailbox. About an hour later, the Financial Director came actually running into my office demanding to know what the letter meant? I explained it was a CYA letter. She demanded to know what that meant and I explained to her that it was a "cover your ass" letter and meant what it said: I was placing the letter in my file and if we received a federal audit, it would come to light. She stomped out of my office and I never heard any more about it.

J. Terry Hall,
Scott Mountain, Buncombe County, 3/3/11

THE DOOR MUST STAY OPEN

When the superintendent that was before me left, he just came in and said he was leaving. He knew he felt bad, but he didn't know he had cancer. He died a short time later. Well, I applied as did some others and a person from out of state called and asked if he should apply. They were told by someone that they didn't need to bother, because it was pretty much understood that they were going to hire from within the county. Boy, was that a mistake. It was reported to the federals and I had to spend several months on that issue after I got the job.

Lowell Crisp,
Robinsville, Graham County, 6/15/11

PARKING LOT MAFIA

Office politics can truly take the focus away from our students. As a Principal, I expected staff members to not be part of the "parking lot mafia." I encouraged them to center their energy to making sure our students were well taken care of both academically and socially. Even today, office politics and the disbanding of it, becomes one of the main focal points faced by the Principal.

Charles Cutshall,
Sodom Laurel, Madison County, 7/14/11

A BALANCING ACT

I never really had a problem with office politics during my career. Although, for seven years my husband, Everette, served on the Asheville City Schools Board of Education, the last six as Chairman of the Board. I was careful not to make any waves that would cause him any concern during that time. I tried to work in such a manner that no one would accuse me of being granted privileges because he was on the Board. But I really didn't have any problem with that issue.

Julia Clark,
Biltmore Lake, June 2, 2011

KEEP YOUR HEAD DOWN AND DO YOUR JOB

I always attempted to stay out of office politics. I tried to do what was expected of me and to show respect to whoever was in charge. This behavior became much more difficult once I became a principal. There were times when I could not obtain what my teachers needed, or do what they wished to happen, due to situations going on behind the scenes. The hardest part was not being able to tell my teachers why I could not do or act in the manner they wished. This put me in a position in which I felt very uncomfortable, but it had to be done at the time in order for other events to come to play. I always tried to respect every superintendent with which I worked whether I agreed with them at the time or not.

Sue Harris,
Hominy Valley, April 26, 2011

ONE IS NOT ALWAYS POLITICALLY CORRECT

When I started teaching at Erwin Middle School, I had the attitude that I needed to make a major difference in the way teaching took place. I found it was not a politically correct idea for a young teacher to attempt to change older teachers who had been there for many years. Some of those teachers started stories about me in the community and throughout the school that were not true in order to hurt my influence. The principal, realizing the situation, made some changes in the schedules of some of those teachers which did not allow them as many opportunities to get together in the teachers' lounge to further their rumors. In addition, I realized I did not need to be such a mover and shaker in the school, but to concentrate on the students in my classroom.

Darren Barkett,
Canton, Haywood County, 1/23/11

WATCH THAT STARE

I never was caught in a negative office politics situation, but I did work with a superintendent who you had to read. Sometimes one would walk into his office and ask if he could try something or the other and he would say, "Sure, go ahead and give it a try." Other times you would ask him something and all you would get was a "stare." One soon learned that the stare meant, "don't you touch that with a ten foot pole." There was one principal who never learned to read "the stare" and he stayed in trouble with the superintendent all the time.

Thomas Ledbetter,
Hendersonville, 4/13/2011

CHAPTER ELEVEN

Winds Of Change

Home Is Breaking Down Across Our Nation

One reason it was so hard to see the old Fairview School be torn down is that Fairview had always been a close knit community. Most families were very stable and had community roots that went back for generations, but that is not as true today as it was back then. Today we have more families breaking apart, with mom going one way and dad going another. In this environment, children are the ones who feel the most hurt. When I began teaching, you could count on one hand the number of families who were broken, with mom and dad not in the same home. Today, you could probably count on one hand the homes that have mom and dad living under the same roof. I honestly feel that the breakdown of the home is the number one problem in this nation. It seems that today everyone wants what they want when they want it. Many parents seems to be thinking me rather than us when it comes to their family. Another major problem is the lack of discipline in the schools. There are very few consequences for unacceptable behavior. In my opinion, this is one reason we have so many children being classified as special education students and given medication.

I also disagree with the way education is going these days. I realize new innovations are needed, but children need structure in their lives. Due to unstructured homes and the lack of structure in our schools, children are feeling lost. I do not believe that we cannot have structure and still bring in new programs and technology. For example, when I give homework I give work that is easy enough for the child to complete successfully my himself, but even more important, I am trying to teach responsibility. I want the child to be responsible for finishing his work, putting it in his book bag and bringing it back to school. We need to teach children responsibility.

I know many people are downing the Latino families who are coming into our country. I realize many of them are illegal and I don't agree with that, but in most cases Latino parents realize the need for their children to get a good education and they will support the teacher. They seem to realize that education is the ticket for their children to have a better life. I had a twenty something year old Latino dad who said with tears in his eyes, "He is my future." he realized that his child needed a good education in order to make it in this world.

Jan Lunsford,
Averys Creek, Buncombe County, 12/2/10

EDUCATORS CAN NEVER GUARANTEE ONE HUNDRED PERCENT SUCCESS

Two areas that concern me today are politicians and parents. Often political candidates use Education as their platform. However, once elected the platform of Education takes a back seat to their real agendas. School systems today are expected to do lots with very little revenue to do a thorough job. Then when they are unable to live up to this expectation, they are deemed a failing school or school system. One such initiative is "No Child Left Behind." While the title has always been a focal point of teachers, the one size model does not fit everyone. They expect educators to operate under a 100% rule while the other professions don't even come close. I wonder what would happen if the same requirements were put on a doctor where it was clearly stated that 100% of their patients were to be cured and if any died, their license would be revoked.

The second concern I have are parents of today. Parents by large are into the "it's all about me" syndrome. They often expect others to raise their children and not bother them too much. Of course, thank goodness there are pockets of parents who really make a difference in the lives of their children.

Charles Cutshall,
Sodom Laurel, Madison County, 7/14/11

TESTING JUST TO BE TESTING

Education has always gone through cycles. It moves from a concrete skill and drill mentality where we are taught to memorize just the facts, and then it cycles around to no-no we, need high level thinking skills using abstract applications, but I think we are getting to a point where we are going to have both of those at the same time. I think a lot has to do with textbook publications and their cycling of ideals. For example we had "No Child Left Behind" and now we have the "Race For the Top" program. This year we are still doing the "End of Grade" test in North Carolina, but they are taking the word, gateway, out of it so we are no longer going to pretend we retain kids who don't meet the benchmarks. I think what that means this year is we won't have to retest the kids who don't pass the first time. The amount of money that will save and the less stress on kids and teachers will be great. I think next year we are going to go back to "National Standards" test that already exists because with the budget the way it is, it does not make sense to be paying all those test people that don't tell us anything we don't already know. Teachers know from the classroom that the kids are not on grade level and we don't need a test, or retest or a summer school test to tell us. But in my opinion what would be useful is using "National Standards" and comparing kids across the nation rather that just in our schools, our district and our state.

Elizabeth Middleton,
Candler, Buncombe County, 10/21/10

REACH DOWN AND GIVE A CHILD IN NEED A HELPING HAND

Many things have changed over the years in the field of social work and rehabilitation. We have moved more back to what we were doing in the 1970s when we were trying to help the individual child. Over the years we had moved more in the direction of looking at the children as a group and not as individuals. The "Families Together" program is one of the best programs with which I have had the privilege of working. And, the "Oasis program" which is a part of "Families Together" is really making a difference in the lives of many children. I am proud to be a part of the program. I feel it is much better to get the child early and provide the support they need rather than wait until they end up in the justice system and have to be punished for their decisions.

Ron Lytle,
Woodfin School, Oasis program, April 28, 2011

LIFE IS FULL OF CHANGE

One of the major changes I have seen in education during my tenure is state standardized testing. I really had a problem with the fact that the state was forcing me to concentrate totally on achieving a certain score on a standardized test rather than on social development or the whole learning of the child. Over time, I realized that my number one goal was to teach them to read better and anything else that was to go along was just great, but the major goal had to be teaching students to read. I have begun to realize that it is necessary to have standardized testing for the community and teachers to see results. I hope we can still work on the social needs of the child, but I realize that if a child cannot read acceptably he/she cannot function successfully in society.

Darren Barkett,
Canton, Haywood County, 1/23/11

CHILDREN NEED AN ANCHOR

I think the biggest change in the schools of this country is the breakdown of the home. We, in education can not make up for kids not being held and read to by their parents. Children need an anchor, and I believe we have lost our anchor in this country. I remember how people used to be so ashamed at being on free lunch. I had this father back in the 1970s and, due to him losing his job, he was forced to accept free lunch for his child. The very next day after he found a job he came to school and asked to be taken off free lunch. Today people feel it is a right for them to be taken care of by the government. We, in this country are going to have to wake up.

Dorland Winkler,
Malvern Hills, 8/12/11

LEARNING SHOULD BE FUN

We used to do fun things to motivate the children. I remember one time my Title 1 Director Fred Trantham dressed up in tights as a motivation for children to read. We have gotten away from that over the years due to the great amount of stress placed on teachers and administrators to meet a certain benchmark.

Sandy Caldwell,
Waynesville, Haywood County, 11/11/10

WE MUST CLOSE THE GAP

One of the things I feel strongly about is that we must learn to work with our minorities. Whether it is black, Latino, or whatever we now have these students in our schools and we must learn to successfully work with these groups. When I came to Asheville City Schools twenty-five years ago, I was told we have an academic problem with our African American students. We need to close the gap. Throughout the years, we have been told there is a new program in New York go find out about it, there is a new program in LA go find out about it, and so on. We have tried program after program through the years and the gap is still there and it is as wide or even wider than it was twenty-five years ago. We must address this issue in a successful manner and I do not know the answer.

Another issue is the diversity of our academic courses. Our students go on to AB Tech and we are not even teaching the language needed to address these classes.

Larry Liggett,
Skyland, Buncombe County, 7/21/11

CHANGE IS ENVIABLE

There have been many changes that have taken place since I have been in the profession. One of the biggest changes began in 2000 with the Federal accountability requirements. Once the Federal Government got more involved in local education, a great many changes took place. These changes are both positive and negative. On the positive side, it has required us to look at the individual students and subgroups rather than the overall average. On the negative side, many of these requirements are made based on what is happening in the bigger cities of our nation and not on what is needed in local small school systems. At first it was "No Child Left Behind" and now it is the "Race for the Top." Our state has also made many changes over the last several years such as "End-of-Grade Tests" and "End of Course Tests." One thing about public education, change is inevitable.

Fred Trantham,
Waynesville, Haywood County, 11/11/10

We Have Come A Long Way

We had kids in school that didn't even have running water in Haywood County. We look at the economy today and it scares people, but overall, folks are so much better off than they were when I started teaching. I often hear teachers complaining about having eighteen or twenty children in their class when, not many years ago, I had thirty-two kindergarten students in my class and I didn't have space for them to lie on the floor. Over the years, our education system has changed a lot, yet in many ways it is still the same.

Sandy Caldwell,
Waynesville, Haywood County, 11/11/10

Testing, Technology And Home

Change is inevitable. One of the few things a person can depend on is that change will happen. I have seen many changes over the past forty years. Most of the changes have been positive, but a few have been negative. On the positive side, we have much more support for new teachers in the profession than we ever dreamed of in 1965 when I first walked into a classroom. At that time, teachers were more or less on their own and their classroom was their domain. Good teachers have always reached out to more experienced teachers for wisdom gained over the years, but, more often once a teacher entered their classroom, they were pretty much on their own.

One of the biggest changes has been testing. When I began teaching back in the day, testing was not often used. A teacher knew when he or she had done a good job and meeting a benchmark was not even considered. Don't get me wrong, testing and accountability is a good thing, although testing for the sake of testing is useless. Whatever the test instrument used, if testing is only for political reasons it is useless, whereas if it is used to actually measure growth and to modify curriculum based on the results then it is a worthwhile effort.

The second positive change is in the area of technology. It truly is a brave new world in the field of technology. When I started out, we were considered advanced to be using a sixteen millimeter, reel to reel projector or a cassette tape recorder, today's technology was in the same area as Buck Rodgers and the little green men he met on Mars. We have come a long way and, if technology is used effectively it can improve education, although technology alone will not lead to improvement. The most important element in a classroom is a teacher who loves and cares about children.

The one negative aspect I would mention is the lack of parental support. I understand culture changes, although I believe with all my heart that human nature never changes and is the same today as it was in the days of Noah, but cultures change continuously. In the area of education, I feel teachers have lost a great deal of respect and support from the very parents and children they serve. Whether this has been the fault of teachers or parents is a matter of debate, nevertheless it is real.

When I began teaching in Nashville, Tennessee most women stayed at home and took seriously the responsibility of raising their children. I realize that in today's world it is necessary for both husbands and wives to work to make ends meet and even then, their dual paychecks will not suffice to put food on the table in many cases. But, whatever the reason, in 1965 when a teacher had a discipline problem at school with a child they could pick up the phone and call mom who in most cases would be at the school in a matter of minutes and set their child on the right track. Today, so often when the teacher calls, the parent meets the teacher's concerns with a cussing and a threat to take the teacher to court. Whatever the reason this is a situation in which we are moving in the wrong direction in this country.

J. Terry Hall,
Scott Mountain, Buncombe County, 3/3/11

THE UNITED STATES HAS THE BRIGHTEST

AND THE BEST

There have been many changes during the time I have been in the educational profession. I think technology has been the greatest advance of all. Technology is wonderful, but it is not an end to itself. Technology will never take the place of a good teacher.

Another change is the "End of Grade Test." I feel the test puts too much pressure on the student. To require one test to determine whether or not the student is promoted is stress that the students should not have to face. We have, in this nation, the brightest and the best, and we are doing right well. I don't think it is a crisis situation like some people say it is, because we have some fine teachers and fine kids in the state of North Carolina.

Charlie McConnell,
Sylva, 6/17/11

REMEMBER TO DO WHAT IS BEST FOR THE CHILD

When I began teaching we taught everything, art, music, PE. We had no special area teachers and we came to school the day the kids came and we left the day they left. There were no work days to prepare nor to train. We had it all to do and very little time to get it done. Each teacher was allowed to teach the curriculum using methods that worked for him/her, and when we administrated the "California Achievement Test," we had to grade each test by hand. At the end of each school year, we all had to come into the auditorium and bring our attendance book. Our names were placed on the chalkboard and every book had to be checked and balanced correctly before we were allowed to leave for the summer. We had to take courses to renew our certification during the summer since we were not allowed to take those courses during the school year. We were not required to have lesson plans prepared in advance, although we had to have some notes on our desk in case we were out sick. I began teaching before integration and I taught in a neighborhood school. After integration, kids had to be bussed to school.

Today things have changed. Most of the changes were positive, although a few were negative. The "End of the Grade Test" is being stressed more than necessary. Today we find teachers teaching to the test to the point that "The Test" has become an end in itself. We must always remember that we are in this business of education for what is best for the child and not just a score on a test.

Julia Clark,
Biltmore Lake, June 2, 2011

Our Society Has Changed

After I retired from the school system, I had so many people say, "I bet you are glad you are not teaching." I do miss teaching children, but not as much now that the behavior in the schools has gone down hill.

Billie Lewis,
Enka, Buncombe County, 11/15/10

I Have Succeed

There have been many success stories during my career. The following are only a few:

Teaching first grade children to read
Being named Teacher of the Year
Being named Principal of the Year

Completing the Principal's Executive Program in Chapel Hill, NC
Being awarded the School of Excellence at Jones Elementary School
Meeting President Reagan due to being awarded the School of Excellence

Sue Harris,
Hominy Valley, April 26, 2011

I Had A Bond With The Old Building

Things in education have changed so much since I retired. I always enjoyed teaching in the old Vance School building. I told my principal when I came to Vance School all those years ago that I loved being in the old building that had been built in 1922, and, that I wanted to stay as long as I could teach in this beautiful building. I retired the year they tore down the old building. I guess you could say that when they retired the old building, they retired me. For me, building the new Vance Elementary was a bad thing, but I feel that it worked out for the best for the younger teachers.

Billie Lewis,
Enka, Buncombe County, 11/15/10

A Child's Education Begins Before Birth

I suppose we are in need of educational reform. I am a huge huge proponent of early intervention. I feel kindergarten is wonderful but I am concerned that as we get more administrators from higher education into the elementary schools that we will see a move to push first grade curriculum down into kindergarten. I think kindergarten needs to stay kindergarten. Luckily, my "Title 1" person has allowed me to have four pre-kindergarten classes, because I feel that if we had pre-kindergarten classes for all four year old children that want to come to school that we would most likely not need the alternative classes at the high school level. I truly believe in early intervention and that success breeds success. I am excited about the "Even Start" classes that are taking place across the nation where teachers work not only with children zero through eight, but work with their parents teaching them parenting skills and helping develop a foundation for a stable educational environment. In Haywood County we get some "More at

Four" monies from the state and tracking research shows a remarkable improvement in the children who have had this early intervention. There is nothing to compare with a young child coming to school ready to learn. It is such a great opportunity.

Sandy Caldwell,
Waynesville, Haywood County, 11/11/10

Children Will Always Need Love

A lot has changed since I retired. I really would not want to be teaching now. I don't know about changes in the profession, but I am sure drugs and the changes in society would make it harder to work in the schools. The way I look at it is children are still children and they need someone to love them and to care for them.

Billie Lewis,
Enka, Buncombe County, 11/15/10

It Is All About The Child

When I was beginning my teaching career, the teacher had so much parent support. I don't really believe in corporal punishment, but I can remember at the beginning of the school year, a parent would come to school and say, "If Johnny misbehaves, just bust his butt and when he gets home, he will get another one for misbehaving at school." We do have parental support today, but there are more parents who are always ready to go off with only part of the needed information and blame the teacher for the child's misbehavior. I remember telling myself many years ago that I am in education for what is best for the child, not what is best for the parents, teachers or administrators, but what is best for the child.

Sandy Caldwell,
Waynesville, Haywood County, 11/11/10

WE ARE ALL DIFFERENT

I think accountability is good because it causes us to look at the individual child. On the other hand, I feel requiring all children to maintain the same level of success is unreasonable. Every child is different and, even though, every child can achieve success, it is not reasonable to believe every child can reach the same level of success or even the same benchmark or the school system will receive a sanction or have some "expert" tell us we are doing something wrong.

Sandy Caldwell,
Waynesville, Haywood County, 11/11/10

BUILD A FIRM FOUNDATION

I am excited about the new math curriculum. Research compares the United States with countries who have higher test scores, although, what they fail to realize is in the United states we have a curriculum that is a mile wide and an inch deep, whereas other countries are stressing foundations. The new math curriculum is placing more emphases on getting the foundation necessary to succeed through the years.

Sandy Caldwell,
Waynesville, Haywood County, 11/11/10

Never Change For The Sake Of Change

The education profession is always changing and this may be good, but as the profession moves more and more toward technology, I am afraid we may be losing the personal touch to some extent. What brothers me more than anything is, in some cases, the student gets the right answer to a problem but has no earthly idea how they got there. So, when they need to apply one situation to another they cannot transpose their learning to the new situation. Also, I feel that one of the biggest enemies of the school system are the judges. Many times, judges make a decision and the school system has to live with it. The judge may have all good intentions, but in reality, the decision may not work in the real world, or may hurt somebody down the road.

Another thing I am opposed to is the idea of Charter Schools being increased. It is now before the General Assembly to increase the limit on Charter Schools. This takes funds away from public schools when there is no hard data showing that Charter Schools are making more progress than public schools where all students are being served.

Thomas Ledbetter,
Hendersonville, 4/13/2011

BIOGRAPHIES OF STORYTELLERS

Darren Barkett was born at Vandenberg AFB, Lompoc, California on September 28, 1971. He attended college at the University of Boulder and graduated in 1995 with a BA in English with teaching certification. His teaching experience consisted of one year as a fourth grade teacher at Mabel Elementary in Zionville, North Carolina, four years as an eighth grade teacher at Erwin Middle School in Asheville, North Carolina, four years teaching eighth grade at Enka Middle School in Enka, North Carolina, and he is currently teaching eighth grade at Canton Middle School in Canton, North Carolina. He was selected as "Teacher of the Year" in 2007, and is also serving as a teaching consultant through his business called *Helping Teachers Grow.* He is the author of a book entitled *Take Back That Class,* which is designed to help teachers with managing student behavior. He is married with two girls as well as the owner of four dogs.

Dot Bryson was born in Glenville, North Carolina and attended Glenville Elementary and High School. She served as secretary at Asheville Hosiery Company for sixteen years before moving to Doctor Daniels' Medical Office and worked as secretary. Mrs. Bryson then served as secretary at Hill Street School in Asheville,

North Carolina before moving to South French Broad Middle School in Asheville and from there to Vance Elementary School also in Asheville. Following retirement from Asheville City Schools, she served as secretary at Asheville Pre-School in West Asheville.

Sandra P. Caldwell was born in Haywood County, North Carolina and attended Elementary and High School in Haywood County. Following graduation she obtained her BS in Early Childhood Education at Appalachian State University, receiving her MA in Early Childhood Education from Western Carolina University as well as certification in Administrative and Supervision also from Western Carolina University. Ms. Caldwell, served as teacher in Haywood County Schools, teaching Kindergarten for seventeen years, Kindergarten-grade two teacher and first and second grade combination. She served as a Title 1 teacher for four years during which time she was selected as Lead Teacher and successfully completed a rigorous Reading Recovery Teacher training program. Ms. Caldwell currently serves as Elementary Curriculum Supervisor for Haywood County Schools. She has made presentations at the National Association of Curriculum Development Conference on Site Based Decision Making in 1992, at the North Carolina Association of Young Children on Phonemic Awareness in 2000, at the Association of Teacher Educators Association on the power of Public School-University Partnerships in 2001, at the North Carolina Association of Compensatory Educators meeting on Balanced Literacy in 2003 and at the National Title 1 Conference in 2004 on *Hey, What's in my Name.*

Donald L. Carter was born in Lubbock, Texas and attended elementary and high school on army bases throughout the world. Following graduation he attended East Carolina University where he graduated with a masters degree in Adult and Community College Education. Donald was employed by Bladen Technical

Institute, Elizabethtown, North Carolina, in 1968 where he served as a teacher for four years. In 1972 he was employed at Southern Nash Junior High School in Nashville, North Carolina where he taught for two years before moving on to Durham Community College. In 1978 he was promoted to a Title 1 Consultant position at the North Carolina Department of Education in Raleigh, North Carolina where he served until retirement. Since retirement he has served on a contractual basis as North Carolina State Director for the Federal Even Start Program which works with parents and children between birth and eight years old.

Mary Bulluck Carter was born in Rocky Mount, North Carolina. Following elementary and high school she attended East Carolina College. Mrs. Carter drove a special education school bus for Wake County Schools before being employed by Data General Corporation for twelve years. In 1992 she was employed by Dorothea Dix Hospital where she served as Administrative Assistant at the school for children for fifteen years. She currently lives in Garner, North Carolina with her husband Donald.

Julia Ann Fox Clark was born in Asheville, North Carolina where she attended elementary and high school. Following graduation she attended Woman's College, (now University of North Carolina at Greensboro) receiving a BA degree in Primary Education. Upon graduating she taught in Danville, Virginia, Henrici County, Virginia, Chesterfield, Virginia, and Pleasant Gardens, North Carolina before returning to Asheville, North Carolina and teaching in the Asheville City Schools until retiring in 1995 after thirty-four years serving in elementary education. Mrs. Clark, was selected as Teacher of the Year at Vance Elementary School in 1995.

Phillip Odell Cochran was born in Polk County, North Carolina and attended elementary school in High Point, North Carolina and Henderson County, North Carolina. Following graduation he attended David Lipscomb College in Nashville, Tennessee where he received a degree in Business Administration. Mr. Cochran taught school in Paint Rock, Alabama and Hendersonville, North Carolina. Throughout his tenure in education he has continued his work as minister of the Church of Christ. He is currently serving as minister at the Tryon, North Carolina Church of Christ.

Lowell Crisp was born in Graham County, North Carolina. Following graduation from high school he attended Western Carolina University receiving a B.S. degree in Business Administration. Mr. Crisp received a double Masters of Arts in Elementary Education and School Administration before earning his Ed.S. in Educational Administration in 1990. He served two years in the National Peace Corps before teaching at Robbinsville Elementary School in Robbinsville, North Carolina. He went on to serve as Principal at Stecoah School and Robbinsville High School before being appointed Superintendent of Graham County Schools. He served as Superintendent of Graham County Schools for thirteen years before retiring in 1996.

Charles Cutshall was born in Asheville, North Carolina and attended Asheville City Schools. Following graduation he attended Montreat Anderson Junior College majoring in Elementary Education. He received his B.A. Degree in Elementary Education before attending Western Carolina University and receiving a M.A. Degree in Educational Administration. Mr. Cutshall has a long list of work experiences in the field of education, serving as both teacher and principal in the following schools: Hermitage Middle School in Henrici County, Virginia, Jones Elementary School, Claxton Elementary School, Hall Fletcher Middle School and Vance Elementary school in Asheville, North Carolina. Mr. Cutshall also served as Curriculum Specialist at Asheville Middle School.

In 1998 he was appointed Executive Director of Elementary Education/Title 1 of the Asheville City Schools. He retired from Asheville City Schools in 2003 and was employed as Principal of Laurel Elementary School in Madison County, North Carolina. He is now serving as English Coordinator of Madison County Schools. His awards consist of being designated as a Master Teacher by the University of North Carolina at Asheville in 1979, Assistant Principal of the Year in 191983, Wachovia Principal of the Year in 1992 and the Jack McCall Leadership Award from the University of North Carolina in 1993.

W. E. B. Du Bois was born in 1868 and was an intellectual leader of the black community in America. He served as civil rights activist, Pan-African, sociologist, historian, author, and editor. Du Bois graduated from Harvard where he earned his Ph. D. in history making him Harvard's first African-American to earn a Ph.D. (From Wikipedia, the free encyclopedia)

Elizabeth R. Hall was born in Larue County, Kentucky in 1915 and moved to Monroe County, Kentucky as an infant. She attended Mill Creek School, a one room schoolhouse from grades one through eight. She had the same teacher the entire eight years by the name of Miss Alice Paterson. Following graduation from eight grade she attended the city school at Tompkinsville, Kentucky in order to obtain a City School certificate along with her County certificate. Many years after graduating from Tompkinsville High School she received her Library Certification and became the first librarian at the William B. Harlan Public Library in Tompkinsville, Kentucky. In this capacity she met on many occasions with different Kentucky governors over the years seeking and obtaining funding for the county Library. In 1970 Mrs. Hall was honored with the title of Kentucky Colonel awarded by the governor of Kentucky and is considered in the highest of esteem. In 1984 she received a Congratulatory Award presented by the Kentucky House of Representatives.

Dr. James Terry Hall was born in Glasgow, Kentucky and attended Tompkinsville, Elementary and High School in Tompkinsville, Kentucky. Following graduation in 1961 he attended the following colleges and universities: Lindsey Wilson College receiving an A.A. Degree in Elementary Education, David Lipscomb College receiving a B.S. Degree in Elementary Education, Western Kentucky University receiving a M.A degree in Elementary Education, Western Carolina University receiving an Ed. S degree in Public School Administration and the University of North Carolina at Greensboro where he received his Doctor of Education degree. Dr. Hall has spent forty years in public education serving as teacher and administrator in Nashville, Tennessee, Barren County, Kentucky and Asheville, North Carolina. In 1988 he was appointed to the position of Elementary Curriculum Supervisor/ Title 1 Director for the Asheville City Schools in Asheville, North Carolina where he served for nine years before retiring. Following retirement he moved to Bowling Green, Kentucky where he served as administrator at Warren Elementary School. Dr. Hall received a North Carolina Teaching Fellows Award in 1989, He was mentioned in *Who's Who in American Education* in1989-1990. He also received an Educators Program Committee award in 1996 and an Award of Recognition presented by the Asheville City Schools Title 1 staff in1997. During his tenure as Title 1 Director he made presentations at the International Reading Association Conference in San Francisco, California, the National Reading Recovery Conference in Columbus, Ohio and several North Carolina state conferences on his longitudinal study of the Asheville City School's Reading Recovery Program of which he was instrumental in bringing to Asheville City Schools. Since retirement he has written three books; *Time Marches On, A Matter of Conscience and Notes*

From the Chalkboard: Teacher *Tales from the Mountains of North Carolina.*

William Frank Hall was born in Monroe County, Kentucky in 1915. He attended elementary school at Mt. Zion one room schoolhouse in Monroe County before attending Tompkinsville High School in Tompkinsville, Kentucky. His first hand descriptions of life in rural one room schools provide a stark contrast to the educational systems of today.

Mary Sue Cooke Harris was born in Asheville, North Carolina. She attended elementary and high school in Asheville before attending Mars Hill College and obtaining an Associate in Education degree. Mrs. Harris then enrolled at Woman's College, (now University of North Carolina at Greensboro) where she received a B.A. in Primary Education. Following graduation she attended Western Carolina University at Cullowhee, North Carolina receiving a Masters in Education, Masters in Administration and an Ed. S. degree in Education. Mrs. Harris served for many years as teacher and principal of McIver School in Greensboro, North Carolina, Number Three School in Shelby, North Carolina, Vance Elementary School in Asheville, North Carolina, Hall Fletcher Middle School in Asheville, and Jones Elementary School, also in Asheville. During her career Mrs. Jones was selected as Teacher of the Year at Vance Elementary School in Asheville, Principal of the Year at Jones Elementary in Asheville and led Jones Elementary to become a School of Excellence.

Ollie Hutchens was born in Falls of Neuse, North Carolina, (now inside the city of Raleigh), but grew up in Rutherford, McDowell and Mitchell Counties in western North Carolina. After graduating high school she attended Appalachian State Teachers College in Boone, North Carolina where she earned her B.S and M.A degree in Education. She then attended George Peabody College for Teachers in Nashville, Tennessee and then back to Appalachian State University where she received her Ed.S. degree. Mrs. Hutchens served as teacher and administrator in both public and private schools across North Carolina. The schools in which she served consisted of; Walkertown Elementary School in Walkertown, Alexander School, Inc., in Union Mills, Western Carolina College in Cullowhee, Forsyth Technical Community College, Baptist Children s Home, Winston Salem/Forsyth County Schools, Chesterbrook Academy all in Winston Salem, and Statesville Christian School in Statesville. During her career Mrs. Hutchens was selected "Teacher of the Year" at Walkertown Elementary School in Walkertown, and Statesville Christian School in Statesville. Mrs. Hutchens has also been honored to have been Division Vice President, President of North Carolina Education Association in 1967-1968, officer(s) in Winston Salem/Forsyth County Reading Association, Secretary, Vice-President-elect, Vice President, President of North Carolina Reading Association in 1983-1986.

Dr. Thomas Allen Ledbetter was born in Sylva, North Carolina. He attended Jackson County Schools and graduated from Sylva High School. Following graduation he attended Western Carolina University for two years before moving on to David Lipscomb College where he received a B.A. Degree in Bible. Moving back to the mountains of North Carolina he once again attended Western Carolina University and earned an M.A. in Education. Moving back west he attended the University of Tennessee where he earned his Ed. D. in Education, and has since has been a fan of Tennessee Volunteers football. Dr. Ledbetter began his career as a minister at the Andrews Church of Christ in Andrews, North Carolina. His introduction into public education began as a teacher in Macon County Schools before moving on to serve as Assistant Principal in Haywood County Schools. He then moved to Henderson County where he served as Principal of East Henderson High School for many years before being appointed Assistant Superintendent of Henderson County Schools where he served until retirement. Dr. Ledbetter has been active in many community organizations including Hendersonville Church of Christ, Kiwanis Club, American Association of School administrators,State and National School Planners Association and a charter member of Phi Delta Kappa at Western Carolina University.

Billie P. Lewis was born in Vivian, West Virginia. She attended Virginia Intermont College in Bristol, Virginia before completing her B.A. Degree at West Virginia University. Mrs. Lewis taught music in Jacksonville, Florida for ten years before moving to Asheville, North Carolina. She attended Western Carolina University and received her North Carolina teaching certificate before being hired to teach fourth grade at Vance Elementary School in Asheville where she spent the next nineteen years.

Dr. Lawrence R. Liggett was born in Cleveland, Ohio. Following graduation from high school he attended Baldwin Wallace College in Berea, Ohio where he received his B.A. degree. Moving to North Carolina he attended the University of North Carolina at Chapel Hill earning an M.A. in Science and continued on to earn his Ph.D. in Education. Dr. Liggett began his teaching career as a teacher in Parma, Ohio before moving to western North Carolina. He was hired as Director of Environmental Education for western North Carolina through Madison County Schools. After spending three years working at Asheville City Schools Central Office serving as Middle School Coordinator for the school system he was moved to Asheville High School where he served as Principal for the next eighteen years. Dr. Liggett has received numerous awards throughout the years. A few of the honors are as follows: Arts Education Award presented by the North Carolina Arts Education

Council, State President of the North Carolina Association of School Curriculum Development, western North Carolina Principal of the year, led Asheville High School to become one of the top ten schools in America, co/founder of Caring for Children which has been in existence for over twenty-eight years, President of the Asheville Civitan Club and is currently serving on the loan council for the North Carolina State Employees Credit Union.

Jan Lunsford was born in Shelby, North Carolina in Cleveland County. She attended Western Carolina University receiving her B.S. in Education. Mrs. Lunsford served Buncombe County Schools for thirty-three years teaching at Fairview Elementary and Reems Creek Elementary Schools. She was selected as "Teacher of the Year" in 1997.

Ron Lytle was born in Kingsport, Tennessee. He attended Warren Wilson College and graduated with a degree in Sociology. Following graduation Mr. Lytle was placed in charge of the recreation department at Hillcrest Apartments in Asheville, North Carolina. Later he was hired as a teacher at Asheville High School Optional School and from there moved to the North Carolina Juvenile Evaluation Center in Swannona, North Carolina where he served for the next thirty-two years. Following retirement from the Evaluation Center he became a counselor with the Families Together Program in Ashville. During his career he has received a Certificate of Appreciation from the Eckerd Screening Committee as well as a Long Leaf Pine Service Award for years of service above and beyond the call of duty.

Dr. Charles McConnell was born in Cullowhee, North Carolina. Following high school in Jackson County he attended Western Carolina University where he received his B.S. degree in Elementary Education as well as his M.A. Degree in Educational Administration.

He attended Winthrop College and earned an Ed. S degree before attending the University of North Carolina at Greensboro and receiving his Doctorate in Educational Administration. Dr. McConnell began his career in education working at the Camp Lab School on the campus of Western Carolina University. He then moved to Rock Hill, North Carolina and served with the Rock Hill School District. Moving back to North Carolina in 1981 he was appointed Superintendent of Haywood County Schools where he served for the next nine years. In 1990 he was appointed Superintendent of Jackson County Schools and served until he retired in 1997. Following retirement he worked with Southwest Community College for three years. Dr. McConnell received many awards and honors during his career including being presented the Superintendent of the Year award in 1988.

Eulala Phillips McCraw was born in Burnsville, Yancey County, North Carolina. She attended school at Bee Log School in Yancey County. Years later, she graduated from Spartanburg Nursing School in Spartanburg, South Carolina and served as a nurse in Polk County North Carolina. Her experiences in a one room schoolhouse in the mountains of North Carolina in the 1930s provides us with a wonderful contrast with the educational system of today.

Elizabeth Middleton was born in Philadelphia, Pennsylvania. After graduating from high school she attended Clemson University in South Carolina before moving to Asheville, North Carolina to attend the University of North Carolina at Asheville and earning her B.A. in Paschology as well as obtaining her North Carolina K-6 Teaching Certificate. In 2010 she entered Western Carolina University where she earned her AIG Licensure and her M.A in Special Education. Ms. Middleton is currently serving at Candler Elementary School in Buncombe County, North Carolina.

Dr. Judy Pierce was born in Dunbar, Kanawa County, West Virginia. Following her elementary and high school in the mountains of West Virginia she enrolled at West Virginia State College where she earned a B.A. in Elementary Education. She moved to North Carolina and attended Marshall University where she was awarded her Master's Degree in Elementary Education. Moving on to Appalachian State University she obtained her Ed. S. in Educational Leadership before once again attending West Virginia University to receive her Doctorate in Curriculun and Instruction, Reading, and Educational Administration. After obtaining her Doctorate she completed Postdoctorate work in Middle School Education at both East Tennessee University and the University of Pittsburg. Dr. Pierce has had a variety of work experiences throughout the years. She taught school in Kanawha County Schools in West Virginia, and Winston Salem/Forsyth in Winston Salem, North Carolina before being appointed Reading Coordinator in Winston Salem. She then moved back to West Virginia and taught at West Virginia University before accepting a position as Reading Specialist at Monongalas County Schools also in West Virginia. In 1983 she was appointed Coordinator for Reading/Language Arts/ Social Studies at the West Virginia Department of Education. Moving on she served as Elementary Supervisor in Johnson City, Tennessee before being appointed to the position of Assistant Superintendent for Curriculum and Instruction for Galax City Schools. Dr. Pierce eventually moved to Bowling Green, Kentucky and is currently serving as an instructor in the Department of Education at Western Kentucky University. Awards received during her career include: North Carolina Scholarship, Taught with Laura Bush at the Abraham Lincoln Birthplace, served on the Kentucky Abraham Lincoln Bicentennial Advisory Council, Kentucky Civil War Sesquicentennial Commission and the Kentucky Historical Society Teacher Advisory Council.

Fred E. Thantham was born is Haywood county, North Carolina. He attended Western Carolina University earning a B.A. in Education, an M.S. In Educational Media and School Administration and an Ed. S. in School Administration. Mr. Thantham began his career in education by serving five years teaching in Haywood County. He was then appointed Director of the Instructional Materials Center, Library Program and Library Media Coordinator. The following eight years was spent as Supervisor and Personnel Coordinator for Haywood County Schools. He then filled the position of Assistant Principal before becoming Director of Federal Programs, Health Searvices and School Board Policies where he had served for the past eighteen years.

Dorland Winkler was born in Lenoir, North Carolina. He attended Western Carolina University earning his B.S and M.A. in Education and Educational Administration. Mr. Winkler began his educational career as a teacher at Vance Elementary School in 1969. Due to the integation of Asheville City Schools in 1969 he was transferred to Hill Street School which had been an all African-American school where he proved successful in the mist of a tense situation. He was appointed Assistant Principal of Hill Street School in 1972 and served there as Assistant Principal and Principal until 1990 when he was transferred to Claxton Elementary to serve as Principal. In 1993 he was promoted to Asheville City Schools' Central Office to serve as Testing Coordinator and Director of Personnel Services. Mr. Winkler was honored in 1988-1989 by being named North Carolina Association of Educators District 1 Principal of the Year.